D0591902

Campaigns and Elections
American Style

TRANSFORMING AMERICAN POLITICS

Lawrence C. Dodd, Series Editor

Dramatic changes in political institutions and behavior over the past three decades have underscored the dynamic nature of American politics, confronting political scientists with a new and pressing intellectual agenda. The pioneering work of early postwar scholars, while laying a firm empirical foundation for contemporary scholarship, failed to consider how American politics might change or to recognize the forces that would make fundamental change inevitable. In reassessing the static interpretations fostered by these classic studies, political scientists are now examining the underlying dynamics that generate transformational change.

Transforming American Politics brings together texts and monographs that address four closely related aspects of change. A first concern is documenting and explaining recent changes in American politics—in institutions, processes, behavior, and policymaking. A second is reinterpreting classic studies and theories to provide a more accurate perspective on postwar politics. The series looks at historical change to identify recurring patterns of political transformation within and across the distinctive eras of American politics. Last and perhaps most important, the series presents new theories and interpretations that explain the dynamic processes at work and thus clarify the direction of contemporary politics. All of the books focus on the central theme of transformation—transformation both in the conduct of American politics and in the way we study and understand its many aspects.

BOOKS IN THIS SERIES

Campaigns and Elections American Style

THIRD EDITION

Edited by James A. Thurber
and Candice J. Nelson
American University

A Member of the Perseus Books Group

Copyright © 2010 by Westview Press

Published by Westview Press,
A Member of the Perseus Books Group

All rights reserved. Printed in the United States of America. No part of this book may be reproduced in any manner whatsoever without written permission except in the case of brief quotations embodied in critical articles and reviews. For information, address Westview Press, 2465 Central Avenue, Boulder, CO 80301.

Find us on the World Wide Web at www.westviewpress.com.

Westview Press books are available at special discounts for bulk purchases in the United States by corporations, institutions, and other organizations. For more information, please contact the Special Markets Department at the Perseus Books Group, 2300 Chestnut Street, Suite 200, Philadelphia, PA 19103, or call (800) 810-4145, ext. 5000, or e-mail special .markets@perseusbooks.com.

Library of Congress Cataloging-in-Publication Data

    Campaigns and elections American style / edited by James A. Thurber and Candice J. Nelson.—3rd ed.
        p. cm.—(Transforming American politics)
    Includes bibliographical references and index.
    ISBN 978-0-8133-4419-5 (pbk. : alk. paper) 1. Political campaigns—United States. 2. Campaign management—United States. I. Thurber, James A., 1943– II. Nelson, Candice J., 1949–
    JK2281.C353 2009
    324.70973—dc22

                                            2009015957

10 9 8 7 6 5 4 3 2 1

To my wife Claudia
And to my family Mark, Kathryn, Greg,
Tristan, Bryan, and Kelsey
—JAT

To David, Kuniko,
Peter, and Michael
—CJN

Contents

Acknowledgments

The rich lessons and knowledge from American University's Campaign Management Institute (CMI) was the genesis of the first edition of this book. CMI was started in 1981 by campaign professionals and academics to bring together academic and practical knowledge of campaigning. It is offered twice a year at the Center for Congressional and Presidential Studies (american.edu/ccps) at American University. It is an intense two-week hands-on learning experience organizing actual election campaigns. Students receive professional guidance and evaluation from campaign professionals, pollsters, media specialists, campaign strategists and managers, and academics.

We thank the thousands of students who have taken CMI and the dozens of campaign professionals who lectured in CMI for their insights and inspiration to write this book. All of the campaign professionals who contribute chapters to this book have spoken at CMI. Thanks to those authors and the many CMI speakers for sharing their invaluable practical knowledge and the strategy and tactics of winning campaigns in America. They have also been wonderful mentors to our students and alumni who are working in the campaign management field. We also thank the many readers of previous editions for their helpful comments and reactions that have helped us improve this edition.

Thanks for our colleagues at the Center for Congressional and Presidential Studies, Olga Gallardo and Alicia Prevost, who provided invaluable research assistance at various stages of the project. We have special thanks for the support of the Center and this project from

William LeoGrande, Dean of the School of Public Affairs at American University.

We thank our friends at Perseus Books/Westview Press. Anthony Wahl, Annie Lenth, and Kelsey Mitchell deserve special appreciation for their encouragement and help in producing this edition.

Clearly this is a collective effort. We thank all the contributors for their chapters. We take full responsibility for any omissions or errors of fact and interpretation.

—*James A. Thurber*
—*Candice J. Nelson*

1

Understanding the Dynamics and the Transformation of American Campaigns

James A. Thurber

This book, a study of campaign management and elections, marries academic wisdom and the practical knowledge of professional political consultants, although the two worlds rarely overlap. Academics use explicit hypotheses and scientific methods for making systematic observations about campaigns and elections, whereas professionals draw generalizations based on direct experience. Campaign consultants "test hypotheses" by winning and losing elections. Both use theoretical perspectives about campaigns and voters, although one is academic and one practical. The common dimension to both worlds is the major changes that have occurred in the way campaigns are waged and elections won or lost in the last twenty years, as especially shown in the 2008 election campaign of President Barack Obama.

Academics use large data sets and systematically test hypotheses to make careful statements about voters and elections. They attempt to explain individual and collective political behavior and try to answer questions about who votes and why. When political scientists write about campaigns and how candidates get elected, their approach is based on scholarly analysis rather than experience (Thurber 1998; Thurber and Nelson 2000).

Campaign professionals also focus on who votes and why, but to develop a winning strategy to attract voters to their candidate. When they write about campaigns, it is often in the form of how-to-win manuals (Napolitan 1972; Shea 1996). They are hired activists who develop strategies and tactics to influence voters and election results (Thurber 2001; Thurber and Nelson 2000). They focus solely on how to win. Political scientists try to understand voters, candidates, elections, and the consequences of electoral battles for governing and developing public policy. Campaign professionals have knowledge gained from their previous campaigns. They know what works through their experience of winning or losing elections and are seasoned by their involvement with campaigning (Thurber and Nelson 2000).

Campaign professionals often assert that the academic literature on campaigns and elections is either obvious or wrong (Thurber and Nelson 2000), while also admitting that they lack time to read the latest political science research findings. Academics often argue that campaign professionals promote the latest folk wisdom about campaign tactics and do not know what works or not until it is too late. The winners possess the "truth," creating new "geniuses" of campaign management each election cycle depending on who wins and loses. All successful consultants try to learn from their mistakes. Winning consultants pick up more clients and business volume and the losers often leave the business. Academics study campaigns and elections but rarely talk with campaign professionals about what they believe regarding their electoral track record. Academics may not be aware of the latest developments in campaign strategies, tactics, and tools until an election is over (recent exceptions to this are the studies of Dulio and Nelson 2005; Nelson, Dulio, and Medvic 2002; Johnson 2007; Thurber 2001; Thurber and Nelson 2000). Political scientists study campaign professionals but rarely enter the world of political campaigning. Mutual distrust characterizes relations between campaign professionals and academics. Many professionals feel that academic research is not applicable to the real world of election campaigns. On the other hand, academics consider professionals' practical how-to knowledge unscientific—not based on the systematic collection of data and tests of hypotheses that are part of a broader theory. And when commentary from political pundits, journalists, and retired political leaders is added to the mix, it becomes difficult to distinguish reality from myth, marketing, and political spin.

When the worlds of academics and professionals do converge, however, insights result, as shown in this book. Whether explaining or managing campaigns, or treating campaign management as a science or an art, academics, professionals, and pundits all agree that American election campaigns have been transformed especially in the last twenty years. Every campaign cycle reveals new strategies and tactics, as shown so clearly in the 2008 election.

In these pages campaign professionals and political scientists confront each other's perspectives. They examine changes in the organization, operation, and impact of campaign strategies and tactics at the local, state, and national levels that have had a significant impact on American elections in the last three decades. Political consultants are using recent technological advances and the Internet to make campaigns operate faster and often more cheaply. Chapters by campaign professionals and political scientists are paired to cover the major elements of campaign advancements from two viewpoints. Our contributors do not always agree. Professionals and academics often have different perspectives on the same campaign topic. The disagreements reveal distinct bodies of knowledge. Dialogue between campaign consultants and political scientists offers a new, more complete view of election campaigns that is essential to an understanding of twenty-first-century American campaigns and elections.

Election Campaigns Are Wars

The word "campaign" comes from military usage: "a connected series of military operations forming a distinct phase of a war" or "a connected series of operations designed to bring about a particular result." Winning an election is like winning a war, complete with "war rooms" and campaign managers. Campaigns battle for the hearts and minds—and the votes—of the American people.

Candidates and campaign organizations compete to capture government and advance policies. Campaigns are battles to define public problems and develop policy solutions and, of course, to persuade voters to support those ideas.

For candidates and professionals, campaigns are zero-sum games or even minus-sum games: there are always winners and losers, and more campaigners are disappointed by the election outcome than pleased by it. For academics, campaigns are objects of analysis; they do not represent a personal gamble, a deeply felt ambition, or a commitment to the objective of winning. Campaigns are not political causes but rather a focus of intellectual interest. Academics are interested in why people vote; professionals are interested in how to get them to vote for a particular candidate. Academics study who contributes money to campaigns and why; professionals persuade people to give funds to their candidates. This book joins these two worlds and shows how both perspectives are needed to manage election campaigns as well as understand and explain them.

Those who manage election campaigns, be they presidential, congressional, or down ballot races (local and state candidates), evaluate the existing political environment, develop strategies and plans within that political environment, pursue a strategic theme and message for a candidate, establish an organization, solicit and use campaign money, buy advertising and attempt to use free (news) media, schedule candidates, organize and use a field organization, use opposition research, and conduct survey research and focus group analysis among a variety of other activities. The basic elements of campaigning have changed dramatically in the last three decades because of the decline of political party organization, the increase in nonvoting, the growing power of interest groups, the power of the media (especially television), technological advancements, and the professionalization of campaigns. What has not changed is that successful campaigns need to develop an explicit strategy, theme, message, and tactics.

Campaign Strategy, Message, Organization, and Planning

Campaigns do not happen in a vacuum and they are not predetermined by economic and political circumstances. Prevailing economic and political conditions influence a campaign, and candidates and campaigns in turn have an impact on those conditions, as was the case with 2008 presidential candidate Barack Obama.

There are three fundamental elements of campaigning: strategy, organization, and message. On these three elements, Barack Obama ran a perfect campaign. His focused strategy and message, contrasted with John McCain's lack of discipline and wavering message, showed that campaigns can determine election outcomes. Obama's campaign presented a clear vision to voters about the failing economy, the wars in Iraq and Afghanistan, and the need to end the policies and partisan deadlock of the Bush presidency. The 2008 campaign was a "change election," and the change theme was used very effectively by the Obama campaign. Historic crowds gathered to witness Obama's inauguration, and the president received high approval ratings in his first weeks in office as well as outpourings of support from around the world. Yet this outcome was not a foregone conclusion in early summer 2008.

Some analysts have suggested that widespread disapproval for Republicans' handling of the economy, the midsummer Wall Street meltdown, and dismal approval ratings of the incumbent president predetermined the outcome of the 2008 election (Lewis-Beck 2009; Campbell 2009; Abramowitz 2009). But this analysis underestimates the effects of both candidates' campaigns on the outcome, especially since Obama was the first African American to obtain the presidential nomination and race has historically been a strong factor in American politics (Lewis-Beck 2009). The effect of Obama's race, given that the United States had never nominated an African American to a major national party ticket and that Obama was the only African American in the U.S. Senate, was uncertain. It is true that President George W. Bush suffered historically low approval ratings, and voters frequently turn out a party that has controlled the White House for two consecutive terms.[1] But John McCain was seen as a "maverick" in the Republican Party with bipartisan leanings; John Kerry had even explored the idea of choosing McCain as a running mate in 2004. McCain ran a heated campaign against Bush for the 2000 Republican nomination, so he may have been the best-positioned Republican to challenge the Bush legacy. In June 2008 McCain led with the up-for-grabs voters, 48 percent to 36 percent, who were crucial to the outcome of the election (Lizza 2008). Obama strategists viewed McCain as the one Republican with the potential to steal the "anti-Washington" message that Obama used effectively during the Democratic primaries. But instead of embracing his centrist potential, McCain lurched to the right by picking Sarah Palin for his vice president, who appealed to the Republican base. Ironically, his choice of Palin made him less of a maverick, at least in terms of appearing to be independent of the Republican Party. Key Obama strategist Anita Dunn said, "What we knew at the start of the campaign was that the notion of John McCain as a change agent and independent voice did not exist anywhere outside the Beltway" (Lizza 2008).

The McCain campaign could have used his stance against the Bush tax cuts as evidence that McCain's economic plan and principles differed from Bush's. But the McCain campaign did not find a salient economic argument until late in the campaign, when he seized on Obama's "spread the wealth" comment, referring to a willingness to raise taxes. This seemed to resonate with the Republican fiscal conservative base, but it was too little, too late. Earlier McCain had wavered on his economic message and offered no clear leadership while the Senate considered the bailout package. Subsequently voters who were "very worried" about the economic crisis chose Obama over McCain, 62 percent to 36 percent (2008 National Exit Poll, available at CBS.com).

Campaigns matter because they give voters information about the candidates. Samuel Popkin's influential study of campaign effects found that "campaign communications do affect choice, and that they generally make voters more, not less, accurate in their perception of candidates and issues" (Popkin 1991, 40). A winning campaign pays close attention to campaign fundamentals (Thurber and Nelson 2000; Medvic 2001, 2006). The most important elements of a campaign are strategy, theme, and message. Raising money, setting the candidate's schedule, doing opposition research, linking resources to campaign tactics, preparing for debates, advertising on television and radio, and mobilizing supporters to vote all follow from the campaign's strategy, theme, and message. In a well-run campaign, the message is expressed in all communications with voters: television and radio ads and the direct mail campaign.

Campaign Strategy and Message

Obama's campaign rarely wavered from its theme and message, "Change We Can Believe In." When the Obama campaign faced challenges, such as the Reverend Jeremiah Wright story during the primaries and Obama's "spread the wealth" statement to Joe the Plumber, it always returned to the central theme and message: change. During the long primary campaign, Hillary Clinton was winning big states like California, Texas, and Ohio. Some campaigns might have wavered from the change message in favor of experience in an attempt to sway Clinton voters and lock up the nomination, or with an eye to the general election campaign (since McCain was already the Republican nominee, a candidate who was perceived to have experience). The Obama campaign could not have known it at the time, but when the financial crisis hit in midsummer, the change message became the most attractive to voters, and the campaign was well served by sticking to it. The McCain campaign, on the other hand, was not served well by its theme, "Country First." When McCain actually tried to put his country before his campaign, there were no results. Before the Republican convention, with a hurricane imminent (which never realized its predicted strength), McCain almost canceled the convention and two days of planned speeches and programming were called off. In this way McCain avoided President Bush's appearance at the Republican National Convention and even with the truncated convention schedule he still received the traditional bump in the poll. According to the *New York Post*, "Senator John McCain pulled five points ahead of Barack Obama today, reinforcing a post-RNC bounce felt over the weekend, according to one poll. . . . Gallup poll put McCain at 49 percent and Obama at 44 percent, while their weekend poll put McCain at 50 percent and Obama at 46 percent."[2] These daily poll results were based on interviewing done Friday through Sunday, after the RNC concluded Thursday. McCain was at 43 percent before the RNC, meaning the GOP party gave him a six-point boost overall.

However, McCain's willingness to "put country first" did not go over as well when he decided to suspend his campaign two days before the first scheduled presidential debate. When the economic crisis exploded in September with the federal takeover of Fannie Mae and Freddie Mac, followed by the fall of Lehman Brothers and the bailout of AIG, McCain announced that he was suspending his campaign. This was not the steady leadership in a time of crisis that voters were looking for. McCain's erratic decisions to suspend, postpone, and then restart the campaign revealed a lack of leadership at the highest levels of the campaign.

Obama's strategy encompassed a commitment to the fundamentals of campaigning (Thurber and Nelson 2000)—a clear strategy, theme, and message linked to appropriate tactics. Running a campaign involves a variety of functions such as scheduling and advance work, press arrangements, issue research and debate preparation, speech writing, polling and focus group analysis, voter targeting and mobilization, print and electronic media advertising and placement, finance, legal analysis, and party and interest group action. These demands require a highly disciplined campaign organization (Thurber and Nelson 2004). A campaign must know how many votes it needs to win and where these votes will come from. This isn't as simple as it may sound. Many pundits thought Obama would not make it past Super Tuesday, but the Obama campaign's focus on the delegate count—the votes it would take to win the Democratic nomination—put them in caucus states that the Clinton campaign ignored. The Obama campaign used to its advantage the Democratic Party's system of proportionally allocating delegates. The Democratic primaries, uniquely in the U.S. election system, use proportional representation. Most elections are determined by winner-take-all, first-past-the-post single-member districts. The Democratic presidential primaries and caucuses, which are governed by the rules of the Democratic National Committee, award delegates based on the vote a candidate receives statewide and by congressional district. National convention delegates choose the party's nominee, so delegates equal votes. A presidential candidate must reach 50 percent plus one delegate. By methodically focusing on the delegate count, no matter how small the state or how complicated the caucus procedures, the Obama campaign was able to overtake the Clinton campaign in the delegate race and ultimately win the nomination. The Clinton campaign was criticized for ignoring caucus states because they tend to be smaller and have fewer delegates. In the general election, the Obama campaign made the same commitment to not taking a single vote for granted.

Obama also ran a perfect campaign in terms of message discipline and quick response to criticism or attack (Thurber, Nelson, and Dulio 2000). The campaign never let a news cycle go by without responding, often within hours or even minutes. The campaign strategy and message was driven by the faltering economy, President Bush's unpopularity, and the war in Iraq. The controversies surrounding Reverend Wright or Bill Ayers arguably could have done more damage to Obama if his campaign had been less disciplined in bringing the discussion back to economic and policy issues. David Axelrod, the Obama's chief strategist and David Plouffe, the campaign manager, had an obsessive focus on the message of change that could be summarized in the term "Bush." Obama was the clear alternative to Bush; McCain was not. Axelrod often said that America was looking for anyone but Bush, for "the remedy, not the replica." It worked in the primaries as well as in the general election. "That allowed Obama to finesse the perpetual problem of presidential politics: having one message to win over a party's ardent supporters and another when trying to capture independents and the up-for-grabs, the voters who decide the general election" (Lizza 2008).

At the November 2008 postelection campaign managers' conference at the Kennedy School of Government at Harvard (held every 4 years since 1972), Axelrod argued that the election was decided between September 15, the date that Lehman Brothers collapsed, and September 26, the date of the first presidential debate, two days after McCain "suspended" his campaign to address the financial crisis (Scherer 2008). Obama's public statements during that period, as well as his solid performance in the debate, allowed voters to see that he was a "safe change" candidate, even though he was inexperienced on the national level of government.

The Strategic Raising and Use of Campaign Funds

How a campaign spends money is just as important as how much money is raised. Much has been written about the fund-raising prowess of the Obama campaign, how Obama became the first "billion dollar" candidate.[3] In many ways, Obama has changed the way that money will be raised in future campaigns. Any serious campaign for federal office will require an online fund-raising component. Future presidential candidates are unlikely to participate in the current system of public campaign financing that limits the amount of money that can be raised and spent. A presidential candidate from either of the two major parties can get a grant from the federal government to cover campaign expenses, as long as the candidate does not spend more than the amount of the grant and does not accept any additional private contributions. In 2008 the amount available to each candidate was $84 million. Accepting it ensured that the campaign would have $84 million, more than Bush and Kerry had in 2004 (when the amount available under public financing was $75 million); declining it meant that the campaign might fail to raise $84 million—or it might raise more. Obama bet that he could raise more, and as it turned out, he raised much more. While McCain was limited to $84 million during the entire general election (which formally begins during each party's national convention), Obama raised more than $150 million in September alone. Ultimately Obama raised a record $742 million (which includes money raised during both the primary and general election). The decision to forgo public financing allowed Obama to outspend McCain by more than 5 to 1. In some states, the margin was even greater: in Indiana Obama's spending advantage was 7 to 1 (Rove 2008). Obama's total is more than what all of the candidates combined received in donations in the 2004 presidential race. For the general election campaign, Obama raised around $300 million, compared to $84 million that McCain was allotted under public financing. From October 16 to October 24, Obama spent more than $136 million while McCain spent just $26.5 million during the same time period. The RNC spent $31 million on advertising for McCain during the same time, not quite enough to make up the deficit with Obama's airtime (Malbin 2009).

Although some public advocacy groups criticized the Obama campaign for not participating in the public finance system (which these groups view as important for reining in the influence of a small number of wealthy donors), others pointed out that the large number of small donors produced something like a publicly financed campaign, in the sense that many members of the public were voluntarily contributing. The Obama campaign reported close to four million individual contributors (Luo 2008). It is difficult to calculate the number of small donors, since the FEC does not require personal information on donors who contribute less than $200. Michael Malbin of the Campaign Finance Institute found that many donors who contributed $200 or less did so repeatedly, in effect becoming larger donors (Malbin 2009). For example, a person could have contributed $100 on five separate occasions. Each individual contribution was under $200, so the Obama campaign was not required to report details about this donor to the FEC (although the campaign collects this information for its own use, including legal vetting, future solicitations, and mobilization messages). Even though many small donors contributed multiple times, 57 percent of Obama's money came from contributions that were $200 or less, and only 35 percent of McCain's money came from these small donors (Center for Responsive Politics 2008). In the campaign's final two months, the Obama campaign spent $170 million on TV ads and the McCain campaign spent $61 million.

During the 2004 campaign allied organizations, called "527s" according to their place in the federal tax code, were influential. Even though these organizations (including Democratic allies America Coming Together and Move On in the 2004 campaign) have the same end goal as the party they are allied with, by law they are not allowed to coordinate with the campaign on matters of strategy. This complicated efforts for the Kerry campaign in 2004, since the campaign was not able to keep tight control over the theme or message of advertising campaigns by its allied groups. In 2008 the Obama campaign reduced the influence of interest groups and 527s by asking contributors to give to the campaign instead of outside organizations. This strategy worked because Obama was not subject to the fund-raising limits that constrained Kerry in 2004. Because of the limitations imposed by the public financing system, Kerry was not able to raise or spend beyond the $75 million federal grant. Donors who wanted to contribute to the campaign sent money to allied organizations, including the party committees and the 527s. Even though the Democratic 527s were allied with the Kerry campaign, they were barred (under federal campaign finance law) from officially coordinating with the campaign. Consequently, when America Coming Together sent canvassers into swing states to mobilize support for Kerry, they were not allowed to say Kerry's name. Instead they were instructed to encourage voters to "vote Democratic." Television ads by the liberal organization Move On focused on the Iraq war, which might not have been the best message for Kerry, given that in 2004 Bush was still seen as a strong commander in chief. But since the Kerry campaign did not control Move On's message, his campaign had mixed messages. In 2008 the Obama campaign controlled all the money that it needed and consequently controlled the message and mobilization on the Democratic side.

Campaign Organization

Obama's money advantage allowed him to dominate all aspects of the media "air war": television, cable, radio, direct mail, and even advertising in video games.[4] He also dominated in the "ground war," including the organization of field staff and offices. Obama had more staff and offices in more states than McCain. Table 1.1 shows Obama's field office advantage.

Obama's staff (paid and volunteer) advantage allowed him to get his message out to more people and organize more supporters than the

Table 1.1 Number of Campaign Offices in Selected Battleground States

State	Obama	McCain
Florida	58	75
Minnesota	27	11
Montana	19	5
Ohio	81	52
Pennsylvania	78	30
Virginia	71	20

Source: Obama and McCain campaign websites as of October 27, 2008. Includes coordinated campaign offices.

McCain campaign did. Campaign staff members worked in local offices that served as gathering places for local volunteers and supporters. Some campaign offices operated phone banks, some served as the gathering point for volunteer door-to-door canvasses, and many served as storefronts where locals could get campaign literature, buttons, and stickers. The campaign's field staff (which typically makes up the bulk of a campaign's in-state operation) identified and contacted potential voters and persuaded them to become supporters and then gots them to vote. To accomplish these goals, the field staff recruited volunteers to make phone calls and knock on the doors of potential voters.

The Obama campaign organization at the national level was made up of experienced, disciplined people who acted as if they knew each other well, although for the most part they had never worked together. Their internal organizational discipline meant that there was "no drama with Obama." The message discipline of the campaign was directly linked to the candidate and a group of well tested professionals. Chief strategist David Axelrod and campaign adviser Valerie Jarrett knew Obama well. They came from Chicago and had worked on earlier races with him. Axelrod's partner, Plouffe, had worked for former House Democratic leader Dick Gephardt. Steve Hildebrand, who had worked for Senate majority leader Tom Daschle, was the deputy campaign manager who oversaw the field organization. Robert Gibbs, the campaign's communications director who came from Obama's Senate office, had national experience working for John Kerry's 2004 presidential campaign.

The online organizing tools that had been honed by Howard Dean in the 2004 primary and by John Kerry and George Bush in the general election set an example for Obama in 2008 to recruit volunteers even before paid staff arrived in a state. The Obama campaign advanced the use of technology and used new forums to communicate his message and to recruit volunteers. Obama's website served as a recruiting tool for volunteers and donors, and the campaign was constantly reaching out to supporters through its email list and social networking sites, including Facebook, MySpace, and BlackPlanet. These techniques helped turn out volunteers and also crowds at his rallies. In the closing weeks of his campaign, "crowds of fifty, sixty, and seventy thousand people greeted

Obama at every stop . . . almost as if there were pent-up demand to see him" (Lizza 2008). Campaign staff and volunteers positioned themselves at these events to get names of supporters and to recruit them to volunteer.

The Obama campaign also exceeded expectations for organizing volunteers. Zack Exley, an adviser to Howard Dean's 2004 presidential bid, commented that "the Dean campaign had Internet gurus; the Obama campaign has community organizing gurus" (Exley 2007). Obama's own community organizing experience in Chicago likely influenced his campaign's early efforts to train volunteers in the fundamentals of organizing and mobilizing voters. Community organizing veteran Marshall Ganz, a Harvard professor who organized farm workers with Caesar Chavez, helped design the Obama campaign's organizing model. By late summer 2007, more than a thousand volunteers had been trained through Obama's organizing school, Camp Obama. They were trained to organize canvasses and phone banks, recruit volunteers, and develop a local organization. They were also schooled on the campaign's message, according to Jocelyn Woodards, the director of Camp Obama (Schaper 2007). Anita Dunn, Obama senior campaign adviser and partner in Squire, Knapp, Dunn Communications, reported that the volunteer turnout in the battleground states was on average 130 percent, compared to 70 percent in past campaigns. Obama's online operation served as a conduit for money and organization. Online organizing allowed the campaign to collect an estimated 14 million email addresses, and it sent millions of messages over the course of the campaign to raise money, recruit volunteers, and get more people to sign up online. About 1 million supporters signed up for text message alerts, which the campaign used to organize attendance at local events and recruit volunteers.

The Obama campaign outperformed the McCain campaign in voter contact. Studies of voter contact efforts indicate that mobilization works. Randomized field experiments have shown that door-to-door canvassing increases the likelihood that individuals will turn out to vote by 8–10 percent (Gerber and Green 2000). Professional phone banks have been shown to be less effective than canvassing, but per-

Figure 1.1 Voters Contacted in 2008 and 2004

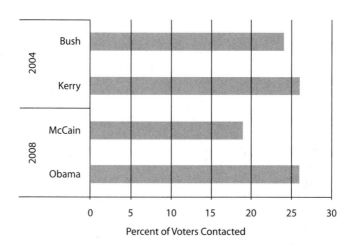

Source: Brian F. Schaffner, Pollster.com, December 2008.

sonal phone contacts among peers can be as effective as canvassing. The technical skill and efficiency of the Obama campaign allowed it to expand on traditional voter contact techniques, such as phone banking. Instead of relying on a traditional phone bank operating out of a union hall or law firm conference room, the Obama campaign hosted parties where supporters brought their cell phones and were given lists of voters to call in targeted states, including nearly 400,000 volunteers in California alone. The McCain campaign's rate of voter contact fell below that of the Bush campaign in 2004, according to exit polls that asked, "Did anyone call you or talk to you in person on behalf of either major presidential campaign about coming out to vote?" Figure 1.1 shows the differences in voter contact by the Republican and Democratic campaigns in 2004 and 2008.

In 2008, 19 percent of voters reported being contacted by the McCain campaign, whereas in 2004, 24 percent reported being contacted by the Bush campaign. Table 1.2 shows the differences in contact rates

Table 1.2 Voter Contact by Presidential Campaigns, 2008

	Contacted by Obama Campaign	*Contacted by McCain Campaign*	*Obama Advantage*
Nationwide	26	18	+8
Ohio	43	36	+7
Florida	29	21	+8
North Carolina	34	26	+8
Iowa	42	30	+12
Virginia	50	38	+12
Indiana	37	22	+15
Colorado	51	34	+17
Nevada	50	29	+21

Source: National exit poll and state exit poll data are from CBS News, available at http://election.cbsnews.com/election2008.

between the Obama and McCain campaigns in selected states where this question was asked in the state version of the national exit poll. Nationwide, Obama's advantage in voter contact was eight points. Obama's contact rate was seventeen points higher in Colorado and twenty-one higher in Nevada, two states that Obama flipped from red to blue (meaning that these states went Republican in 2004 but turned Democratic in 2008).

Measuring the Organizers' Performance: Voter Turnout Numbers

Over 61 percent of eligible voters, or more than 132 million, cast ballots nationwide (McDonald 2009). Turnout was slightly higher in battleground states, with a combined rate of 65.9 percent in Colorado, Florida, Indiana, Iowa, Missouri, Nevada, North Carolina, Ohio, Pennsylvania, and Virginia (McDonald 2009). Around 30 percent of all votes were cast early (McDonald 2009). According to exit polls, 26 percent of voters said they had been contacted by Obama's campaign, compared to only 18 percent who said they had been contacted by the McCain cam-

Table 1.3 Turnout by Group

	Obama	McCain	2008 % of electorate	Kerry	Bush	2004 % of electorate
Women	56	43	53	51	48	54
Men	49	48	47	44	55	46
African American	95	4	13	88	11	11
Hispanic	67	31	9	53	44	8
Asian	62	35	2	56	44	2
White	43	55	74	41	58	77
18–29	66	32	18	54	45	17
30–44	52	46	29	46	53	29
45–64*	50	49	37	48	51	30
65+**	45	53	16	46	54	24
College graduate	53	45	44	49	49	42
No college degree	53	46	56	47	53	58
Liberal	89	10	22	85	13	21
Moderate	60	39	44	54	45	45
Conservative	20	78	34	15	84	34
First-time voter	69	30	11	53	46	11

*In 2004 this category included 45- to 59-year-olds.
** In 2004 this category included voters age 60 and older.

Source: National exit poll results, available at www.cnn.com/ELECTION/2004/ and www.cnn.com/ELECTION/2008/.

paign. Although the historic turnout that some predicted did not materialize, certain groups of voters did see increases, such as young voters. According to CIRCLE, an organization that tracks turnout among voters age 18–29, there was a 4–5 percentage point increase in this age-group, or about 3.4 million more than voted in 2004. Of these voters 66 percent chose Obama, according to exit polls, compared to only 54 percent who chose Kerry in 2004. Table 1.3 shows voter turnout among key demographic groups according to national exit poll figures.

Instead of a "seventy-two-hour project" like the get-out-the-vote (GOTV) campaign Republicans famously waged in 2000 and 2004, which focused on contacting supporters in the last seventy-two hours before Election Day, the Obama campaign ran a "three-month project." Obama's organization put paid field staff and extensive volunteer networks in every battleground state and even some states that were not. The extended battle for the Democratic nomination gave Obama the opportunity to organize in traditional battleground states such as Ohio and Pennsylvania, and it also gave him the opportunity to organize early in states like Indiana and Virginia, which had never been battleground states and few predicted would switch from red to blue in 2008. The long Democratic primary battle allowed Obama to organize in more states than ever before. It was a competitive battle that toughened him and his organization for the general election campaign.

Campaigns are dynamic and combative, as seen in the 2008 election. They do not happen in a vacuum, and they are not predetermined by economic or political circumstances. Successful campaigns develop a clear message that focuses on groups of voters that will help the candidate win—party loyalists (the base) and swing voters (often moderate and ideologically in the middle). Candidate Obama understood this. He had the organization, strategy, and money to run a perfect campaign. The political environment undoubtedly benefited the Obama campaign, with a historically unpopular president, two ongoing wars, and a damaged economy all tied to Republicans and their president. But the Obama campaign overcame a massive historical hurdle in American politics by electing the first African American president. Obama's unwavering message discipline and outstanding organization innovated and used technological advancements to target and mobilize voters on the ground and inspired voters through the air war using Obama's charismatic communication skills. All of this combined to elect the first African American as president of the United States. It was the best run campaign in modern history, and students of campaign management will study its strategy and tactics for years to come.

The 2008 Obama campaign shows clearly that candidates and their campaign managers must evaluate environmental conditions early and develop campaign strategies and plans that take advantage of them, but revise their plans when events (like a failing economy) call for it. Campaign strategy, planning, and tactics must take objective economic and political facts into account. Some think that a campaign plan must be adhered to with almost military discipline and precision. Campaign strategy simply charts a path to win the election and recognizes that campaigns are dynamic and react to events and opponents. Campaigns are frequently underfunded, disorganized, and understaffed, and their personnel lack enough information to make rational decisions. In order to start with a strategy and plan, it is essential to develop a campaign theme and message, making the best use of campaign resources, reducing liabilities, and establishing a set of objectives whose achievement will maximize the probability of winning an election or attaining a plurality—50 percent plus one of the total votes cast. The campaign plan to achieve this is a program of specific activities designed to accomplish the set of objectives and eventually to win the election within a given political and economic environment. Campaign strategies and plans must take into account a vast number of factors, such as the candidate, the constituency, the level of office being sought, the nature of the electoral system, the party organization (or lack of it), the economic situation, the financial and political resources available, and the nature of the voters.

Campaign strategy and tactics were the sole realm of political parties up to the mid-1960s. Today they are the domain of professionals: campaign managers, media consultants, campaign finance specialists, pollsters, field (get-out-the-vote) specialists, television producers, schedulers, and many others (Dulio 2004; Johnson 2001; Thurber 2001; Thurber and Nelson 2000; Sabato 1981). In the past three decades campaigns have evolved into complex organizations featuring distinct divisions of labor and elaborate teams of (usually) outside professionals who coordinate with party organizations (Thurber, Magleby, and Patterson 2002). However, recent studies that examine the impact of political party organizing and funding on campaigning suggest that local parties may be playing important roles in campaigns (Thurber, Prevost, and Bohne 2008).

An Overview of This Book

Successful campaigns develop a clear strategy and message focused on groups of voters that will help the candidate win the base (party loyalists) and swing voters (often moderates). All campaigns analyze the political environment, choose tactics or tools to implement the campaign strategy, and establish the campaign budget (the allocation of money, time, and personnel to each element of the campaign plan). Campaign tactics are the specific activities designed to achieve the strategic objective: victory in the election. Campaign tactics, managing the message to target groups of voters, are at the operational level of the campaign.

The critical elements of campaign strategy and plan have evolved with each election cycle, amid dramatically changing methods and tactics for achieving strategic goals, as shown in the 2008 presidential campaign. David Winston, a Republican Party campaign professional with more than twenty-five years experience in the field, describes how to develop a successful campaign plan in Chapter 2, "Creating a Winning Campaign Strategy." He argues that a campaign without a plan is a journey without a map.

A campaign must be organized into a plan (often written) to present a message to voters about a candidate, but that plan is always subject to change and debate, a dynamic and endless series of dialogues within the campaign to sharpen the focus of the message to the voters. It is the compass that points toward victory. Campaign strategy answers the questions of who will vote for the candidate and why. The principles of sound campaign strategy are the same whether the candidate is running for a seat on a school board or for the presidency of the United States. Without a strategy, a campaign becomes a series of unplanned reactions to unanticipated events. There are four major dimensions of campaign strategy: (1) dividing the electorate into three groups in any given contest (supporters, opponents, and the vast majority of voters who are generally uninterested in the candidate and the campaign); (2) using political research to identify the voters who fall into each of the three groups, (3) selecting a large enough subset of undecided voters to create victory; and (4) allocating resources to targeted voters or identifying how to win the necessary numbers of voters by directing campaign resources (money, time, effort, message) to those key voters. Resource allocation is defined by campaign strategy, the necessary steps to attract the critical voters needed to win. Winston argues that a campaign begins and ends with the campaign plan and strategy. The campaign begins with a written plan of the strategy, and it ends with the achievement of that plan: winning the election. To execute a winning strategy, a campaign must communicate one message to voters. It must be clear, concise, connected, compelling, contrasting, credible, and consistent.

Glen Bolger, the author of Chapter 3, "The Use of Survey Research in Campaigns," is a well-known Republican pollster who for twenty-five years has advised hundreds of federal candidates and is a partner of Public Opinion Strategies. Bolger describes how surveys are used in election campaigns. He offers a concise history of polling in campaigns, and he explains why and how polling is done, the methodology of polling, and how to understand polls. He argues that survey research (public opinion polling) is most important to a campaign as a planning tool. Campaigns use polling to make a whole host of decisions throughout the race such as targeting voters, modifying their message, and reallocating resources. Polling helps a campaign team put together a road map to win. It helps the campaign make decisions about allocating resources of time and money. Polling helps provide message discipline and voter targeting.

Campaign Finance

"Money is the mother's milk of politics," as the late speaker of the California Assembly, Jesse Unruh, said in the mid-1960s. It has become even more important in twenty-first-century politics, as shown by the precedent-setting $745 million dollars raised (over half from small donors) by the Obama campaign in the 2008 election cycle. A series of campaign finance reforms have been enacted beginning in the early 1970s to the passage of the Bipartisan Campaign Reform Act (BICRA) of 2002 and the campaign finance reforms of 2007 and 2009. Chapter 4, "Strategies and Tactics of Fund-raising in 2008" by Candice J. Nelson, and Chapter 5, "Fund-raising Strategies in the 2008 Presidential

Campaign" by Anthony Corrado, political scientists who study campaign finance, offer complementary perspectives on the importance of the money chase in 2008 and in campaigns generally. Both scholars describe how the two campaigns organized their campaign finance efforts, focusing on where the campaign financing came from, how it was collected, and how it was spent. How does a campaign successfully get its second most important resource, financial backing (the first being the candidate)? The methods of raising money and the amount of money collected and used in a campaign can raise ethical questions that may become an issue in a campaign, something Obama avoided through raising small contributions and something McCain avoided by accepting public financing for his general election campaign. Skillful use of money is central to a campaign strategy. Money can be allocated for staff, advertising, television time, survey research, and so on.

Nelson documents the fund-raising strategies and tactics that were most important in the 2008 presidential election. She analyzes Obama's strategy of building on the Internet fund-raising success of the Dean campaign in 2004 as well as employing traditional fund-raising techniques such as bundling. Obama raised more money than McCain and any previous presidential candidate through small contributions obtained online; he also raised more money in large donor contributions than any previous candidate. The record $745 million raised by the Obama campaign speaks to the wisdom of his campaign fund-raising strategy and tactics.

Anthony Corrado characterizes the 2008 election as an "unending chase for campaign dollars, spurring candidates to use any means available to try to raise money." However, he concludes by identifying contradictory lessons in regard to the money chase in the presidential campaigns. The Democratic nomination contest followed the patterns of the past. The candidates who raised the most money early on emerged as the clear front-runners and were confirmed as the leaders in the race once the voting began, leading to a competitive, high-spending race. Obama, the candidate who had the most money, was able to wage a better funded, more extensive campaign, and ended up winning the nomination. Obama then outspent McCain by a substantial margin and won the presidency.

Campaign Advertising and the Media

Paid advertising and earned media are cardinal elements in a modern election campaign. Most Americans rely heavily on the news media—television, radio, print media, and the Internet—for information about candidates and issues in a campaign. Candidates who have enough money to buy significant amounts of advertising and who attract positive free media (earned media/news coverage) benefit by becoming better known, which in turn positions them to frame issues and influence voters to support them. The media projects the theme and message of the campaign and is critical to success.

In any electoral system, political communication has several basic functions. The first, name identification, is critical because few voters will vote for a name they do not recognize. The second function, candidate image, may be defined as the answer to the question, What kind of person is this candidate? Competent media consultants do not force their clients into a predetermined mold but seek ways to present the real person in a positive light. The third function, issues, forms the basis for discussions of the differences between the candidates. If name identification is carried in signage and headlines, and image identification through pictures, issues are the body copy. The two tests of legitimacy for the fourth function, attacks, are truth and relevance, with the voters as ultimate judges. The fifth function, defense, often employs the same medium used in the attack and at the same level. Defense tactics include denial, explanation, apology, and counterattack.

Political advertising simplifies complex issues and takes them out of context. Political ads are simply another product of our mass culture, no better or worse than the rest of the media. We must be cautious about condemning ads when they merely reflect our larger media culture. More importantly, we need to understand the role of ads in politics and give Americans the tools to decode them and avoid being manipulated by them. Both positive ads and attack ads prey on people's emotions—attack ads on fear, positive ads on hope.

Campaigns ads must conform to the rules that govern the rest of the mass media culture, and accommodate themselves to the

conventions of television. In devising ads, candidates and their strategists understand that most undecided and swing voters make up their
minds based on televised impressions, symbols, and cues. Political
advertising in the television age is more about projecting a likable
persona than communicating ideas about governance. Campaigns
must find ways to differentiate their candidate from rivals and thus
question the one quality that seems to matter most with voters—
character.

Political campaigns shape their candidates to reflect personal dreams
and national myths. Conveying a narrative the public relates to and un-
derstands becomes a primary goal of political ads, for example, narratives linking the candidate to the American Dream, narratives drawn
from our distrust of accumulated power, narratives of the candidate as
common man, and leadership narratives, all used in the 2008 presidential campaigns.

Two communications specialists with decades of experience as-
sisting campaigns and covering campaigns for the news media,
Leonard Steinhorn in Chapter 6, "The Selling of the President in a
Converged Media Age," and Dotty Lynch in Chapter 7, "How the Media Covered the 2008 Election: The Role of Earned Media," analyze
the role of campaign advertising and media in campaigns, with a special focus on 2008.

Steinhorn's history of campaign advertising put the transformational 2008 campaign into the context of many election cycles. He argues that television ads alone will not win an election. He shows that
types of media come and go; the predominant form today must share
the stage with others tomorrow. Political campaigns have always been
integrated marketing campaigns that use a variety of techniques to
reach voters. With media converging and transforming almost daily, as
shown in the 2008 campaign, with a newly dominant visual medium—
YouTube—barely a few years old, with online interactivity changing
our experience with politics, news, information, and media, the old
ways that seemed so magical a few years ago no longer apply. Steinhorn
shows that Barack Obama understood this from his announcement to
his election.

Ironically, Obama spent nearly twice as much on television advertising as John McCain did during the general election and Hillary Clinton did in key primary states. Steinhorn concludes that Obama figured that TV advertising was not sufficient in a converged media era for building a brand and creating an icon. Obama did what successful presidential candidates before him had done—create and nourish his brand. But he was the first to understand how the new media environment so thoroughly changed the strategic calculus for getting elected.

"Earned media" is a public relations term that means positive coverage of an event, issue, or person by the news media, initiated by a campaign. One of the most efficient and cost-effective ways to reach a large audience is through earned media. Earned media is positive news coverage that you actively work to get. By creating newsworthy stories or events and offering the stories to news outlets in your area, you can generate effective media coverage that targets specific audiences with your specific message.

Chapter 6 looks at the history of earned media and its evolution in political communications theory, discusses the news environment of 2008 (which formed the backdrop for presidential campaign communications), and examines how the attempts at earning positive media, controlling the message, and setting the news agenda were executed, how successful they were, and what lessons candidates and political professionals can learn for the future.

In Chapter 7, "How the Media Covered the 2008 Election: The Role of Earned Media," Dotty Lynch defines "earned media" as "positive coverage of an event, issue or person by the news media, which has been initiated by a campaign." Lynch analyzes the history of earned media and its evolution in political communications theory. She describes the news environment of 2008 and examines how the attempts at earning positive media, controlling the message, and setting the news agenda were executed. Finally she evaluates how successful the 2008 campaigns were in generating earned media and what lessons candidates and political professionals can learn for the future.

Field Organization, Grassroots Campaigning, and the Digital Campaigns

Election campaigns rely on thousands of volunteers and party activists to get out the vote during the critical last few hours that the polls are open. The functions of these field organizations—voter registration, targeting, literature distribution, and get-out-the-vote drives—have been integral elements of campaigns and elections since the 1990s. As Karl Rove and President Bush reminded campaign professionals in the 2000 election and in the 2002 congressional races, there is no substitute for a well-organized, focused field operation. A strong field operation works the phone banks and streets to identify supporters, reinforce the candidate's message, persuade voters to support the candidate, and get out the vote (GOTV) for the candidate. Field operations need to be linked to the campaign strategy and plan. These operations were formerly performed primarily by the party organization. The party organization is still the most important building block for a campaign, but modern campaigns often obtain the assistance of a field operations specialist.

The purpose and activities of a successful field organization focus on voter contact, the heart of the field operation. The structure, duties, and size of a campaign field operation depend on the strategy and plan of the overall campaign. Few successful campaigns have no field operation. Some campaigns that have a field operation still cannot overcome the odds against a particular candidate.

Political scientist Paul Herrnson in Chapter 8, "Fieldwork in Contemporary Election Campaigns," describes the goals of fieldwork: to identify, communicate with, and mobilize campaign supporters. Although the techniques have changed dramatically over the last fifty years, especially in the 2008 Obama campaign, these goals have not. One of the first activities conducted by a campaign organization is voter research: determining which groups of voters are inclined to support them, support their opponent, or are undecided. After classifying voters into relevant groupings, campaign strategists determine the intensity of each group's support. In addition to group loyalties, campaigners also consider group size and turnout level when designing their targeting strategies. Once the target audiences are determined, demographic, geographic, and polling information is used to create a campaign plan that determines where voter mobilization activities will be conducted, the content of the candidate's message, and where and how that message will be communicated to voters.

Getting the message out is central because a campaign that is unable to define itself risks being defined by its opponents. The basic goals and strategies of campaign communications are to introduce the candidate to voters, give them a reason to support that candidate, discourage them from supporting the opponent, excite supporters enough to get them to vote, and demoralize opponents' supporters so they will be less inclined to vote. Personal contact with voters in the form of candidate-citizen interactions in the field allows for spontaneous learning and expressions of concern. Field activities are also used to generate free media coverage. Because they are labor-intensive, cheap, and often involve volunteers, field activities play a big role in campaigns for state and local offices.

Herrnson argues that although isolating the effects of fieldwork is difficult, it has been found to affect election outcomes. He concludes that campaign fieldwork is good for democracy because it helps increase political participation, efficacy, and support for government by encouraging people to get involved in politics, something shown by the Obama campaign and presidency.

Alan Rosenblatt, digital guru at the Center for American Progress, describes the latest developments in the use of the Internet and digital networks in modern campaigns in Chapter 9, "Dimensions of Campaigns in the Age of Digital Networks." Although the vast majority of the electorate spends little time going to political sites on the Internet, key constituents do. Several lessons emerge from the study of its use in 2008. First, campaigns must include the Internet in their tactics, maintaining websites, blogs, and meet-ups, and developing innovative ways of contacting voters through the Internet. Second, innovative use of the web in campaigns can provide the volunteers and finances to play a critical part of a candidate's strategy, as shown with John McCain in 2000 and Obama in 2008. Third, Rosenblatt argues the Internet has revolutionized campaigns and has become an essential part of all successful campaigns. The diversity and range of digital networking tools and strategies for using them in political campaigns will continue to make a big impact on electoral politics, as they did in the 2008 presidential campaign. Rosenblatt concludes that these tools are in the hands of voters as well as campaigns. This creates a more chaotic environment for spreading campaign messages than in the past. Digital tools provide new solutions to getting the message out and organizing voters and volunteers. He argues that election campaigns must now develop strategies that take into consideration all of the strategic dimensions created by these new technologies. Rosenblatt shows that while strategy, message, and organization remain most important in a campaign, digitally networked technology has altered the playing field, not just in scope and scale but in more fundamental ways.

In Chapter 10, "Election Law Is the New Rock and Roll," Chris Sautter, election law and recount expert, describes how election laws have an impact on campaigns. Election rules matter for all levels of elected office, well beyond the presidential nomination process. Sauter analyzes how the regulations and laws governing elections affect how votes are counted. He discusses the passage and content of the Help America Vote Act (HAVA), which was enacted in response to the 2000 presidential election and the subsequent Supreme Court decision in *Bush v. Gore*. Sautter describes discrepancies among the states and localities in registration, voting procedures, and other key aspects of election administration. Election laws have an impact on election outcomes, as clearly shown in Michigan and Florida in the 2008 primaries, as well as the 2008 Minnesota U.S. Senate general election.

Political science campaign management expert David A. Dulio analyzes the Michigan primary and general election campaigns in Chapter 12, "Madness in Michigan: A Microcosm of Elections American Style." Dulio helps the reader see the dynamics and combative nature of American campaigns. He demonstrates that during the 2008 election cycle, the state of Michigan had just about everything one might expect in terms of a typical American-style campaign. From the early discussions of moving the primary date to Barack Obama's overwhelming victory on November 4, things did not turn out as they typically do in Michigan. There were spirited debates between candidates, large amounts of money, wall-to-wall television advertisements, volunteers, and paid staffers knocking on doors, as well as party infighting, bitter disagreements between voters, political maneuvering and calculation, and in the end, even a little disappointment. Dulio's analysis reveals several useful lessons. The political context of elections matters a great deal. McCain's misfortune of sharing a party affiliation with an unpopular president severely damaged his prospects from the start in Michigan. In addition, McCain could not keep up with the spending power of the Obama campaign. McCain was always behind in Michigan with television ads, paid staffers, direct mail, or any other campaign tactics that need money. Messages candidates communicate to potential voters matter as well. McCain took unpopular stands on issues related to the economy and jobs in Michigan and ultimately the nation. Dulio argues that the Michigan presidential illustrated very clearly that our process of choosing candidates for the general election needs an overhaul. He asks, Will Iowa and New Hampshire continue to have a prime place at the beginning of the line? Will states like Michigan be able to attain the relevancy they crave? Will there be a national primary?

Ethics and Campaigns

The American voter increasingly distrusts politics and politicians, even with the popularity of Obama in the 2008 campaign. The public believes that political campaigns are often conducted in an unethical way. Indeed, political scandal is no stranger to contemporary campaigns. Candidates and staffers may act in unethical ways that cause great damage to a campaign (e.g., associating candidates with public figures of questionable character, questionable campaign financing and spending). Sometimes this comes from going negative (misuse of campaign funds, unethical campaign solicitation, or perceived character flaws of a candidate, for example). The laws and norms of ethical behavior in campaigns and elections have changed dramatically since the days of Tammany Hall when George Washington Plunkett "saw his opportunities and took advantage of them." Watergate and the campaign finance activities of Richard Nixon's Committee to Reelect the President changed campaign ethics fundamentally. Every campaign must set a high standard of proper behavior or all the plans and strategies of a campaign will be for naught.

The ethical dilemmas in political campaigns are discussed by Carol Whitney in Chapter 11, "Campaign Ethics in a Changing World." Whitney is a campaign professional and professor with a long-standing concern about increased public cynicism regarding campaigns, campaign professionals, and candidates for public office. In 2008 Barack Obama convinced voters that he too was tired of negative, partisan politics. He pledged to change our political process for the better, and voters turned out to support his election. Whitney describes the ethical dilemmas and temptations from her experiences in campaign politics and draws lessons from the 2008 campaign. She advocates requiring candidates to sign a code of ethics and outlines the elements of such a code. Whitney argues that ethical codes should govern the actions of every candidate and campaign professional, and the media and voters should do more to promote civility in campaigns and politics.

Conclusion

Candice J. Nelson concludes the book with Chapter 13, "Campaigns Matter," a historical perspective of what is known about campaigns from the viewpoints of professionals and academics. She describes what political scientists know about campaigns and what professionals know. The rivalry and collaboration between political scientists with their scientific knowledge and professionals with their campaign experience are themes that complete the analysis.

The principles and process of campaign management described in this book contributed mightily to the outcomes of American elections in the last three decades and to the "perfect campaign" of Barack Obama. The basic thesis of this book is that election campaigns influence voter behavior. Few changes have transformed American elections more in the past three decades than the professionalization of campaign management and the evolution of new strategies and tactics. What began in the 1960s as the waning of political parties evolved into the increased importance of campaign professionals, which has become a major industry involving several billion dollars being raised and spent in each election cycle (Thurber and Nelson 2000; Dulio 2004). Campaign professionals are a staple of contemporary elections. This book describes and evaluates this crucial development—the professionalization and transformation of twenty-first-century American political campaigns.

Acknowledgments

I am grateful to Alicia Prevost, research director of the Center for Congressional and Presidential Studies, for her excellent research assistance, astute knowledge of campaigns, and her careful substantive work for this chapter. I am also grateful for her outstanding assistance as the assistant director of the Campaign Management Institute, which helped improve this edition in a multitude of ways.

Notes

1 Since World War II, every two-term president's party has lost control of the White House in the next election, with the single exception of George H. W. Bush, who was elected after Ronald Reagan's two terms.

2 www.nypost.com/seven/09082008/news/nationalnews/reuters_poll__mccain__obama_tied_at_48_p_128107.htm.

3 The total amount raised by the Obama finance team will be close to $1 billion, when totals from the campaign, convention, transition, and inauguration are included.

4 The Obama campaign was the first to advertise in a video game. The advertisements consisted primarily of billboards and other signage posted with online sporting events including the American football game Madden'09 (Barrett 2008).

References

Ambramowitz, Alan I. 2009. "Time-for-Change Model Again Right on the Money in 2008." *PS: Political Science & Politics* 42, no. 1: 22.

Barrett, Devlin. 2008. "Video Games Feature Ads for Obama's Campaign." Associated Press, October 14. www.mlive.com/entertainment/index.ssf/2008/10/video_games _feature_ads_for_ob.html.

Campbell, James E. 2009. "The 2008 Campaign and the Forecasts Derailed." *PS: Political Science & Politics* 42, no. 1: 22.

Dulio, David. 2004. *For Better or Worse: How Political Consultants Are Changing Elections in the United States.* Albany: State University of New York Press.

Dulio, David A., and Candice J. Nelson. 2005. *Vital Signs: Perspectives on the Health of American Campaigning.* Washington, D.C.: Brookings Institution.

Exley, Zack. 2007. "Obama Field Organizers Plot a Miracle." *Huffington Post,* August 27. www.huffingtonpost.com/zack-exley/obama-field-organizers-pl_b_61918.html.

Gerber, Donald, and Alan Green. 2000. "The Effects of Canvassing, Telephone Calls, and Direct Mail on Voter Turnout: A Field Experiment." *American Political Science Review.*

Johnson, Dennis W. 2001, 2007. *No Place for Amateurs: How Political Consultants Are Re-shaping American Democracy.* New York: Routledge.

Lewis-Beck, Michael S. 2009. "Race Blunts the Economic Effects? The 2008 Obama Forecast." *PS: Political Science & Politics* 42, no. 1: 22.

Lizza, Ryan. 2008. "Battle Plans: How Obama Won." *New Yorker*, November 17, 46–55.

Luo, Michael. 2008. "Obama Hauls in Record $750 Million for Campaign." *New York Times*, December 5.

Malbin, Michael J. 2009. "Small Donors, Large Donors, and the Internet: The Case for Public Finance After Obama." Washington, D.C.: Campaign Finance Institute.

McDonald, Michael. 2009. "The Return of the Voter: Voter Turnout in the 2008 Presidential Election." *The Forum* 6, no. 4. www.bepress.com/forum/vol6/iss4/art4.

Medvic, Stephen K. 2001. *Political Consultants in U.S. Congressional Elections.* Columbus: Ohio State University Press.

———. 2006. "Understanding Campaign Strategy: 'Deliberate Priming' and the Role of Professional Political Consultants." *Journal of Political Marketing* 5: 11–32.

Napolitan, Joseph. 1972. The *Election Game and How to Win It.* New York: Doubleday.

Nelson, Candice J., David A. Dulio, and Stephen K. Medvic. 2002. *Shades of Gray: Perspectives on Campaign Ethics.* Washington, D.C.: Brookings Institution.

Popkin, Samuel. 1991. *The Reasoning Voter: Communication and Persuasion in Presidential Campaigns.* Chicago: University of Chicago Press.

Rove, Karl. 2008. "Obama's Money Advantage." *Polling News and Notes*, December 11.

Sabato, Larry J. 1981. *The Rise of Political Consultants: New Way of Winning Elections.* New York: Basic Books.

Schaffner, Brian F. 2008. "Obama's Ground Game Advantage in Key States." Pollster.com, December 8. www.pollster.com/blogs/obamas_ground_game_advantage_i.php.

Schaper, David. 2007. "'Camp Obama' Trains Campaign Volunteers." National Public Radio, June 12. www.npr.org/templates/story/story.php?storyId=11012254.

Scherer, Michael. 2008. "A Campaign Postmortem at Harvard." *Time*, December 12. www.time.com/time/politics/article/0,8599,1866093,00.html.

Shea, Daniel M. 1996. *Campaign Craft: The Strategies, Tactics, and Art of Political Campaign Management.* Westport, CT: Praeger.

Thurber, James. 1998. "The Study of Campaign Consultants: A Subfield in Search of a Theory," in *PS: Political Science & Politics* 32, no. 2 (June): 145–149.

———. 2001. *The Battle for Congress: Consultants, Candidates, and Voters.* Washington, D.C.: Brookings Institution.

Thurber, James, and Candice J. Nelson. 2000. *Campaign Warriors: Political Consultants in Elections*. Washington, D.C.: Brookings Institution.

Thurber, James, and Candice J. Nelson, eds. 2004. *Campaigns and Elections American Style*. Boulder: Westview.

Thurber, James A., David B. Magleby, and Kelly D. Patterson. 2002. "Campaign Consultants and Responsible Party Government," in John C. Green and Paul S. Herrnson (eds.), *Responsible Partisanship? The Evolution of American Political Parties Since 1950*. Lawrence, KS: University of Kansas Press.

Thurber, James, Candice J. Nelson, and David A. Dulio, eds. 2000. *Crowded Airwaves: Campaign Advertising in Elections*. Washington, D.C.: Brookings Institution.

Thurber, James A., Alicia Kelor Prevost, and Maik Bohne. 2008. "Campaign Consultants and Political Parties Today," in *The Routledge Handbook of Political Management*. New York: Routledge.

2

Creating a Winning Campaign Strategy

David Winston

Introduction

More than twenty years ago, I was sitting at my desk at the National Republican Congressional Committee watching a show on C-Span. It was a lecture on targeting by Democrat Mark Gersh at American University's Campaign Management Institute. Later I discovered he was the Democratic Party's leading expert on redistricting and targeting. For the next two hours, I sat fascinated by what Mark had to say; by the time he finished, I had learned the fundamentals of targeting through the prism of the opposition party. This turned out to be a valuable perspective indeed. For the past three national elections, Mark and I have been the Democratic and Republican analysts for CBS, calling races on election night. We've become friends and colleagues, and I laugh about the origins of my targeting education. He doesn't find it quite as funny.

My point is that strategy, like targeting and other elements of campaign management, is partisan in terms of implementation but not definition. The principles of good strategy apply equally to Republicans and Democrats. The harder question to answer is, What is strategy? A lot has been written and said about this sometimes confusing but central component of a winning campaign, whether the strategy is designed for the beaches of Normandy or for a congressional district in Long Beach.

My favorite maxim about strategy was written by Sun Tzu, the fifth-century author of the *Art of War*: "Strategy without tactics is the slowest route to victory. Tactics without strategy is the noise before defeat." Two thousand years later, when it comes to strategy, not much has changed.

There are as many definitions of strategy as there are strategists, but here is mine:

> Strategy is achieving a desired outcome using a structured approach based on understanding existing and potential environmental elements.

This chapter focuses on the foundation of a winning campaign: strategy. Crafting a successful strategy takes good instincts; an understanding of politics; historical context; and detailed, quantifiable, and qualitative research.

Driving the process are four key steps that the campaign manager must undertake with support from the candidate, the campaign's consultants, and other key players.

- Define a desired outcome
- Develop situational awareness
- Define a winning coalition
- Create a strategic communications plan

After taking these steps, this same group must agree on the final strategy and get behind it to achieve success.

"Think New"

Before leaping into the process of putting together a winning strategy, every campaign manager must avoid the natural tendency to think as we have always thought. Remember the early critics who scoffed at the

Obama campaign's decision to change the dynamics of the presidential race by expanding the pool of participants? That was a strategic decision that took some new thinking.

History backs up this idea. In the 1930s, the French General Staff hoped to discourage a German invasion by building the Maginot Line. The French embraced a "static defense" that was based on what they had learned in World War I. The Germans, focusing on the future, outthought them by developing a strategic doctrine based on mobility, which completely overwhelmed the French strategy.

Now, fast-forward to the 2008 election. While the McCain campaign was busy running a base strategy, as George W. Bush had done successfully in 2000 and 2004, Barack Obama understood that the political environment had changed dramatically over the past four years and crafted a strategy that would leave the GOP scratching its collective head, wondering what happened. In both examples, the losers clung to the past while the successful strategists beat their opponents by "thinking new."

Break the Rules

One of the ways to think new is to break the rules. Here's what I mean. See if you can solve the following puzzle, but be warned. Solving it takes some new thinking.

Here's the task: Connect the nine dots with three lines but do it without lifting your pen or pencil from the paper.

Here's the answer.

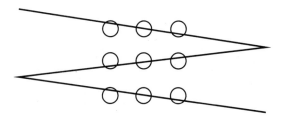

This is tritely but accurately called the "outside the box" solution. Most people fail to find the answer because they instinctively view the nine dots as a box and internally create a rule that says, "stay in the box." An important structural element is at work here. To solve the puzzle, you have to consciously decide to break rules and do things differently. Breaking rules is one of the critical elements of being creative.

For example, before Bill Frist became a U.S. senator, he was one of the preeminent heart research surgeons in the world. He was part of the extraordinary team at Stanford that found the answer to how to implant a heart and keep the body from rejecting it. Other researchers had managed to implant hearts before, but the patients lasted only days or weeks. The Stanford team decided to break the rules. They asked, How do we ratchet down antibodies so they don't do what they are supposed to do long enough for the body to accept the new heart and then restore the antibodies back to working capacity? No one had tried it before. It was outside the box thinking. It worked and changed medicine and many people's lives forever.

Change Perspective
Another way to think new is by changing your perspective. Here's another puzzle to try. Remove three sticks and leave four.

If you look at this puzzle as a group of objects, you won't solve it. If you can transition your thought process to view it as a graphic, you can find the answer. Here it is.

Thinking new is often the crucial missing component in failed strategies. The McCain presidential campaign lost, in part, because of a dated perspective that was especially ineffective up against an opposing campaign that embraced all things new.

The McCain campaign looked at the country as a collection of red, blue, and purple states, each with its own potential as a McCain victory state. The campaign focused on the 2000 and 2004 presidential contests when it should have been analyzing what happened in the 2006 elections. The answer would have led them to adopt a different kind of strategy.

In 2006, the Republican majority coalition fell apart. The GOP lost ground with a number of key constituencies—married women with children, middle income voters, independents, and Catholics. The impact of these demographic losses in important states was obvious. For example, Republicans lost Catholics by eleven points nationally. That kind of margin meant that reelecting Senator Rick Santorum in Pennsylvania and Senator Mike Dewine in Ohio were uphill battles.

The results in 2006 should have set off alarm bells. Instead, the McCain people decided to run a tactical, base-focused campaign. The strategy was to get out the base in large numbers everywhere, appeal to certain targeted constituencies in key electoral states like Catholics in Ohio and Pennsylvania, and cobble together an Electoral College victory much as Bush had done.

The campaign failed to understand that voters in what I call the "big middle" had abandoned the GOP in 2006 and nothing had happened in the interim to bring them back. A nationalized campaign to reach and attract those voters was their only hope of victory. The McCain campaign should have changed perspective, looked beyond the base, and found a strategy to rebuild the Republican coalition.

Even with a great direct mail operation, a world-class voter turnout effort, and smart television buys, if a campaign can't put together a majority coalition, it doesn't know how to win. It's like building a house. Without a blueprint, a great crew and first-rate tools don't matter.

Finally, when it comes to new thinking, it's important to understand that every manager embarks on a campaign with personal biases.

That's not necessarily good or bad. It's just a fact. We all grow up in different places, in different families with different views and values, go to different schools, and have a variety of friends and influencers.

The key is to recognize your biases and incorporate them in a way that expands your options but does not limit your decisions. For example, I was once a senior fellow for statistical analysis at the Heritage Foundation, so I view issues through the prism of conservative economics. That perspective would be in total sync with most Republican candidates I might work for. But if I were a campaign manager for a Republican running on the Upper West Side of Manhattan, I would have to factor that bias out of my decision making because most people in that area probably wouldn't agree with me. It's important to remember. The campaign manager is not the candidate. The manager's job is to help get the candidate elected.

Step 1:
Define a Desired Outcome

Now that you have your head in the right place, ready to think new and act differently, the first step on the journey to a winning strategy is settling on a "desired outcome": your goal. In the business world, it could be increasing sales by 10 percent. In college, it might be getting a 4.0 grade point average. In political races, it usually means winning the election by a 50 percent plus one margin. Political outcomes are a little easier to determine (if not to achieve) than most. Your goal could be a number higher than 50 percent, but in most political contests, the desired outcome is no more complicated than setting a winning percentage. But whatever the strategy—in politics, business, the nonprofit sector, or even war—the key to defining a successful outcome is to ask the right questions. Do you define your goal clearly and does your strategic plan go on to achieve it?

In politics, the goal may seem obvious but sometimes we ask the wrong questions.

A good example is the Gore 2000 campaign. Its goal was winning the majority of the popular vote. It achieved the goal but lost the election be-

cause it lost sight of the electoral map. It didn't consider a what-if scenario for a popular vote win but an Electoral College loss.

In 2008 the Hillary Clinton campaign's desired outcome was winning the delegate-rich primary states. The campaign succeeded but didn't count on the cumulative numerical advantage of the caucus states, the proportional nature of Democratic Party nominating rules, and the media attention Obama gained with caucus victories.

Here are some examples of asking the right questions.

In 1994 Newt Gingrich decided to ask why the GOP should continue to run campaigns based on the notion that "all politics is local." After all, it was Democratic Speaker Tip O'Neill who coined the phrase. Gingrich answered his question by deciding to nationalize the 1994 congressional elections. He broke all kinds of Republican doctrine that dictated candidates win locally, one race at a time. He picked up over fifty seats in one election.

In 2006 DCCC Chair Rahm Emanuel looked at the playing field and said, in essence, "If there are only thirty competitive seats, we can't win." Democrats won that election because Emanuel asked the right question: "How can we turn forty more seats into competitive contests?" He tasked Mark Gersh with finding them. Ultimately, expanding the field, coupled with a favorable political environment, allowed Democrats to win back the Congress. Other factors were important—fund-raising, candidate recruitment—but Emanuel changed the dynamics of the election cycle when he asked the key question.

Step 2:
Develop Situational Awareness

For most nonpresidential races, the bottom line is pretty simple: get the strategy right by developing a winning coalition, which takes us back to the second half of my definition of strategy: using a structured approach based on an understanding of the existing and potential environmental elements.

To do that, campaigns must engage in something called "situational awareness." The U.S. Navy defines it as "the degree of accuracy by which one's perception of his current environment mirrors reality." In politics, your ability to assess the environment will determine, in large part, whether your campaign succeeds or fails. To understand situational awareness, a campaign manager must begin with an analysis of the *existing* elements that impact the political environment.

Assessing the Existing Elements

Party Registration/Identification

First and foremost, you must know the party registration and identification numbers for your race by heart. This is an absolute necessity. The numbers tell you the size of your voter pool—how many Republicans, Democrats, and independents—and where to find them. Without these basic numbers at the core of your strategy, you cannot win.

The wider the gap in party registration/identification numbers, the less chance a party has to compete. Maryland is a good example. There the party registration is about 2 to 1 Democratic. Even a good Republican Senate candidate like Michael Steele in 2006 couldn't overcome the Democrats' registration advantage in a bad Republican year.

There can be rare exceptions. In the 2006 election, Florida congressman Mark Foley's solidly Republican seat, which under normal circumstances would not have made Emanuel's target list, was won by a Democrat thanks to the sex scandal that broke just before the election. Similarly, in 2008 Louisiana's 2nd District, a solid Democratic seat, was won by a Republican, when incumbent congressman William Jefferson was caught with $90,000 in his freezer.

But in races with a narrow registration gap, party registration/identification numbers become all-important.

Previous Political Behavior

Both parties focus on reaching and turning out their base, as they should. But nationally and in most states, neither party has a sufficient electoral majority to win without looking at the big middle. One way to do that is to analyze previous political behavior.

Voters' past political behavior provides a gold mine of information to help develop strategic targeting. This data can answer questions like,

What was the historical turnout in past elections? How has that turnout differed in presidential and nonpresidential election years and how has one party benefited from these patterns? What kinds of candidates have generally won in this area? Is this a ticket-splitting area?

Answering this last question is particularly important because certain areas in the country have a history of ticket splitting. Ticket splitters, who may be registered Republicans, Democrats, or independents, vote for candidates in both parties. They make up the big middle and should never be taken for granted. Virginia has a large number of ticket splitters. Over the past few years, voters in Virginia, which had been reliably Republican, have elected Democrats as governor and more recently to both Senate seats. Anyone looking at previous political behavior wouldn't have been surprised to see Virginia, or Indiana, become a battleground state in the 2008 presidential contest. In 2006 Indiana voters gave three Republican-held congressional seats to the Democrats. Obviously something was happening with Indiana voters, and it paid off when Obama won the state, the first Democrat since 1964.

When looking at past political behavior, remember that any targeting strategy should reflect ticket splitters. Years of election data and exit poll results have shown that most Republicans get at least 10 percent of the Democratic vote and most Democrats get at least 10 percent of the Republican vote. When you include independents, nationally ticket splitters are somewhere in the neighborhood of 25–30 percent of the electorate.

Precinct data can show where swing voters are found. But that's only half the analysis. The next step is to discover who the voters in your election are and what they care about.

Demographics

A demographic analysis of an election district provides "up close and personal" information on voters by such factors as race (e.g., African American, white, Asian, Latino), income level, sex, age, and religion. The importance of demographics varies according to the nature of the election district, the candidates, and current key issues.

In Florida districts, for example, age is a significant demographic. In urban districts and, more recently, in southwestern and western areas, race is a key demographic. The demographic makeup is critical because these groups tend to share common experiences, values, and issue positions. For example, Latinos are concerned about education, jobs, and immigration policy. Women may be concerned with security, the economy, education, and health care. Analyzing demographics helps you identify issues that concern target voter groups and connect your candidate with these key voters.

There are two main sources for demographic information. The Census Bureau can give you information on everything from the number of women 55+ in your area to the number of low income voters. It can provide data on race, age, sex, income, and union participation, to name a few. It does not have information on religious affiliation.

The other source for good demographic information is your state's voter files as well as files made available by the two parties at both the national and state level.

These sources will become your references of choice as you put real numbers behind your target groups.

Issues Currently in Play

The 2008 presidential contest was overwhelmingly about one issue: the economy. The McCain campaign, however, argued that the contest wasn't about issues but experience and in so doing forgot one of the cardinal rules of campaigns and elections: issues matter. In the 2008 election, voters wanted a president who understood their concerns and offered solutions to address them. The McCain campaign thought the election was about defining Obama. The Obama campaign thought it was about the economy. Is it any surprise, then, who won?

In developing a winning strategy, campaigns and candidates must address the issues people care about or risk irrelevancy. A party that is overly focused on its base, especially in races other than presidential campaigns, often only emphasizes issues that don't reflect what the majority of voters worry about on a day-to-day basis.

That doesn't mean base issues aren't important, but to put together a majority coalition requires an issue matrix that focuses on broader issues that matter to both the base and the big middle. This is where survey research can provide crucial issue information by political areas, by demographic categories, and by geography to help you reach your winning coalition of targeted voters.

Strengths and Weaknesses:
Your Candidate and Your Opponent
Every candidate has strengths and weaknesses that must be identified and agreed upon before a campaign strategy is crafted. This takes both courage by campaign managers and a sense of reality. Again, look at the last presidential race. An honest assessment of Obama would have found his speaking ability a great strength; his lack of experience, a weakness. A similar critique of McCain would have shown his experience as his main strength and his self-admitted lack of knowledge about the economy as his weakness. Putting together a candid assessment of the candidate's and the opponent's strengths and weaknesses is the final but critical last step in understanding the *existing* political environment and its likely impact on the campaign. If you don't know that, you don't know how to win. It's like a fighter pilot who says, "I don't care what the enemy does. I'm going to fly as effectively and efficiently as possible." How long would that pilot last in combat? A campaign isn't much different.

Assessing the Potential Elements

Once you have analyzed the existing elements impacting the political environment, it is time to assess the *potential* elements that may affect the political environment. This critical exercise in making knowledge-based assumptions begins by asking the right questions. Start with these.

What Are Future Issues Likely to Be?
In assessing the current political environment, survey research provides the most reliable and current analysis of voter concerns. The issue mix, however, can change over time. Who would have guessed a couple of years ago that by the fall of 2008 the war in Iraq would rank behind a housing crisis, high gas prices, and a collapse on Wall Street? As you write your campaign strategy, you should focus on two or three major issues. But it's also important to make assumptions about whether that current issue mix is likely to stay the same or change and explain why.

As with current issues, survey research can give you some sense of where the electorate could move. All of us have gut feelings about major issues. We can also get a sense from news coverage and listening to the opposition about potential issues. Early in the campaign cycle, it's wise to think about other potential issues, have a "plan B" in the desk drawer, and be ready to pivot if a new issue arises.

What in the Environment Is Likely to Change
or Is an Unknown and What Will Remain the Same?

Crystal balls don't work, but we can make some educated assumptions about the political environment. For example, last spring, assuming that George Bush's high negative job approval ratings would remain a significant factor in the fall election was a pretty good bet. The McCain campaign should have accounted for this likely situation by making a painful but necessary strategic decision to separate the candidate from an unpopular president.

In the same race, the African American turnout and the youth vote were other unknowns. Both groups were important to an Obama victory. It was safe to assume they would go to the polls in higher numbers. But how high was the key question. Republicans failed to understand the importance of the youth vote, once again relying on television to reach voters. Had they assumed a higher youth vote, their strategic communications strategy would have included the kind of new technologies that are the conduits for conversations with this voter group.

In 2004 the Kerry campaign assumed his war record would not be a major issue and could be dealt with tactically. Had they assumed the opposite, they might have handled the situation strategically and changed the dynamic of the race.

What Weaknesses and Strengths in
Both Candidates Are Likely to be Important?

By this point, you have put together what is likely to be a long list of strengths and weaknesses for your candidate and your opponent. At this point the manager must pare down the list to the strengths and weaknesses that are likely to matter in the election.

In 1992 Bill Clinton's admission that he smoked marijuana was a weakness. So was his inexperience, but only the inexperience became a serious issue. For his opponent, President George H. W. Bush, his strength was his foreign policy experience, but it gained him little in the election because voters were focused on the economy.

Your campaign must hone in on the two or three strengths and weaknesses of each candidate that will be most important to voters, given the political context of the election. This is crucial to a winning strategy.

What Is the Impact of the National Brands of Both Parties and Other Political Races?

A bad national party brand or a tsunami of a campaign like Barack Obama's can have a major impact on other campaigns. In 1980 Jimmy Carter's disastrous economy gave Ronald Reagan a huge win as Republicans won the Senate and picked up thirty-four seats in the House. In 1994 Democratic congressional scandals and Bill Clinton's policy mistakes in his first year as president combined to form the perfect political storm, and Republicans gained control of the House for the first time in forty years. The negative national Democratic brand simply overwhelmed many of their candidates that year.

In 2006 it was the Republicans' turn. Hurricane Katrina, the faltering war in Iraq, congressional overspending, and Republicans' inability to get things done downgraded the GOP brand to a point where Democrats were able to regain both the House and the Senate. Winning in a difficult environment is possible, but a realistic assessment of the impact of these outside factors must be part of the situational awareness process.

Step 3: Defining a Winning Coalition

Once you have a comprehensive picture of the political environment, you have achieved situational awareness and it's time to move to the next step: defining a winning coalition.

Start by precisely defining your coalition. This means more than simply coming up with vote totals. A precise definition requires knowing how many voters it will take to win, but you must also know who those voters are and where they are found. How many married women with children? How many Hispanics? How many Catholics? You must put both percentages and hard numbers behind the target groups.

Next, determine which groups are reliably in your column and how you will hold them. Past political behavior and survey research are critical here. For Republicans, at the moment, this is more difficult because of losses among swing voters in the past two elections. Conservatives fall into this category, which remains a larger group than self-identified liberals, according to the 2008 exit polls. Evangelical Christians also remain reliably Republican. For Democrats, liberals, African Americans, and, at least for the moment, eighteen- to twenty-nine-year-olds make up their most reliable voters.

Then, determine which groups are key swing groups and how to attract them. If you don't know who these groups are, find out. Survey research can tell you which groups offer your campaign the best opportunity and which the biggest challenge. It can also tell you what issues are of greatest concern to these voters and what messages will have the most resonance.

These are not mutually exclusive steps. One of the most difficult challenges campaigns face is appealing to both their base and the swing voters needed to reach a winning coalition.

Finally, predict what your opponent's coalition will look like and identify the friction points between the two campaigns. The single most important factor that will impact your strategy is your opponents' strategy. So, figuring out how they might win and how you think you can win will give you the overlay—the playing field where the contest will take place.

For example, in 2008, when Obama began talking about a middle class tax cut, he was going after voters who made $50,000 to $75,000 per year. In 2004 Republicans had won this group by ten points. The Obama campaign decided to pursue a GOP key target group, realizing the move would play on Republican turf. But Obama's strategic message on the issue *won the day. Exit polls showed that despite his liberal record and views, the Obama tax message worked with these voters and took away what had been a solid Republican advantage for decades.*

You must put your plan to build a winning coalition on paper. Your chart or spreadsheet should list the target groups, numerical and percentage vote goals, and the issues/message that will bring those voters into the fold. For a Republican congressional race, an abbreviated hypothetical coalition might look something like this:

Target Group	Goal (%)	Issue/Message	Vote Total
Reg. Republicans	92	Economy/national security	121,400
Independents	52	Economy	58,240
Women 55+	50	Health care	44,000
50–75K	55	Economy	48,400

For Democrats, those boxes might include registered Democrats, African Americans, single women, union workers, or a host of other possible targets. Geography can be a target "group" (i.e., selected counties or precincts) if a particular area behaves in a unique fashion. But remember that other demographics may have more impact on voters' political behavior than where they live. For example, eighteen- to twenty-nine-year-olds in Tampa probably have more in common with eighteen- to twenty-nine-year-olds at Ohio State than with the eighty-year-old couple across the street. Given the current communications environment where political discourse has become nationalized thanks to cable and the Internet, geography is becoming a lesser factor in targeting. When putting together a coalition, remember that there will be overlap. Many voters will be found in more than one group. Many independents will be in the $50,000 to $75,000 group as well. Don't overcount.

The Weakness of a Base Strategy

Thanks to redistricting, a significant number of congressional districts, both Republican and Democratic, are relatively safe seats. In those races, a base strategy, in which the base is large enough to provide the numbers needed to win, may work. But for many races—local, congressional, statewide, and presidential—neither party's base is large enough to win outright. The voters who will push a campaign into the win column will be found in the middle. Don't make the mistake of assuming that the base alone can win the race.

Create a Strategic Communications Plan

Strategy Versus Tactics

Once the campaign has identified the groups that make up a winning coalition, the next step is to develop an effective message. But don't mistake tactics for strategy. Strategy includes elements like defining the political environment, understanding the opponent's strategy, developing messages to reach them. Tactics are methods for delivering the message and reaching voters like direct mail, phone banks, social networks, scheduling, advertising, and Internet. Think of the process as a little like building a home. Strategy is like an architectural plan that reflects the wants and needs of the buyer and the environment in which the house will be built. Tactics are the tools to build the house.

Strategy creates context for tactical decisions. Don't buy an ad because you think you should buy an ad. Do it for a reason.

Survey Research: Reaching Voters with an Effective Message

During your situational awareness phase, survey research can be a major source of crucial information about voter concerns. You may also be able to gather information from public polls and other resources. But as you put together strategic messaging, internal survey research is critical because it helps you listen to voters, learn what they're thinking, figure out how to help them at a policy level, and then develop a message for the candidate so he or she can lead. All candidates have a series of issue positions. Surveys should not be used to decide a candidate's position on issues but to assess the strength of a particular issue with a particular group. If one of your target groups is married women with children, survey research can identify their number one issue and the components of that issue. For example, it could be gas prices or the cost of health care. It could be worries about how to pay for college when falling stock prices have decimated the college fund. Survey research can tell you which issues to emphasize with each of your target groups and gives you the ability to test the effectiveness of your candidate's issue messages and those of your opponent.

Strategic Communications

David Ogilvy, a giant of modern advertising, said, "The results of your campaign depend less on how we write your advertising than on how your product is positioned." Ultimately, it is a candidate's positions, not money, not consultants, and not campaign managers, that will make or break a campaign. Does anyone think that Barack Obama would have won the Democratic nomination if he had supported the war in Iraq? Equally interesting, two of the Republican candidates in the primaries who raised and spent the least came in first and second—John McCain and Mike Huckabee. Positioning matters.

When developing a strategy, it's important to do an analysis comparing the strategic messaging for your campaign and your opponent's. It's called a communications matrix, and it's an exercise to help you predict what the debate will look like in the months ahead. The matrix looks like this.

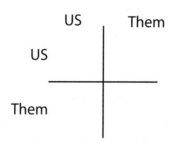

The first quadrant is what are you are going to say about your candidate. What are you going to emphasize about his or her issue positions with the key groups identified in your winning coalition? The second quadrant reflects what you are going to say about your opponent. The third quadrant is what the opponent will say about your candidate and finally what the opponent will say about himself or herself.

This tool gives you a starting point for a campaign discussion, based on the issues you want to talk about. Once the communications matrix is completed, you take the potential messages from each quadrant and test them using survey research to determine who wins the battle of strategic messaging. If candidate A says, for example, "The economy is on the verge of catastrophe. We need the $800 billion stimulus bill," and candidate B says, "The country is facing tough economic times, but tax cuts for small business to create jobs is the answer, not spending billions for pet projects," what happens? Strategic communications is the single most important element of your strategy because winning campaigns are all about delivering a well-constructed argument as to why voters should choose their candidate.

Voter's Memory Process

Political strategic communications are impacted by what is called the voter's memory process. Average people respond to three triggers that determine whether something is remembered or not. First, issues that interest them. Recently the economy has swamped all other issues, and voters remember what candidates have to say or not say when it comes to their economic plans for the country.

The second type of memory is what I call a sudden dramatic change; 9/11 is a good example of a searing memory that results from a highly emotional, vivid experience. Politically, we saw soccer moms suddenly become security moms as they watched people die in real time on television. Polls at the time showed the national security/defense issue, which had been at 4 or 5 percent, jump to 25 percent. The Breslan school terrorist in September 2004 incident is another example of a dramatic moment that voters, especially women with children, remembered as they cast their vote for president that fall.

The third memory trigger is, in reality, no trigger at all. The very fact that the vast majority of voters simply aren't consumed by politics while many politicians run ads based on what interests them rather than the voters explains the failure of so much political advertising/messaging on both sides. People don't remember what doesn't interest them.

For example, I am not interested in quilting. You could create the most compelling ad about quilting ever made and I wouldn't remember the message. A lot of political messages are the advertising equivalent of a quilting ad. When the ads don't work, campaigns simply crank up the buy or pump up the volume with a harsher tone.

It's a little like the storied American tourist traveling in France who doesn't speak the language. So he talks slowly and loudly, and then is frustrated when the locals still don't understand him. Too much of what passes for strategic campaign communications today is based on this methodology. Moreover, too many campaigns don't understand why they're not getting through to voters and as a result spend even more money to fund ineffective messages.

If the challenge of every campaign is to develop a communications strategy and message that engages voters, then it must reflect the most important element of strategic communications—getting the issue mix right. Here is an example of a Republican strategic communications effort that worked because it addressed high gas prices, a key concern of voters in the summer of 2008.

With the ban on offshore drilling scheduled to be lifted at the end of the fiscal year, the question facing the House was whether to extend the ban or let it expire. The Democrats' liberal leadership had a record of inflexibility when it came to drilling and maintained its antidrilling views even with gas prices going through the roof. Democrats had the votes to extend the ban, but they didn't count on a concerted strategic communications effort by House Republicans who had long opposed the ban as a roadblock to energy independence, lower prices, and national security.

Republican leaders argued for an "all of the above" energy policy that included drilling along with more funding for other energy sources like wind, solar, and biofuels. They drove home the point with assistance from vocal advocates for the policy like Newt Gingrich; and within weeks, polling data showed the majority of Americans now favored off-shore drilling.

Democrats got the message, and despite their antidrilling views and the fact that they had the votes in Congress to extend the ban, they decided to quietly let the ban expire. They didn't even take a vote. While 2008 wasn't a good year for Republicans, exit polls showed that Republicans did win voters for whom energy was the top issue. The Republican victory on the energy issue didn't result from an attack campaign against the Democratic leadership but rather a strategic campaign to offer voters a positive policy alternative on an issue that interested them. If you've got the right issue, the right position, and the right message, it is possible to win even as the minority.

Means End Theory of Communications: Laddering

Engagement is the name of the game in strategic communication. But how do you make a personal connection with a voter who may be interested in the campaign but more likely is not? One method is called laddering. It is a process of seeing issues in a way that connects your campaign and candidate with voters and their values through language. On paper, it looks like this:

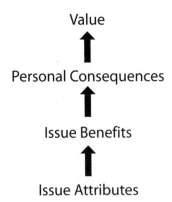

- Issue attributes are various policy components of the issue.
- Issue benefits are the results of the policy—the outcome.

- Personal consequences are the ways in which the outcome affects voters personally.
- Value is how the consequences mesh with voters' life goals.

In practice, here's how laddering works with a real issue: a 5 percent tax cut. To reach a more conservative voter, the language laddering might go like this:

Issue	Favor a 5 percent tax cut.
Issue benefit	"You will have more money in your pocket."
Personal consequences	"You can afford your child's education."
Value	"You are a good parent."

For a more liberal voter on the same issue, the laddering might go like this:

Issue	Oppose a 5 percent tax cut.
Issue benefit	"The government gets to keep more resources it needs to help people."
Personal consequences	"More low-income elderly can get better health care."
Value	"You're a good citizen."

Both of these examples show how to approach issues in a way that goes far beyond a policy discussion to create a personal connection between an issue and a voter's values, something that is important to him or her.

Allocating Resources

Reaching voters is not inexpensive. Whether it's through TV ads, paid television media, earned media, or new technologies, making that personal connection to voters through shared values is likely going to be the most costly part of any campaign budget. As you do your targeting, as you put together a potentially winning coalition, put a dollar figure on the cost of reaching each target group. You must know not only who you are going to reach and what you are going to say to them, but how you're going to reach them, how much it will cost, and whether you can raise the necessary funds. If not, go back to the drawing board.

Managing Strategy

Once a strategy is defined, too many campaigns assume that is how it's all going to play out. Winston Churchill said of strategy, "However beautiful the strategy, you should occasionally look at the results."

The military has a useful management tool that can help you manage your strategy. It's called an OODA loop:

- Observe
- Orient
- Decide
- Act

After you've begun to implement your strategy, the next step is to observe how your strategy is performing. This often begins by doing survey research, which provides a statistically based analysis of the campaign's impact and progress. From those observations, you move on to the next stage: orienting, determining what has worked and what needs changing. Orienting is the process of developing options that move your strategy forward.

From those options, you decide which actions to take and then you execute. Then you return to observation to see the impact of your actions and repeat the process. The faster a campaign can employ an OODA loop kind of self-assessment, the greater chance the campaign has to stay a step ahead of its opponents.

Campaigns that lack an effective strategy based on the elements I have described in this chapter are unlikely to be successful. In 2006 Republican leaders operated on the assumption that it would not be a national election and success depended on turning out the base. Strategically, they couldn't have been more wrong. It was obvious months before the election that it was going to be nationalized and that a base turnout would not be sufficient to win. It didn't matter if the GOP turnout operation was better. It didn't matter if the television ads were better. The strategic assumptions were wrong, and Republicans lost badly.

Once again, "Strategy without tactics is the slowest route to victory. Tactics without strategy is the noise before defeat." Without a viable strategy based on a winning coalition, a campaign can make a lot of noise but is unlikely to make the kind of progress needed to win.

3

The Use of
Survey Research
in Campaigns

Glen Bolger

Introduction

In a campaign, the most important use of polling is as a planning tool, not as a predictor. The predictive value of polling generally gets the most attention from the press, but campaign operatives use polling to make a whole host of decisions throughout the race. Tweaking targeting, modifying message, and reallocating resources are all decisions made with the help of polling.

This is not to slight the predictive capabilities of polling. In 2008 the remarkable aspect of the predictive abilities of polling was not the few instances where it was wrong (such as the New Hampshire Democratic presidential primary), but how often it was right. For instance, of the fifty-four races I polled in October 2008, the last survey in those races was on the mark in fifty-three of them. As I look back, the only race that I felt the polling was off the mark had the right winner, but the campaign was much closer than expected given the polling.

Most of the polling that I'm aware of from 2008 (either from public polls or postelection discussions) was very accurate. That's remarkable given the difficulty in projecting turnout in the truly unique 2008 campaign, and the rise in cell phone–only voters.

This digression into the predictive nature of polling is not to pat the industry on its collective back. There are times when polling fails to pick up late movement in a campaign or incorrectly models turnout of different partisan or ethnic groups. Instead, the digression is to ensure that the topic of accuracy is not ducked. After all, pollsters who work for campaigns have a huge economic incentive to be accurate. Inaccurate partisan pollsters will soon run out of clients as word of their inaccuracy gets around.

A Brief History . . . And a Look Ahead

A brief history of political polling underscores that the industry is still scarred by a pair of seminal events early in its history. The first—the *Literary Digest* fiasco of 1936 predicting the election of Alf Landon over Franklin D. Roosevelt based on a postcard survey of its readers— happened around the same time that George Gallup was honing the techniques of random polling that used a more demographically representative sample. So, at the same time a huge "sampling" was wrong, a much smaller but statistically based sampling was on the mark.

The second infamous event is the prediction that Thomas Dewey would defeat Harry Truman. The prediction was based on a survey done by Gallup three weeks prior to the 1948 election and is still cited by critics as an example of the inaccuracy of polling. Indeed polling can be inaccurate. However, the 1948 debacle taught pollsters and campaign operatives that campaigns matter, that undecided voters are crucial, and that the campaign isn't over until the last ballot has been cast. There is little doubt that Truman was behind for most of the 1948 election, but that he garnered momentum by hitting on a focused message just about the time swing voters were really focusing on the choice. The Gallup poll may have been right at the time, but events during the campaign caused opinion to shift. Of course, the "Dewey Defeats Truman" photo is one of the most famous touchstones in American political history.

At the same time as Gallup was developing his methods and reputation, Elmo Roper was improving polling techniques. Political polling was boosted by Lou Harris, who became the first truly national political pollster by working for John F. Kennedy's presidential campaign in 1956, the first time a presidential campaign had ever hired a pollster to work for it. Up until that point, the campaigns had followed the polls in the press. Harris worked mostly for Democrats, but also polled for a few Republican candidates.

Harris veered away from polling for campaigns and focused on polling for nonpolitical clients and for the press. The next step in campaign polling took a few more years, when Republican pollsters like Richard Wirthlin and the late Bob Teeter, as well as Democratic pollsters like Peter Hart and Pat Caddell, became known as crucial parts of a campaign team. These were the fathers of the modern political polling firm. They also did nonpolitical work, but their bread and butter was as polling gurus for their respective partisan clients. For example, Richard Wirthlin created the modern tracking poll, and Bob Teeter created dial testing of ads and debates.

Many of the polling firms in the political business today can trace their roots back to those earlier firms, as entrepreneurial people got experience there before leaving to start their own companies.

Nowadays, fifty-seven firms are listed as being in the business of polling in the *Political Pages*, a reference guide for campaigns published by *Politics* magazine (in the interest of full disclosure, my firm, Public Opinion Strategies has one of those listings).

Going forward, political pollsters face a myriad of challenges. Declining cooperation rates are driving up the costs of polling, which worries budget-conscious campaign managers. Voters who have cell phones only are a growing percentage of the electorate. These cell phone–only voters are much more expensive to survey (when even done at all). For example, surveying a cell phone–only respondent with a certain area code and prefix phone number (the first three digits after the area code) does not mean that respondent necessarily lives in the state legislative or congressional district that a pollster is sampling. The industry is spending a great deal of time and effort figuring out the direction that political polling is headed.

A number of political polling firms are testing blended methodologies, where they might do 85–90 percent of their sampling with traditional landline interviewing, and then the remaining 10–15 percent with either cell phones or on the Internet. The challenge with Internet polling is that Internet users are not reflective of the electoral as a whole. The Internet appears to be ubiquitous in American life, but it has not quite reached the penetration levels of television, for instance.

So, as in 1936, 1948, and 1960, political polling stands at a crossroads. The direction it is headed is difficult to predict, but it has become such a staple of modern campaigns that political survey research will adapt to the changing times.

The Four Elements of a Winning Campaign

There are four key elements to a winning campaign:

Candidate Quality

In a swing seat where both political parties have a roughly equal chance of winning, the better candidate generally wins the election. That's not necessarily true in a district that tilts more heavily to one party over the other, but in a bundle of toss-up races, where for instance partisan control of Congress is decided, the better candidate wins. The tricky part is understanding how voters decide who is the better candidate. Some years, such as 1994, 2006, or 2008, the decision is heavily weighted to the party perceived to not be totally screwing up Washington. In other years, such as 2000, 2002, and 2004, it is based primarily on voter judgment as to who is the better person and is more in tune with their values.

A variety of factors go into that sizing up, and it's clearly not the same standard of measure from race to race. If you watch C-Span, you'll note that few members of Congress look like the caricature of the media's typical blow-dried congressman. For every member of Congress with movie star looks, there are ten who look much more like ordinary Americans. Some members of Congress are articulate, while others are not. But somehow, either through working harder, hitting the right issue notes, or having a focused message that resonates, they convinced their voters that they were the better choice.

A Focused Message

Few campaign components matter more than focused messaging. Unfocused campaigns rarely win. In 1996 the popular Nebraska governor Ben Nelson started out as a heavy favorite over Chuck Hagel in the U.S. Senate race. However, Hagel and his campaign team had a disciplined message focused on fighting for lower taxes and Nebraska values. Nelson never had a message other than "you like me as governor, so send me to Washington." Hagel's message discipline allowed him to slingshot past Nelson. The Democrat's campaign began to flail, putting up a new ad with a new message seemingly every other day. To be fair, sometimes a campaign flails around for a message because nothing is working. Its opponent has run over it like a freight train, and nothing can fix that.

Candidates get off message in different ways. They may feel they need to talk about every issue to show how smart they are, or they take advice on their message from too many people and keep switching it up. It's okay early in a campaign to tinker with the message, but by Labor Day the campaign needs to exercise message discipline for the home stretch.

The need for a focused message is simple: campaigns never know when voters are going to pay attention to the race. Thus when swing voters tune in, it is best if they hear your strongest message. Do not use the presidential race as a model for other campaigns. The amount of attention that a presidential campaign receives is freakishly outsized. No campaign for any other office can come close to that level of attention. So don't assume voters know what you are trying to tell them as to why you should be elected. Instead, stay focused in your messaging.

Enough Money

The Bible notes that the race is not always to the fastest nor the battle to the strongest (Ecclesiastes). Noted writer Damon Runyon noted that may be true, but the fastest and the strongest is the way to bet. In politics the campaign with the most money usually wins, but not always. It is a rare challenger who wins by outspending the incumbent. (If so, it is simply the sign of a lazy or corrupt incumbent. Lazy because incumbents should never be out-raised, or corrupt because the incumbent is on the brink of going to jail and can't raise funds from anyone worried about associating with such a problem person.) But challengers do win occasionally. Similarly with open seats: generally the campaign that spends more wins, but not always.

A Strong Grassroots Operation

The volunteer component of a campaign often gets overlooked by political professionals, but a grassroots operation that combines the latest technology and old-fashioned voter contact is crucial in a close race.

Good polling helps shape the first two elements of the four elements of a winning campaign—candidate quality and having a focused message. Before conspiracy theorists shout "aha, I always knew polling is evil because it helps candidates be chameleons and hide their true nature," let me clarify. Good polling helps shape candidate quality by better understanding what aspects of a candidate's background and issue priorities resonate most with voters. It is very difficult to change a candidate's basic personality and charisma. Voters tend to see through phonies. However, given that nearly all campaigns have limited ability to communicate with voters, it is always best to highlight aspects of a candidate's background that matter most. Why spend money (a finite, very precious resource in most campaigns) highlighting something that doesn't matter to the voters?

So, while disappointing conspiracy theorists, polling helps a campaign winnow down a candidate's number of background points, thus improving the presentation of candidate quality to the voters. Polling can't give a candidate charisma, intelligence, or that innate ability to connect with people. But it can help keep the candidate and the message focused.

Why Do Campaigns Poll?

Good polling helps a campaign spend its resources more intelligently. A campaign faces many decisions, but it boils down to a simple formula: delivering the right message to the right target groups. Nearly every decision in a campaign revolves around one of those questions:

- What's our message (what do we say)? Thus polling is done to develop the communications and message strategy. HOW does the campaign get to 50 percent plus one (or whatever the goal is)?
- Who are our target groups (who do we say it to)? Thus polling is done to define the campaign's target audience. WHO does the campaign need to get to 50 percent plus one?

Rather than just guessing at target groups or hoping they've picked the right message, campaigns use polling to help refine those decisions. Just as the business adage says, "You've got to spend money to make money," a campaign must spend money on polling to better allocate the rest of its money in the long run. In a theme that will be revisited later in this chapter, why would a campaign spend money pushing a message that does not work, or why would a campaign spend money targeting groups that it either can't win over or already has? Polling helps avoid those mistakes.

There is a perception that politicians use polling excessively, leading them to make decisions they might not otherwise make. There is also a concern that politicians use polls to manipulate public opinion. Some of that may occur. However, it is far more limited than many may fear. In the twenty-four years I've been a pollster, there has only been a handful of times a member of Congress has ever called to talk through an issue before voting on it in the House or Senate. And even then, it wasn't to make the decision, but to gather more information to factor into a decision.

Incumbents use polling to help them make decisions about the campaign. Early polling is used to identify target groups, test themes and messages, and test accomplishments.

How Campaigns Use Polls

Here are eight good reasons to do polling in a campaign. They don't always apply all the time, but across a campaign, they generally do.

Measure the Mood of the Electorate

As both 2006 and 2008 showed, sometimes the political environment is far more powerful a factor than anything else in the campaign. However, trends are trends until they change. The political environment will be different in 2010 and other election years. The question is, What is the political environment, and how does it impact the campaign? Is there a mood for change? What is the partisan split in the electorate? What impact are the other races on the ticket having on your campaign? For example, in 2008 it was very important to profile Obama voters who were voting for the Republican incumbent. In the 6th Congressional District of Illinois, freshman Peter Roskam won reelection with 58 percent of the vote, despite the fact that Barack Obama won the district with 56 percent.

When we profiled the Obama-Roskam voters, we found:

- Thirty-three percent were GOPers, 30 percent were independents, and 36 percent were Dems.
- The majority (58 percent) were women.
- More than half (57 percent) were age 54 or younger.
- Ideologically, 47 percent were moderate, 29 percent were somewhat conservative, 24 percent were liberal, and just 4 percent were very conservative.
- Fully 54 percent were college graduates.

Questions that measure the political environment include:

"Would you say that things in the country are going in the right direction, or have they pretty seriously gotten off on the wrong track?"

"If the election for U.S. Senate were being held today, for whom would you vote . . . the Republican candidate . . . or . . . the Democratic candidate?"

"Do you approve or disapprove of the job Barack Obama is doing as President?"

"Do you approve or disapprove of the job the United States Congress is doing?"

Confirm Issues/Measure Intensity

It is rare that a survey will discover a "magic issue" that has not been part of the public debate thus far. Instead, issue questions are good for measuring:

- Overall attitudes
- Intensity
- Wording nuances
- Key target groups for those issues

Overall attitudes are important. If your candidate is on the right side of a 70 percent issue and your opponent is on the wrong side of that issue, usually it is a good one to drive. Highly polarized, 50-50 issues aren't nearly as good, unless the intensity is stronger on your side.

Sometimes with issue questions, it is good to split-sample (ask half the respondents one wording, and the other half a slightly different version) to see which framing of an issue resonates more.

Key target groups are important, because analyzing the cross-tabs tells campaigns which issues allow the campaign to be fought on their strength issues, and which issues benefit the opponent.

Examples of issue questions:
"Which ONE of the following issues is currently MOST important to you in deciding how to vote for U.S. Senate?"

Education

Taxes and spending

Social security and Medicare

Transportation and roads

Terrorism and national security

Health care reform and
    prescription drugs

The economy and jobs

Moral values

Illegal immigration

The war in Iraq

Gas and energy prices

The environment and
    global warming

"Which one of the following statements regarding the U.S. involvement in Iraq do you MOST agree with . . . "

The U.S. should immediately withdraw its troops from Iraq.

The U.S. should set a strict timetable for withdrawing troops from Iraq.

While I don't agree that the U.S. should be in the war, our troops should stay there until civil order is restored and the Iraqis can govern and provide security to their country.

... or ...

The Iraq War is the front line in the battle against terrorism and our troops should stay there until civil order is restored and the Iraqis can govern and provide security to their country.

"Now I would like to talk to you about the state of the economy. Would you describe the state of the nation's economy these days as ... Excellent ... Good ... Not so Good ... Poor?"

"How concerned are you about the issue of illegal immigration?"

Measure Name ID and Images

Many decisions about campaign strategy revolve around the name identification and images of the two candidates, as well as the images of other key players in the race.

The opening strategy in a race depends on whether the candidate is unknown, well-known, well liked, known but not well defined, or polarizing. It's helpful to ask an open-ended question about candidates who are well-known because it provides the campaign with the building blocks of a message. It's always easier to reinforce a perception voters already believe than to create a new perception.

Name ID/image questions:

Example 1

"Now, I would like to read you some names of different people active in politics here in South Dakota. For each one, please tell me, first, whether you've heard of the person; then, if so, please tell me whether you have a favorable or unfavorable impression of that person. If I name someone you don't know too much about, just tell me and we'll go on to the next one. The first name is . . . John Thune. The next name is . . . Tom Daschle. The next name is . . . Stephanie Herseth."

Example 2

"Thinking now just about John Thune . . . what are the first two or three things that come to mind about John Thune, that is, what is it you like MOST about him and what is it you like LEAST about him? What else can you tell me about that? Anything else?"

Test Potential Themes and Messages

Given the importance of having a focused message, surveys should test themes that the campaign is considering. There are a variety of ways to do this, but surveys can test everything from broader messages to specific slogans to see what resonates best.

Example 1

"Thinking some more just about Jim McCrery . . . I am going to read you a few statements, and after I read each one, please tell me if you think it describes Jim McCrery . . . VERY well, SOMEWHAT well, NOT VERY well, . . . or . . . NOT AT ALL well.

Is ethical and honest

Cares about people like you

Is out of touch with most people"

Example 2

"Now I would like to read you some of Chuck Hagel's accomplishments in the Senate, and for each one, using a ten-point scale, with ten being VERY IMPORTANT and one being NOT IMPORTANT AT ALL, please tell me how important each is to you personally. Of course, you can choose any number between one and ten.

Increasing local control of education and providing greater opportunities for our young people.

Increasing agricultural exports, reducing regulatory burdens on farmers, and providing assistance to farmers and ranchers to better manage their operations.

Providing for a strong national defense and improving our military, especially the quality of life for the men and women of the Armed Forces and their families."

Determine the Impact and Intensity of Vulnerabilities

This is the testing of both self and opposition research. Generally there are a lot of opposition research points to test; the survey can help discover which issues move voters. The cross-tabs will show which hits sway undecided voters, and which issues shore up support among weaker groups. Testing self research allows the campaign an advance peek at strategy—which hits they will absolutely push back on, and which attacks they will ignore.

Example 1

"Now I am going to read you some statements you might hear about Jerry Weller. And after I read each statement, please tell me if the statement makes you MORE likely or LESS likely to vote for Jerry Weller, or if it would make no difference to your vote.

Jerry Weller wrote the legislation that redeveloped the Joliet Arsenal. That legislation has revitalized and attracted jobs and businesses to the area. In fact, Walmart recently announced they will build a large warehouse facility there that will create another one thousand jobs.

Jerry Weller has authored alternative fuel legislation that will help move America away from dependence on foreign oil by replacing some of those imports with domestically produced ethanol made from corn and other renewable sources."

Example 2

"For whom would you vote if you learned that . . . (ROTATE)

Republican Jerry Weller supports making the recent tax cuts permanent, including repealing the death tax, ending the marriage penalty, cutting tax rates, and keeping the per child tax credit.

. . . while . . .

Democrat John Pavich opposes making the recent tax cuts permanent because he says the country is running a huge deficit and the tax cuts help only the rich, not the middle class."

Chart Movement During the Race
Overall and Among Subgroups

As the great boxer Joe Louis once said, "Everyone has a plan until they get hit in the face." When the battle is joined, it is imperative to track the race (whether it is monthly, weekly, or nightly depends on the race and the budget). It's important to know how much movement there is, which direction the movement is going, and among what target groups the campaign is gaining or losing ground with, so that assessments can be made about how to allocate remaining message and dollar resources.

In a 2008 U.S. Senate incumbent campaign in a conservative state where we had a comfortable lead, we polled almost weekly in September and then weekly in October. Our opponent was making gains with his positive TV ads, positioning himself as a conservative change agent. The movement by his campaign led us to switch gears and tell voters about the very liberal parts of his record that he was neglecting to talk about. Once he was fully exposed, his unfavorables skyrocketed, and his support dropped back down. We also shifted from weekly tracks to more often, just to ensure that the overall movement and key groups were where we needed them to be to ensure an easy victory.

Seen/Read/Heard Series

"Thinking some more about the upcoming election for United States Senate . . . Has what you've seen, read, or heard recently regarding Pete

Domenici or his campaign for the U.S. Senate given you a more favorable or less favorable impression of him? And, what was the source of this information?"

Table 3.1 Image Trend: Pete Domenici

Date	Name ID	Fav	Unfav
10/07	99%	80%	13%
08/29	98%	76%	16%
06/13	98%	81%	13%
05/16	97%	77%	14%
02/06	98%	81%	12%

Table 3.2 Ballot Trend: 2002 Election

03/01	02/06	05/16	06/13	08/29	10/07	10/28	
68%	71%	67%	71%	66%	67%	67%	TOTAL DOMENICI
18%	21%	25%	24%	25%	25%	27%	TOTAL TRISTANI

Determine the Impact of a Major Hit on Either (or Both) Candidates

Is an attack by your opponent hurting your campaign, or can you ignore it and keep the pressure on? What subgroups you are hurting with? When a heavy blow hits the campaign, it's important to get in the field quickly to decide how to handle it—respond or ignore, shift to defense, or stay on offense are key questions that face campaigns when a major punch has been thrown.

In a 2002 congressional race in a truly toss-up open seat district in Nevada, county commissioner Dario Herrera was the anointed one for the Democrats. A young, aggressive Hispanic who was a good fundraiser, Herrera was saluted by the pundits as all but a shoo-in. The district was new, as Nevada was expanding from two seats to three, and the seat was the product of a compromise between the Republicans who controlled the state Senate and the Democrats who controlled the General Assembly.

In the spring, Herrera was hit hard by corruption scandals in the press. Las Vegas is a difficult area to burn a message in through earned media, so we polled to see the impact of his scandals. Herrera's image had plummeted from 28 percent favorable/11 percent unfavorable in a survey done in January 2002 to 23 percent favorable/21 percent unfavorable. We released the survey, and his campaign tried to minimize it, saying that a bad newspaper story in March wasn't going to affect a November election. Given that we were going to run TV spots, we made sure it did affect the election, as Herrera only got 37 percent of the vote.

Example 1
"As you may know, last year, while he was a county commissioner and candidate for U.S. Congress, Dario Herrera received a no-bid $42,000 consulting fee from a political supporter who is the executive director of the Las Vegas Housing Authority. The Housing Authority's board members were not told about the contract and said that Herrera did little to earn the money. Board members also said the money should have been spent to help house the needy, not on a public relations contract for a politician. Does this information make you MORE likely or LESS likely to vote for Dario Herrera, or does it make no difference to your vote?"

Example 2
"As you may know, Christine Jennings filed an unsuccessful lawsuit and also petitioned Congress to overturn the results of the 2006 election.

Does Christine Jennings's lawsuit to overturn the results of the past election make you MORE likely or LESS likely to vote for her in the 2008 congressional elections, or does it make no difference to your vote?"

Establish Credibility

The campaign team often has to establish credibility with several key players in the race. First and foremost is the candidate. The team should use the survey as a template for the campaign plan, providing the candidate with confidence that there is a reason for the strategy, message, and target groups that the campaign is focusing on.

Second, polling is often useful in establishing credibility with donors. Some donors stroke a check because they are friends with the candidate, others because they believe in the cause or the moment. They write the check out of loyalty or passion. However, some view their check as worth writing only if the candidate can win, so they need evidence of that first.

Third, polling can be used to establish credibility with the media. Campaigns should not always release their polls. That would be like the coach of the New York football Giants releasing his playbook in advance of the game. However, just as there are times a coach says "we are going to establish the run," there are times a campaign can release a poll to show strength and/or momentum—after it spends time discussing and war gaming the possibilities, of course.

In the 2004 South Carolina Republican primary for the U.S. Senate, a poll was released to convince both potential donors and the press that the campaign was more competitive than conventional wisdom had it. Former governor David Beasley led in the polls, but had an underwhelming level of support for a candidate with universal name ID. Given that he was getting only 37 percent on the ballot, there was no way he would survive the runoff as the nominee. So, in my role as pollster for the Jim DeMint campaign, I put together the following for release. The release was controversial, as the other campaigns pushed back against it, but the race played out exactly as expected.

PUBLIC OPINION
STRATEGIES

MEMORANDUM

TO: CONGRESSMAN JIM DeMINT

THE DeMINT FOR SENATE CAMPAIGN TEAM

FROM: GLEN BOLGER

RE: KEY FINDINGS—BENCHMARK SURVEY

DATE: FEBRUARY 5, 2004

The Bottom Line

Both candidates who have previously held statewide office have underwhelming numbers in the primary. Both David Beasley and Charlie Condon have higher than expected negatives, and analysis shows they will collapse like a house of cards. Jim DeMint is well-positioned to be in a runoff with Beasley, and the anti-Beasley sentiment is significant and will likely propel DeMint to victory.

Key Findings
1. Charlie Condon is barely ahead of Jim DeMint—despite having significantly higher name ID.

While David Beasley leads on the ballot (37 percent), he is far below 50 percent. Just so there is no confusion—a former Governor who is below 50 percent on the primary ballot test is in significant trouble. He won't be able to add votes—everyone knows him and 63 percent prefer not to back him. Underscoring his softness is that only 18 percent are definitely voting for Beasley—a vote of no confidence in a former Governor.

Charlie Condon is in second place, with 19 percent, while Jim DeMint is just three points behind with 16 percent. Condon's problem is similar to Beasley—everyone knows Condon, and yet he's only getting support from one in five voters. Conversely, DeMint has half the hard name ID that Condon has, and yet is just three points behind. As DeMint's ID increases, he will easily pass Condon. Thomas Ravenel—who has higher name ID than DeMint—polls just 10 percent, while Mark McBride is down at 2 percent.

2. DeMint's ability to win is highlighted by a telling cross-tab.

Among the voters who are paying closest attention to the race—the 34 percent of voters who have an opinion of both Beasley and DeMint, Jim leads 42 percent–30 percent–10 percent. Thus, given Jim's substantial cash on hand advantage over Beasley and Condon, once the DeMint campaign gets on the air, he will make significant gains with voters who don't yet know him.

Methodology
The survey was conducted January 12–13, 2004, among 500 likely Republican primary voters statewide and has a margin of error of ±4.38 percent in 95 out of 100 cases.

Facts and Myths About Push Polling

Besides questions of accuracy, the most controversial topic in polling over the last number of years is the topic of push polling. It's controversial because there are a significant number of myths and misperceptions about it.

"Push polling" is not polling. Instead, it is the use of negative advocacy phone calls done under the guise of polling. It takes its name from

"push questions," a polling term that refers to testing factual information about a candidate or candidates to see if that information has any
impact on voters.

There are dramatic differences between push polling and survey
research:

Survey research seeks to collect or gather information, *not* to inform
or change it during the process. Push polling is specifically intended to
spread information (sometimes true, sometimes false).

Every survey research firm provides its name or the name of the
telephone research center conducting the interviews. Most push polls
do not name a sponsoring organization.

Survey research firms interview a limited sample of people that is
designed to mirror the entire population being studied, as low as three
hundred interviews in a congressional district to a high of eight hundred or a thousand interviews in a major statewide study. Push polls
contact thousands of people per hour with an objective of reaching
sometimes hundreds of thousands of households. Survey research firms
conduct interviews of between five to over thirty-five to forty minutes
for a major benchmark study. Push polls are generally designed to be
thirty to sixty seconds long.

Survey research firms use different questionnaire design techniques
to assess how voters will respond to new information about candidates
and their opponents. The intent of this process is not to persuade or
change the view of the electorate, but to replicate information that
could conceivably be available to the voter during the campaign. Push
polls are designed solely as a persuasion vehicle.

Push polling in the classical sense is usually done in the last few
days of a campaign to thousands (or tens of thousands) of voters with
a three-question script. Push polling is part of the realm of phone banks
that typically do GOTV (Get Out the Vote), persuasion, and ID phone
calls. Push polling is a type of persuasion call that masquerades as a
poll. Actual polling firms do not do push polling because the firms train
their interviewers to follow certain interviewer methodologies, and because it is outside the realm of the polling field.

One reason for the controversy around the practice is that sometimes in the past the negative advocacy hit calls pushed messages that

were not factual. False information has no room in a campaign, and operatives who knowingly use it deserve to have their candidates lose.

Do negative advocacy calls under the guise of polling work? Sometimes yes, sometimes no. It seems to have fallen out of favor in campaigns, as I've seen fewer and fewer campaigns doing it late in the race, instead using phones for GOTV or to drive a straight negative message (instead of disguising the negative info as poll questions).

However, survey message testing is often mistaken for push polling in a campaign. Typically, a campaign tests opposition research messages in the benchmark survey. Let's say it is a state with an early June primary. After winning the primary, the campaign immediately prepares to go into the field. The benchmark poll is going to test the political environment, the state of the race, perceptions of the candidates and other key players, key issues, as well as opposition and self-research messages.

Campaigns should not be reluctant to test self-research messages. First, testing makes it more difficult for your opponent to level the charge of push polling at your campaign (odds are extremely high that *both* campaigns have tested or will test opposition research [oppo] in their benchmarks). Second, your opponent is almost assuredly going to come after your candidate at some point, and it's better to know how harmful those attacks might be (and with which groups).

Some have argued that there is no difference between negative advocacy calls and legitimate polling that tests oppo messages. Even with all those counterpoint arguments listed above, another commonsense point is that using survey research to drive negative messages would be the least efficient use of campaign dollars possible.

A statewide campaign may spend $40,000 on a twenty-five-minute benchmark in June, testing the impact of messages among six hundred likely voters. *If* spreading a negative message is the goal of the survey, that means the campaign spent $67 per respondent ($40,000 divided by 600) to drive five to seven minutes worth of negative messages that 595 of those participants are going to forget by the next day. That's not much bang for your campaign buck. Instead, opposition research (and also self-research) should be done to help determine what works (and what does *not* work) with which key target groups before spending money on the message. If an opposition research point is received with a collective yawn by voters, why would the campaign ever spend money on it?

For more resources on push polling, use the following links:

http://rothenbergpoliticalreport.blogspot.com/2007/03/
   for-thousandth-time-don't-call-them-push.html
www.cbsnews.com/stories/2000/02/14/politics/main160398
   .shtml
www.ncpp.org/?q=node/41
www.pollster.com/blogs/so_what_is_a_push_poll.php

Questionnaire Design

Questionnaire design (as well as analysis) is part science, part art. There are certain fixed components in questionnaire design, including questionnaire order. The art part of questionnaire design comes in the wording of the message testing questions.

The most important aspect of questionnaire order on a political poll is to ensure that message testing comes after the collection of information about the current state of the race.

There is a saying that surveys should be unbiased. That's true—to a point. Message-testing surveys are done to see how voters react to information they will hear during the campaign. The inclusion of this information will unquestionably bias the respondent. Not every survey tests messages, but many do.

A key to good survey design is to ensure that the information that must be unbiased (political environment, name ID and images, the ballot test, issue agenda) is upfront, ahead of the messages. Putting messages prior to those questions is simply pollster malpractice (yes, I've seen it done). It's as fundamental an error in polling as leaving LeBron James uncovered is in basketball. Think of a poll as a funnel—with the widest point at the beginning; the questionnaire starts to narrow and focuses more and more on specifics.

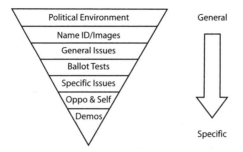

Questionnaires that ask the ballot first have very high undecideds and refusals. The interviewer needs to earn the respondents' trust or they will become skeptical and refuse to answer the key questions.

The art of wording message questions is crucial. Some firms (on both sides of the aisle, as well as some public polls) skew the wording of questions to put the best face forward for their client. Campaigns are ill-served by such work. Instead, they are much better off with an approach that we call "combat message development." That's where we take the messages we want to use in the campaign and test them against what our opponent is going to say. A careful reading of the clips, as well as the opponent's website, generally provides a clear picture of what the other side believes are its strongest messages.

Combat message development allows you to play out the campaign in advance, testing your best messages against the other side's best messages. Like a Civil War general, you find the favorable terrain for your side of the battle and fight on that ground. If your message is stronger and more relevant, not even Pickett's charge can dislodge it. As you develop the wording of the questions, be extremely fair to your opponent. (This makes many clients uncomfortable, but they have to understand if we don't replicate the opposition message in advance, we're not getting a realistic picture of the fight to come.)

Questionnaire development is a crucial phase of the survey process for the entire campaign team. Typically, the campaign team has a conference call with the pollster and throws out images, issues, messages, and oppo/self-research to test. The pollster should have the backup documents (especially for the oppo). The pollster then sends the first draft to the campaign team. That's followed by either edit emails or a conference call to edit/change the draft. Sometimes the candidate is in the process from the start, while other times the candidate doesn't care to be involved until nearly the end of the process. The campaign should *always* have final sign-off on the survey; as the saying goes, it's important to "get the fingerprints on the murder weapon."

The campaign should *never* test opposition research that has not been fully verified. Testing rumors or half-verified research can come back to bite the campaign in the derriere. Early in my career, I received a call from a talented operative who told me a fortuitous piece of oppo that had just occurred, which I added to the survey fielding that night. However, neither he nor I tracked down whether the juicier part of the oppo was true, so we tested a half-truth. The Democratic candidate made a fuss (and rightfully so) about us spreading lies and falsehoods— and the newspapers gave it more life. Fortunately the GOP candidate won (albeit barely) despite the grievous mistake. It was a valuable lesson: make sure the opposition research information is factual before testing.

(Broader political observation: Republicans are *always* held to higher standards by the media in a campaign, so just get used to it. It's not fair to GOP campaigns, but that's the reality under which we operate.)

Targeting Demographic Subgroups

Targeting is another crucial aspect of polling. There are three types of targeting in a campaign—precinct targeting, microtargeting, and demographic targeting.

Precinct targeting is using previous election results to analyze turnout, the base vote, and the swing vote precinct by precinct in order to be able to prioritize persuasion and GOTV efforts. Precinct targeting should be done by every campaign on every level to allow for better use of the candidate's time, the campaign's focus, and the campaign's volunteer and financial resources. Precinct targeting allows a campaign to prioritize by region.

Microtargeting allows campaigns to strictly define groups. It uses analysis of large individual and consumer databases of lifestyle information, voter information, demographic information, consumer behavior, census data, and geographic data. These data are combined to create distinct groups of voters who can be reached with specific micromessages that will resonate with them.

Microtargeting is expensive, but allows campaigns to reach clusters of specific types of individual voters in a more resonant fashion than other forms of media. Microtargeting allows a campaign to prioritize by individual.

Survey targeting focuses on demographic subgroups as well as larger geographic regions. A campaign needs to decide what subgroups and regions to focus on. The easiest ways to target in a campaign are the simplest:

1. Geography   3. Gender
2. Party   4. Age

There are certainly other ways—ideology, church attendance, union membership, race, or ethnicity—but the four listed are generally the first four ways to approach a campaign. (In areas with high minority populations, particularly Voting Rights Act states in which voter lists have ethnicity on them, race expands the above list of four to five.)[1] Use other demographic questions only if the campaign can target those voters. "Nice to know" is not a reason to spend limited survey dollars on a poll question.

The difference between precinct targeting and geographic targeting from surveys is significant. The two are complementary, not at cross-purposes. Survey targeting by geography tends to be in larger increments. For example, in the Mississippi Senate race of 2008 between Roger Wicker and Ronnie Musgrove, we looked at geography on two levels in the polling. (I did the polling for Senator Wicker's successful campaign.) We analyzed and tracked the race by media market (DMA) and by geopolitical region.

During the tracking, for instance, we made decisions about where to put increased media dollars, and what the mix of positive/negative ads should be in each media market. We found that certain ads worked well in certain markets, while in other markets, certain attacks by Musgrove's campaign hurt us more than in other markets. Thus, while we had an overall media message and media buy strategy for the campaign, we tweaked it on the fly based on the trends in the daily tracking.

We used geopolitical region data from the daily tracking to decide where to put volunteers and how to focus the candidate's time. We put a lot of volunteer time and effort into the coastal region based on the tracking. And because of his strength up north, the campaign also worked to maximize turnout in northern Mississippi.

Demographic targeting from the polling is used to make all sorts of decisions for campaigns. I used to say that if Republican candidates have a tie or better with two of the following three groups–women, seniors, and independents—they'll win. In 2008, because of Democratic advantage on party ID, only a draw among women guaranteed a win.

So, on gender, a pollster doesn't just analyze men and women but also younger men, older men, younger women, and older women. I've also done more analysis as of late breaking down gender by education—looking for opportunities for Republican candidates among women without college degrees, or checking to ensure we are doing fine among men with college degrees. While it is difficult to target specifically at that level, media buyers can skew their buys toward those different groups.

When it comes to partisanship, I focus on analyzing five groups, not just three. Instead of just the typical Republican, independent, Democrat cross-tabs, I look at self-identified *base* Republicans, *soft* Republicans, independents, *soft* Democrats, and *base* Democrats. There tend to be significant attitudinal differences between base and soft partisans. Base partisans are hard-core supporters who tend to unite immediately behind their party's candidate. Soft partisans are more open to persuasion. A Democrat who holds a traditionally Republican seat likely won independents by a healthy margin, at the same time making inroads of 25–30 percent into the soft GOP vote. The reverse holds true for Republicans who win traditionally Democratic seats.

In analyzing the results among those subgroups, it is important to make sure the base is united. Ultimately, however, the "base strategy" that some political operatives favor will fail at the slightest sign of trouble for a political party.

Independent voters determine elections in swing areas. Unquestionably, there are too few competitive elections. In 2008, 55 winners in the 435 congressional races received less than 55 percent of the vote—the winning percentage that separates competitive from noncompetitive races. In 2006, there were only 65 winners who received less than 55 percent of the vote. While only 13 percent of U.S. House seats were competitive in 2008, the difference in winning close races generally determines the ability of the controlling party to get policy through the House.

Thus campaign partisan targeting should be run from the middle outward, focusing on (in the case of a Republican campaign) messaging to soft Republicans and independents. The campaign should also try to find ways to pick off some soft Democrats. Anytime you can force your opponents to play defense on their own side of the field, things are going your way in the race.

In a southern state or district, five partisan groups are still key, but the groups change slightly. Instead of soft Democrats and base Democrats, it's important to analyze differences between white Democrats and black Democrats to make more informed decisions about using resources.

Targeting by gender and age allows campaigns to further target their message. This applies to all campaign messaging, not just direct mail. Targeting ads to women (or men), skewing the buy toward a certain age-group, or reaching senior citizens through recorded voice messages are all examples of using cross-tab data to make decisions about which groups need to be moved.

Several years ago in a congressional race in a Big Ten state the campaign for an open seat was tight, and the Republican candidate was underperforming among younger men—winning, but not by enough in comparison to other Republicans on the ticket. Later in the conference call, during discussion of the media buy, the team was kicking around the question of whether or not to buy the state university's football game that upcoming Saturday. It was a very expensive spot to buy because so many people watch that game. I broke into the discussion, noting that the very people we need (younger men) were the ones most likely to be watching the game. So while the spot might be expensive, the investment would have a strong return. The campaign bought the spot. (That's not why the candidate won the race, but it is an example of using polling to help make key decisions.)

Understanding How to Read Polls

Learning to read and interpret polls takes a long time. My business partner of many years, Neil Newhouse, put together a list of rules of thumb that are helpful to an initial reading of the data (I've modified them a bit, but the bulk of the work is his):

- Polls are not very good at predicting the future. They are usually a snapshot of the electorate at a specific point in time in a campaign. The purpose of running a campaign is to either change the numbers (if behind) or solidify the numbers (if ahead). Events can also significantly move the numbers. There are times when an experienced pollster can look at the state of play in the race, know the status of the two campaigns, and suggest what is likely to happen. So polls do sometimes predict the outcome, but it's usually based on knowing the direction the plot of the race is headed.
- The generic ballot is akin to the point spread in a football game. It reflects the degree of difficulty of a race, but the generic ballot does not indicate factors like the quality of the candidates or the strength of their messages.
- A candidate's image (favorable/unfavorable) generally needs to be at a 2 to 1 (or better) ratio, but candidates with images at 1 to 1 do win occasionally (because their opponent has an even worse image!). Evaluate images in comparison to each other, not in a vacuum.
- The "reelect/new person" score for incumbents has declined over the years and is no longer as useful as it once was. Look more at the ratio. A 1 to 1 reelect to new person ratio is problematic, while a soft reelect with a corresponding low new person score simply means the incumbent needs to define herself more aggressively, not so much that she is on the brink of electoral disaster.
- Intensity drives voters. Pay attention to "definite" vote support, "strong" approval scores, "strongly favor/strongly oppose" numbers on issues, and "much more likely/much less likely" on message testing sequences.

- Undecided voters generally break heavily *against* well-known and well-liked incumbents. A 50 percent to 35 percent lead for an incumbent with 90 percent name ID over a challenger with 50 percent name ID is not safe. Assume the race is more like 53 percent to 47 percent (which is why you often see incumbents defining challengers). Remember, there are two kinds of name ID—the good kind and the bad kind. If your campaign has hit a wall, it's imperative to define your opponent.
- "Informed" ballots are nothing more than head-to-head ballot scores after voters have heard information about one or both candidates. Campaigns should not release those informed ballots, and the media should not print them.
- Media takes time to have an impact, so don't expect to see poll numbers move the moment a candidate starts advertising. It usually takes about 1,000–1,500 GRPs (gross rating points) for an ad (or ads) to start resonating with the electorate.

  (Note: One of the worst things a campaign can do is pull down ads before they've accumulated enough points. Unless the ad is over the top or has a factual error, it is best to leave it up for at least 1,000 points so voters start to get the message.)
- Don't discount a poll's result just because the other side released it. More likely than not, the poll was timed to be done after a media buy, so it is possible the race has moved from your initial reading.
- Don't just look at the overall results; look at the state of the race, the issues, and the messages among the key subgroups, especially swing voters. The voters who will determine the difference between winning and losing provide a lot of clarity about what is important when analyzing the poll.

Using Focus Groups

Focus groups are the qualitative method of survey research, and campaigns now do numerous types of focus groups. They are used to add the meat to the bones of polling. They provide additional insight, allow topics to be explored in greater depth, and make it possible to test and refine advertising.

Focus groups allow for the testing of messaging in greater detail than a poll, the testing of language, and positioning of the candidate/campaign.

A focus group discussion is led by a moderator and lasts approximately two hours. The campaign team develops a discussion guide prior to the groups, although the moderator has the discretion to probe further or add questions based on the discussion. Generally there are eight to ten participants who are selected based on their attitudes and demographics (for example, an undecided swing woman is a good participant, while a core partisan who is definitely voting for a candidate is not).

Often two groups are conducted in one night. The first group may consist of independent women who are undecided, while the second group would then consist of independent men who are undecided. Single gender groups are generally more at ease and open than when one gender feels the need to perform or dominate the discussion. The participants are paid for their time, and the group is either held at a local research facility with a viewing room for the campaign team to watch or at a hotel with a camera and TV hook-up in an adjoining room for the campaign team to watch.

Not every campaign does focus groups. In fact, many do not, including some statewide campaigns. Some media consultants disdain focus groups as simply a bunch of wannabe ad critics. Those statewide campaigns that do use focus groups generally are able to separate the wheat of useful information from the chaff of pointless chatter.

Some focus groups don't test ads at all. In a high-profile race with well-known candidates, focus groups are perfect for providing additional context as to how key voter groups perceive the candidates. Typically, general elections only have swing voters participate in the focus groups. Most Democrats are locked in for the Democratic candidate, and there is a similar dynamic on the Republican side. Thus campaigns shouldn't spend limited resources having people in the group who will be very difficult to move. Instead, nearly all general election focus groups are done among independent voters who are undecided.

Questions asked by the moderator include, What have you seen, read, or heard about the campaign for Senate? What do you like most or like least about (candidate name/opponent name)? If you were having dinner at (candidate's) house, what would the house be like, what would he/she serve for dinner, and what would you talk about? Another favorite is, If (candidate name) were an animal, what kind of animal would he/she be and why? While those last two examples seem a little touchy-feely, they get voters to project feelings about candidates in ways that are very illuminating as to their perceptions of those candidates.

In a campaign a few years ago, we found that voters perceived the Republican (who had very high name ID) as a silver spoon, rich candidate who had never struggled. None of that was true. He actually grew up dealing with family tragedies, never made much money, and owned a decidedly middle-class home in a decidedly middle-class neighborhood. We immediately scrapped plans to focus on issues in our opening round of ads, and instead we told his life story—repositioning voters' perceptions about him from a weakness to a strength. Until we did focus groups, the campaign team had no idea voters had such a distorted—and potentially devastating—perception of the candidate!

When candidates are not as well-known, focus groups can still be useful in testing bio points, messaging options, and campaign positioning.

In ad testing, respondents usually use dials to react to the various ads being tested. Typically a campaign will test five or six rough cut ads, a couple of ads that have been running, as well as some ads the opposition has been airing. The dials are used to garner instantaneous feedback from participants. Sometimes dials aren't an option, but it is still important to get quantitative feedback prior to discussing the ads.

There is often a huge difference between how people react to the ads when they first see the spots, and then later during the discussion. The participants tend to be much more critical of the ads during the discussion, suggesting a certain need to be cool by critiquing. However, there are worthwhile nuggets to be garnered from the discussion. The post–dial discussion often helps the campaign avoid going down the wrong path unintentionally.

A few years ago in an open seat U.S. Senate race, the GOP candidate's lead had collapsed down from twelve points to a tie because of a very effective—and potentially fatal—issue attack. After ten days of watching our poll numbers nosedive, we conducted focus groups testing a wide range of options for a response. In the first group, the spot that tested the best was the one the entire campaign team liked the least. "Well," we said to each other after the group, "that was weird. Not sure we should believe what they told us." Then the second group reacted the same way.

So we ran the ad. It was a spot that most political operatives (myself included) doubted could work. It was the candidate talking calmly, and in great detail, about what he really supported. Within a few days after the ad went on the air, the bleeding stopped. A few days later, the Republican regained the lead. Having put the issue to rest, we changed the subject for the last ten days of the campaign, and his poll numbers rose steadily en route to a ten-point win.

In a statewide initiative campaign in California, we only had enough money for one, maybe two ads. So we did a series of four sets of focus groups spaced several weeks apart. The media consultant created eight rough cuts for the first set of groups. Then, based on what we learned in the first set of groups, the media firm created four new ads to test again. They kept some concepts from the first groups for two ads, but came up with two entirely new treatments. Then the media firm took the learnings from that group and further refined the ads (twice more). Finally, we had a finished spot very different from the first eight treatments we started with.

In the campaign, we were working for the "no" side. We went from 60 percent yes/30 percent no in early polls (both public and private) to winning the campaign 39 percent yes/61 percent no. Interestingly, it was not the pollster who suggested the research plan, but the media consultant. The media firm knew it had one shot to get it right. After months of work the media spot killed the proposition, moving the ballot a net fifty-two points!

In a special congressional election held in a district that had been represented by a conservative Democrat until his passing, we had some strong opposition research on the Democratic candidate on a key values issue. However, we were worried voters would explain away the vote and there would be an unintentional backlash in favor of the female Democratic candidate (she was also running as a conservative in a neck-and-neck race). So the media consultant mocked up some ads and we focus-grouped them among the key target group for the race—independent white women. Instead of a backlash, we found that they were even angrier about the vote than we could have dreamed. Needless to say, we put the spot on the air with a satisfactory result.

Focus groups don't always come up with clear answers and simple solutions. Sometimes group participants prefer to play television critic and comment on clothing, voice, or (of course) the horrible nature of negative ads. However, focus groups often work to clarify public opinion, and allow the campaign to make decisions in an environment that helps lift the fog of war.

The Bottom Line: Campaign Polling

Polling helps a campaign team put together a road map for winning the race. It helps the campaign make decisions about allocating the rest of the campaign's resources. It helps provide focus to the message and to the subgroup targeting. Remember, the point of running a campaign is to move numbers; early in the campaign, the ballot test can be among the least important questions.

It is imperative to use early polling to test messages in a way that accurately reflects your potential messages, as well as your opponent's likeliest messages. Early polling also helps provide a firm foundation for the assumptions that the team is making about the campaign. Late polling is important for fine-tuning (or radically shifting) the campaign and the advertising. In a campaign, polling is not dry science; it helps to drive your political strategy.

Notes

1 Voting Right Act states: Alabama, Alaska, Arizona, Georgia, Louisiana, Mississippi, South Carolina, Texas, and Virginia.

4

Strategies and Tactics of Fund-raising in 2008

Candice J. Nelson

Introduction

The presidential elections of 2000, 2004, and 2008 each introduced new and innovative ways of raising money. In the 2000 election, then Governor George W. Bush created the Pioneers, a group of people who each pledged to raise $100,000 for the Bush campaign. In his 2004 reelection campaign, capitalizing on the increased individual contribution limits as a result of the Bipartisan Campaign Reform Act, he created a new category of fund-raisers, the Rangers, who each pledged to raise $250,000 for the president's reelection campaign. The 2004 election also saw innovation on the part of Democrats, as Governor Howard Dean, seeking the Democratic nomination, used the Internet to raise substantial sums of money for his campaign. In 2008, we saw very different fund-raising strategies by the Obama and Clinton campaigns. While Senator Clinton concentrated on soliciting donations from wealthy donors who could contribute the maximum donation of $2,300 to her campaign, Senator Obama focused on raising large amounts of money from small, individual donations contributed primarily through the Internet. The disparate fund-raising strategies of the two campaigns had important consequences for the Democratic nomination process.

Primary Fund-raising Strategies

The Federal Election Campaign Act provides partial public funding during the nomination process for candidates who meet minimum qualification requirements, but candidates who accept partial public funding must also agree to an overall spending limit for the nomination period. For 2008, the total amount of money that was allowed to be spent during the nomination contests for candidates who accepted partial public funding was just over $42 million. Both Senators Clinton and Obama demonstrated early in 2007 that they could raise much more that the $42 million spending limit, and thus both opted out of partial public funding, as had front-runners Howard Dean and John Kerry four years earlier, and George W. Bush in 2000 and 2004.

Going into 2007, Senator Hillary Rodham Clinton was the presumptive favorite to win the Democratic Party's nomination. The Clinton campaign also presumed she was the front-runner and planned a fund-raising strategy based on that assumption. With the front-loading of the nomination process in 2008—four Democratic caucuses and primaries in January, and twenty-one caucuses and primaries on the first Tuesday in February, February 5—many political observers thought the nomination process for both parties would likely be over on February 5. In the past two election cycles the nominees of both parties were known by early March, and many expected 2008 to be no different.

Consequently the Clinton campaign sought to raise the maximum amount of money possible as quickly as possible, so she would have the funds to wage a long and arduous general election campaign, even before the formal general election period began in the fall. During the first quarter of 2007, almost two-thirds, 64 percent, of her contributions came from donors who gave the maximum $2,300. During the second quarter of 2007, 66 percent of her contributions came from maxed-out donors. During the third quarter, almost three-quarters of her donors—74 percent—maxed out, and for the fourth quarter, 70 percent.

When Senator Clinton finished third in the Iowa caucuses, the inevitability of her nomination came into question, and with it the wisdom of her fund-raising strategy. Shortly following the New Hampshire primary, senior Clinton adviser Harold Ickes, who oversaw the campaign's budget operations, announced to both Senator Clinton and her husband, former president Bill Clinton, as well as to the senior campaign staff, that "'the cupboard is empty.' The campaign had burned through its money just getting past Iowa. And the news got worse: despite spending $100 million, it had somehow failed to establish ground operations in all but a handful of *upcoming* states. Now, urgently needing them, it lacked the money."[1] Senator Clinton agreed to lend her campaign $5 million. However, because she had so many maxed out donors, she did not have a ready list of contributors she could resolicit during the protracted nomination fight between February and June. One Clinton supporter described the efforts to raise more money as "like asking me to run a half-marathon after I've run a marathon."[2] Twice more during the primary season she lent money to her campaign and finished the nomination campaign $25 million in debt. In July 2008, Jonathan Minz, Clinton's national finance director, worked to put together fund-raising events to retire her debt but found it slow going because she needed "new donors because so many of her earlier contributors gave the legal limit."[3] It was an ironic ending for a campaign that assumed money would be no object.

Senator Obama, the junior senator from Illinois serving in his first term and having faced no serious challenge in his Senate election, could not assume a large pool of wealthy donors willing to contribute to his campaign. Consequently Senator Obama's fund-raising strategy was to raise money from wealthier contributors where he could find them and build off Howard Dean's success in 2004 in raising smaller donations online. During 2007, when Senator Clinton was raising between two-thirds and three-quarters of her funds from maxed out donors, less than half of Obama's contributions came from maxed out donors. In the second quarter of 2007 over half of Obama's donors, 53 percent, maxed out. For the other three-quarters, less than half of Obama's contributions came from maxed-out donors, 47 percent in the first quarter, 46 percent in the third quarter, and 43 percent in the fourth quarter. As a result, when the nomination continued past February 5, Obama was in a position to go back to those who had contributed to his campaign and ask for more money.

For example, in February 2008 the Obama campaign raised $30.5 million in donations of $200 or less, and $5 million of that came from repeat donors.[4] In March, 60 percent of Obama's contributions came in amounts of $200 or less.[5] In April, and again in June, almost two-thirds of Obama's contributions, 65 percent, came from contributions of $200 or less.[6]

Senator McCain, like others seeking the presidential nomination, assumed he needed to raise $100 million in 2007 to be competitive for the nomination. McCain's strategy was to assume he would raise that much money, and to build a staff and organization accordingly. McCain began the nomination process with a 120-person staff, including a large campaign headquarters just outside Washington, D.C., and field staff in early primary and caucus states.[7] McCain's first-quarter spending in 2007 was promulgated on his fund-raising assumptions: he spent $8 million in the first quarter of 2007, including $1.6 million on staff salaries.[8] However, "the money did not come in. Most campaigns can expect 80 to 85 percent of donors to honor their pledges. In the McCain campaign, fewer than half did. 'They come, they eat our food, they drink our liquor, they get their pictures taken,' said McCain's aide Mark Salter. 'But they don't send a check.'"[9]

When McCain only raised $13 million during the first quarter of 2007, he announced that he was revamping his fund-raising operation and cutting back his staff and some contracts with campaign consultants.[10] When his fund-raising was equally tepid in the second quarter of 2007, despite the restructured fund-raising operation, McCain let go all but a handful of staff and focused exclusively on winning the New Hampshire primary. According to one campaign adviser, "the campaign had overestimated what it could raise, and had overspent . . . We had to make dramatic cutbacks."[11]

With his campaign floundering, McCain briefly considered accepting partial public funding for the primaries and caucuses. While such a strategy would have given the campaign a much needed infusion of cash, it would have limited the amount the campaign could spend, both overall during the nomination process and in the key early primary state of New Hampshire. Because of that, the campaign ultimately decided not to accept public funds. "It would have been almost irresponsible," said Charles R. Black Jr., a McCain adviser. "We knew that this time we would have to persevere without taking the match."[12]

Obama's Fund-raising Tactics

While Senator Obama's success in raising money online and in small (under $200) amounts received considerable attention during the campaign, the Obama campaign was successful in raising money in both small and large dollar amounts. The Campaign Finance Institute found that 49 percent of the Obama campaign receipts were from contributions of $200 or less. Because only donations of $201 or more require disclosure to the Federal Election Commission, estimates of the number of $200 donors are just that, estimates. The Campaign Finance Institute, based on reports from the Obama campaign and CFI's own internal reporting, estimated that "2.5 million undisclosed donors gave a cumulative average of about $62 each . . . Obama's innovation would not be in the amount he raised from each small donor, but in the number of such people he was able to reach."[13]

As already noted, one of the strengths of the Obama campaign was its success in encouraging individuals to contribute over and over again to the campaign. While figures for the total election cycle were not available as of this writing, the Campaign Finance Institute found that while 49 percent of Obama's contributions came in donations of $200 or less, only 26 percent of his contributions (through August 31, 2008) came from donors whose total contributions aggregated to $200 or less. CFI found that many of the donors who initially gave $200 or less to the campaign ended up contributing between $201 and $999 to the campaign.[14] However, very few (CFI estimated approximately 13,000) of these initial small donor contributors ended up contributing more than $1000 to the Obama campaign.[15]

While the Obama campaign was successful in raising both small and medium dollar contributions, it was also very successful in raising money at the opposite end of the fund-raising spectrum. Obama's problem early on was how to tap into the network of large donors. Senator Clinton, through her husband, had a large network of donors to both his presidential campaigns and her Senate campaigns, and most were committed to her presidential run. However, there was one network of potential donors that were not tied to the Clintons—the entrepreneurs in Silicon Valley, California. In a very enlightening study of Silicon Valley donors published in the *Atlantic Monthly* in June 2008, Joshua Green tells the following story:

> The Internet was still in its infancy when Bill Clinton last ran for president, in 1996, and most of the immense fortunes had not yet come into being; the emerging tech class had not yet taken shape. So, unlike the magnates in California real estate, apparel, and entertainment, who all had long-established loyalty to the Clintons, the tech community was up for grabs in 2007. In a colossal error of judgment, the Clinton campaign never made a serious approach, assuming that Obama would fade and lack of money and cutting-edge technology couldn't possibly factor into what was expected to be an easy race . . . As a result, the wealthiest region of the wealthiest state in the nation was left to Barack Obama.[16]

The entrepreneurs of the Silicon Valley were, oddly, a perfect fit for the Obama campaign. While many contributors to past presidential campaigns saw Obama's inexperience in a presidential race as a cause for concern, his potential promise fit perfectly with the mind-set of the tech community. As Green put it, Obama "was familiar to Silicon Valley in at least one way: like a hot Internet start-up in the glory days, he had great buzz, a compelling pitch, and no money to back it up."[17] When asked if Senator Obama's limited résumé had been a concern for potential Silicon Valley contributors, John Roos, the finance chair for the Obama campaign in northern California and a partner in a Palo Alto law firm, said "No one in Silicon Valley sits here and thinks, 'You need a massive inside-the-Beltway experience' . . . Sergey and Larry were in their early 20s when they started Google. The YouTube guys were also in their 20s. So were the guys who started Facebook. And I'll tell you, we recognized what great companies have been built on, and that's ideas, talent and inspirational leadership."[18]

Not only did Obama's message appeal to the entrepreneurs of Silicon Valley, but his tactic of raising money through social networks was also a method that appealed to these new contributors to presidential politics. For example, Steve Spinner, a Silicon Valley entrepreneur, first met Obama at a fund-raiser at John Roos's home early in 2007, and volunteered to raise $25,000 for the Obama campaign. Using social networks such as Facebook, LinkedIn, and MyYahoo, he quickly exceeded the $25,000 he had pledged to raise. He was then invited to join Obama's national finance committee, with an expectation of raising $250,000. He agreed, and "in a period of weeks, Spinner, who had never raised a dime for a presidential campaign, had gone from neophyte to mid-six-figure Obama fund-raiser."[19]

Bundling, the technical term for Spinner's method of fund-raising, was not new to presidential politics. Indeed, then Governor George W. Bush took bundling to a new, systematic level of fund-raising when he developed first the Pioneers, those who pledged to raise $100,000 for the Bush campaign in 2000, and then the Rangers, those who pledged to raised $250,000 for the campaign in 2004. What was different about the Obama campaign was not the existence of bundlers (Bush and Kerry both had bundlers in 2004, as did Hillary Clinton in 2008) but the way bundlers on the Obama campaign were able to use social networks as a tactic for raising money. As a result, they were able to tap into new sources of money in new ways. Joe Rospars, the new media director for the Obama campaign, describes the approach as "to give them the tools and have them go out and do all this on their own."[20] For example, My.Barack.Obama.com allowed supporters to customize the website to fit their interests. In terms of fund-raising tools, contributors could "click on a button and make a donation, or . . . sign up for the subscription model . . . and donate a little every month. [Contributors] could set up [their] own pages, establish target numbers, and watch personal fund-raising 'thermometers' rise."[21]

Encouraging individual fund-raisers, whether large or small, to tap into their own social networks meant the campaign, and Obama himself, needed to spend less time on fund-raising events. In February 2008, the Obama campaign raised $55 million without the candidate hosting a single fund-raiser.[22] Between January 1 and April 1, 2008, Hillary Clinton "attended more than a dozen fund-raisers, and her husband appeared at more than 40, while Obama and his wife attended fewer than 10 during that time."[23] As one Obama fund-raiser described the effect of the social network fund-raising tactic of the Obama campaign, "If the typical Gore event was 20 people in a living room writing six-figure checks, and the [typical] Kerry event was 2,000 people in a ballroom writing four-figure checks, this year for Obama was stadium rallies of 20,000 people who pay absolutely nothing, and then go home and contribute a few dollars online."[24]

While the number of small donors to the Obama campaign is one of the trademark strategies of the campaign, large donors and bundlers played an equally important role. According to the Center for Responsive Politics, almost fifty donors bundled a minimum of $500,000 for the campaign, 276 donors bundled between $100,000 and $200,000, and slightly more than a quarter of a million donors bundled between $50,000 and $100,000.[25] Linda Douglas, spokesperson for the Obama campaign, recognized the importance of large donors. "Although the Obama campaign was unprecedented in its aggressive outreach to small donors, it is a fact in American politics that large donations are necessary as well."[26]

General Election Fund-raising Strategies

What defined the general election fund-raising strategies of the Obama and McCain campaigns was McCain's decision to accept public funding for the general election and Obama's decision to forgo public funding. The 2008 presidential election was the first since public funding of presidential elections began in 1976 that a major party candidate did not accept public funding in the general election. Initial reports predicted that the two campaigns would achieve parity during the general election. The very well regarded Campaign Finance Institute put out a press release in late September entitled "After Holding Financial Advantage in Primaries, Obama Likely to Achieve Only Parity with McCain in General Election." [27] But that did not turn out to be the case.

Declining public funding in the general election was not without risk for the Obama campaign. Though he had out-raised Clinton during the primaries, his fund-raising dropped off during the last three months of the primary season. After raising a record $54 million in February 2008, he raised $40 million in March, $30 million in April, and $21 million in May.[28] It was also still a question mark after the primaries ended if he would be able to tap into the Clinton fund-raising network.

The much touted success of Obama's online fund-raising was reason for concern in the early summer months. One member of Obama's finance committee describes the concern as follows: "The big question was: How would the online stuff do? We had heard this from everyone in the campaign, it wasn't a secret, that the Internet money is event-driven. We were sitting there in June and July realizing this may be a heavier lift for us."[29] When the finance committee met in Denver for the Democratic National Committee, new fund-raising targets were assigned to the members of the committee. "We looked at what we had to do in our regions, and they were pretty Herculean goals, no doubt about it," said one member of the finance committee in describing the meeting.[30]

The event-driven nature of online fund-raising in the end worked in Obama's favor, and the event that turned the tide was the Republican Party's nomination of Alaska Governor Sarah Palin as its vice presidential nominee. The Obama campaign raised $10 million in the twenty-four-hour period after Palin accepted her party's nomination.[31] Palin's nomination also persuaded Clinton supporters who had until that point been reticent to financially support Obama to become engaged in his campaign. "To the extent that there was lingering hesitation in Clinton land, it shut down overnight . . . And not just shut down. They came over in droves," said one member of Obama's finance committee.[32] In the end, the Obama campaign raised $150 million in September and went on to financially completely dominate the McCain campaign in the general election, as Anthony Corrado details in Chapter 5 of this volume.

Conclusion

The fund-raising strategies and tactics that were most important in the 2008 presidential election were the Obama campaign's building on the Internet fund-raising success of the Dean campaign in 2004 while also continuing tried and true traditional fund-raising techniques such as bundling. While Obama raised more money in small contributions online than any previous presidential candidate, he also raised more money in large donor contributions than any previous candidate.[33] The Obama campaign took advantage of the new tools of campaigning in 2008, including social networks, and adapted them to fund-raising. As a result, the campaign had a steady stream of small, medium, and large donors it could return to again and again for contributions. The message of the Obama campaign, described elsewhere in this book, only fueled the interest in contributing to the campaign. The record $750 million raised by the Obama campaign speaks rather dramatically to the wisdom of its fund-raising strategy and tactics.

Notes

1 Joshua Green, "The Front-Runner's Fall," *Atlantic Monthly*, September 2008, www.theatlantic.com/doc/print/200809/hillary-clinton-campaign.

2 Matthew Mosk, "Clinton Campaign Feels Spent, and Outspent," *Washington Post*, April 4, 2008, A6.

3 Anne E. Kornblut and Matthew Mosk, "On the Money Trail, Twice the Challenge," *Washington Post*, July 27, 2008, A10.

4 "February Fund-raising Frenzy for Presidential Candidates," Campaign Finance Institute press release, March 21, 2008.

5 "March Presidential Fund-raising: Small Donations Fueled Democrats, Large Donations Republicans," Campaign Finance Institute press release, April 22, 2008.

6 "April Presidential Reports: Small Donations Continue to Fuel Democrats; McCain Has His Best Month; Clinton's Debts Rise to $19.5 Million," Campaign Finance Institute press release, May 21, 2008. "Obama's Small Contributions Surged in June, but McCain's Party-Based Strategy Gave the GOP Side a Combined Cash Advantage on June 30," Campaign Finance Institute press release, July 22, 2008.

7 Michael D. Shear and Matthew Mosk, "Campaign Financial Reports Show McCain Lagging Rivals," *Washington Post*, April 14, 2007, A3.

8 Shear and Mosk, "Campaign Financial Reports."

9 Evan Thomas, *A Long Time Coming* (New York: Perseus, 2009), 34.

10 Shear and Mosk, "Campaign Financial Reports Show McCain Lagging Rivals."

11 "With Loan, McCain Secured a Last-Minute Lifeline," *Washington Post*, February 1, 2008, A10.

12 "With Loan, McCain Secured a Last-Minute Lifeline."

13 "Reality Check: Obama Received About the Same Percentage from Small Donors in 2008 As Bush in 2004," Campaign Finance Institute press release, November 24, 2008.

14 "Obama Received About the Same Percentage."

15 "Obama Received About the Same Percentage."

16 Joshua Green, "The Amazing Money Machine," *Atlantic Monthly*, June 2008, 57.

17 Green, "Amazing Money Machine," 56.

18 Green, "Amazing Money Machine," 57.

19 Green, "Amazing Money Machine," 60.

20 Green, "Amazing Money Machine," 62.

21 Green, "Amazing Money Machine," 62

22 Green, "Amazing Money Machine," 54.

23 Mosk, "Clinton Campaign Feels Spent."

24 Green, "Amazing Money Machine," 62.

25 www.opensecrets.org/pres08/donordems.php?cycle=2008.

26 Kimberly Kindy and Sarah Cohen, "The Donors Who Gave Big, and Often," *Washington Post*, January 18, 2009, A2.

27 "After Holding Financial Advantage in Primaries, Obama Likely to Achieve Only Parity with McCain in General Election," Campaign Finance Institute press release, September 26, 2008.

28 "Obama's Fund-raising Slowdown: Will It Cause Him to Look More Toward Large Donors?" Campaign Finance Institute press release, June 24, 2008.

29 Matthew Mosk, "Fear of Failure Helped Fuel Obama's Record Fund-raising," *Washington Post*, October 21, 2008, A4.

30 Mosk, "Fear of Failure."

31 Mosk, "Fear of Failure."

32 Mosk, "Fear of Failure."

33 "Obama Received About the Same Percentage."

5

Fund-raising Strategies in the 2008 Presidential Campaign

Anthony Corrado

The 2008 race for the White House was widely expected to be the most expensive presidential campaign in American history. Long before the start of the election year, political observers and editorial page writers were predicting that the election would be the first in which the two major party nominees would spend a total of a billion dollars.[1] This estimate was predicated on the assumption that neither major party nominee would accept public funding—and its associated spending limits—in either the primary or general election, and that each would spend up to $250 million during the primaries and another $250 million during the general election period. These predictions proved to be only partially correct.

The election did turn out to be the first presidential race to surpass the billion dollar mark. As anticipated, both of the major party nominees, Democrat Barack Obama and Republican John McCain, decided to forgo public funding during the primaries and each raised far more than the amount that could have been spent under the public funding primary expenditure limit. But while McCain accepted the $84 million public grant to finance his general election campaign, Obama chose to opt out of the grant and instead rely on private contributions. Even so, these two candidates raised a combined $1.1 billion, with most of this sum, $745 million, the result of Obama's unprecedented ability to raise funds. In his quest for the presidency, Obama raised more than the entire Republican field of presidential contenders, including McCain, and more than the combined total of then-President George W. Bush and his Democratic challenger, John Kerry, in the entire 2004 campaign.[2] In fact, his campaign's total receipts exceeded the amounts raised by the Democratic and Republican National Committees *combined* during the course of the two-year election cycle.[3] In terms of fund-raising, Obama was essentially a party of his own.

At the beginning of the election cycle, no one expected a presidential candidate to raise as much money as Obama did. He set the fund-raising pace throughout the election year, leaving his challengers, including the financially formidable former first lady Hillary Clinton, struggling to keep up. Obama's resources allowed him to build an organization and mount an advertising effort on a scale never before seen in a presidential contest, and none of his opponents would be able to compete with it. Obama was able to outspend all others by substantial margins, and he held a significant financial advantage over McCain during the final weeks of the election. His fund-raising, which was driven by an unprecedented number of donors, particularly individuals who gave small amounts, became a defining feature of the election.

Although Obama's fund-raising efforts differed in scope from those of any other candidate, they were emblematic of the financial activity that took place throughout the election cycle. Republicans and Democrats alike engaged in a frenzied quest for campaign dollars, with the top fund-raisers amassing sizable sums, especially compared to candidates in the past. Overall, those seeking the major party nominations raised more than $1.2 billion for use in the primaries. With general election receipts included, the total reached close to $1.7 billion, which was twice the $844 million total received by the candidates in the primary and general elections in 2004 and almost three times the $566 million received from all sources by the presidential contenders in 2000.[4]

This growth in campaign funding was a result of the diverse strategies employed by the candidates in their efforts to accumulate the resources needed to mount what they considered to be a viable bid for the Oval Office. While many of the techniques were not new, the candidates combined proven approaches with innovative tactics, leaving few options unexplored in the search for funding. The only option most of the candidates passed up was public funding. All of the major candidates—with the exception of former Democratic vice presidential candidate John Edwards—decided to rely on private rather than public funding during the nomination phase of the contest. In the general election, McCain accepted the public grant, but he supplemented this money in a variety of ways, so that the limited public funds proved to be only a part of his total campaign budget. The 2008 election thus signaled the death knell of public funding as an important source of campaign money, since, in the end, presidential aspirants financed their campaigns primarily from private sources. The methods they used and the implications for future presidential elections are the principal subjects of this chapter.

The Demand for Dollars

Presidential candidates always face intense pressure to raise money. A presidential campaign is an expensive endeavor, and those who hope to compete in the early contests in Iowa and New Hampshire typically have to raise millions of dollars in the year before the election year to do so. Because fund-raising totals are one of the few measures available to assess the relative prospects of the candidates before the voting begins, those who hope to be ranked among the front-runners usually have to raise tens of millions of dollars. No matter how well-known a candidate may be, this is a daunting task.

In 2008 the demand for campaign money was especially acute. The presumption that most contenders would forgo public funds and thus face no spending restraints, combined with changes in the primary calendar that exacerbated the "front-loading" of the selection process and the competition created by open nomination contests in both parties, produced a money chase that elevated the fund-raising bar to extraordinary heights. Some pundits estimated that a candidate who hoped to be financially competitive would have to raise as much as $100 million by the end of 2007.[5] To put this figure in some perspective, political scientist Michael Malbin noted that a candidate would have to raise, on average, more than $10,000 "every single hour, every single day, including weekends and holidays, for an entire year" to reach this amount.[6] What was most surprising is that the top fund-raisers almost did just that.

The 2008 election was not the first presidential contest in which candidates chose to rely on private financing and thereby avoid the public funding spending restraints. In 2000 George Bush became the first major party candidate to win the nomination after refusing public funding. By doing so, he was able to outspend his eventual Democratic opponent, Al Gore, by a margin of 2 to 1, and exploited this financial advantage during the summer months leading up to the national party conventions, when Gore was essentially prohibited from spending additional sums due to the spending limits.[7] In 2004 Bush opted out again, which placed pressure on his prospective opponents in the Democratic Party to follow suit. Whether any of the Democrats would do so was an unknown early in the election cycle. Eventually Democrat Howard Dean announced in November 2003 that he would not accept public funds (at the time, Dean led the Democratic field in fund-raising and was successfully raising money through the Internet).[8] John Kerry also decided not to take public funds (although unlike Dean, Kerry opted out in order to spend more than $50,000 of his own money on the campaign, which would not have been permitted under the public funding rules).[9] As a result, in both parties, the winner of the nomination relied on private funding and was able to raise and spend significantly more than the public funding expenditure cap would have allowed. By the end of the primaries, which for the purposes of federal campaign finance law occurs at the time of a party's national nomination convention, Bush had raised $260 million and Kerry, $248 million.[10] Each challenger thus spent five times the $50 million that would have been permitted during the primaries in 2004 under the public funding limits.

What was different in 2008 was that most of the candidates were expected to opt out of public funding from the start. Under the terms of the public funding matching program, a candidate eligible for public financing in the primary election could receive matching public funds on a dollar-for-dollar basis on the first $250 contributed by an individual donor. The total amount an individual could contribute under federal law was $2,300 per election, which meant that an individual could give this sum in the primary and again in the general election. Any amount received from public funds was thus likely to constitute a relatively small share of a candidate's total primary receipts. In exchange for this subsidy, a candidate had to abide by an aggregate primary spending limit of $54 million and agree to limit any personal loans or expenditures in support of the campaign to no more than $50,000. Most candidates were unwilling to accept this trade-off.

Presidential contenders based their fund-raising strategies on the lessons they drew from the 2004 election, which had demonstrated that front-running candidates could raise and spend much more than the amount permitted by the spending limit. In addition, previous races had demonstrated that the cap was wholly inadequate given the costs of a presidential campaign. Any candidate who accepted public money was likely to be significantly outspent by a privately funded opponent, and was certain to be at a severe disadvantage during the months bridging the effective end of the primary race—which was expected to occur as early as the end of February or beginning of March—and the formal end of the primary season, which occurred at the national conventions at the end of the summer.

So in 2008, public funding was no longer a viable fund-raising option for the nomination contest. Given the changes that had occurred in the presidential selection process, it was unrealistic to assume that $54 million would be an adequate amount for a winning campaign. A number of large states, including California, New York, New Jersey, and Illinois, had moved their contests forward to the beginning of February, while Florida and Michigan, hoping to draw more attention from the candidates, scheduled contests in January. This in turn led Iowa and New Hampshire to move their traditional "first in the nation" events to the beginning of January. The result was the earliest start in any presidential race and a heavily front-loaded primary schedule, which included a Super Tuesday the first week of February, when more than twenty states held primaries or caucuses in both parties. Consequently, in the year *before* the election, candidates had to raise the money needed to compete in Iowa and New Hampshire, as well as the sums required to build organizations in other states.

Moreover, for the first time since 1952, no incumbent president or vice president was competing for a party nomination. Both parties therefore promised open, highly competitive contests, which attracted strong fields of candidates. Few believed that a candidate could run a viable, competitive campaign in such a resource-intensive process and still have much money left to spend by the end of February under the provisions of the spending ceiling.

It is therefore not surprising that almost all of the candidates chose to forgo public funding. In January 2007, a year before the first voting was to take place in Iowa, Democrat Hillary Clinton, who began her bid for the presidency with a list of 250,000 previous donors and $10 million in available cash in her Senate campaign bank account that could be used in her presidential campaign, indicated that she would not accept public funding during the primaries.[11] Within a few months, it was evident that the other top contenders on both sides of the aisle would also forsake public funds. The only notable exception was John Edwards, who lagged behind the front-runners in the Democratic fund-raising race throughout the campaign, and ended up receiving $12.9 million in public money as part of his campaign's $49.6 million total by the end of his campaign. In any previous presidential election, $50 million would have been considered an impressive sum. But the 2008 fund-raising race proved to be different from any other.

Fund-raising in the Primary Campaign

Freed from the constraints of spending limits and confronting a financially demanding process, the presidential candidates began building their campaign war chests early and tried to capitalize on every opportunity to raise money. By the end of the first quarter of 2007, the challengers had already taken in more than $157 million, or five times the $30 million total that candidates had received in the first quarter of 2003.[12] The Democrats reported more than $95 million in first quarter receipts, while their Republican counterparts reported close to $62 million. By the end of 2007, the total had reached $552 million, or more than double the previous off-year fund-raising record of $273 million, which was achieved in 2003.[13] The Democrats raised the most, taking in $292 million by year's end, as opposed to $260 million for the Republicans. But as these figures indicate, both parties featured unprecedented levels of fund-raising.

To raise such large sums, the candidates made use of an array of fund-raising devices and techniques. As in the past, most of the money was raised through high-dollar fund-raising efforts, including traditional fund-raising dinners, celebrity galas, and special events. Some candidates even held fund-raisers in locations overseas.[14] The top candidates also relied heavily on volunteer fund-raisers, commonly called "bundlers," who were capable of soliciting large sums of money on a candidate's behalf. But a major difference from past campaigns was the extent to which the leading fund-raisers relied on the Internet as a means of soliciting small-dollar donations. The growth of the Internet as a fund-raising tool, combined with the voter outreach facilitated by online social networks and campaign websites, provided candidates with a means of seeking small donations that was more efficient and less expensive than direct mail or telephone programs, although these more traditional methods also continued to be used by most of the contenders.

Perhaps the best indicator of the intensity of the fund-raising race was the panoply of unique or innovative means candidates used to solicit money. These ranged from phone-a-thons conducted with the help of corporate CEOs to direct donations made through cellular phones, from special contests and giveaways offered to online donors to opportunities for large donors to join the candidate at debates, on the campaign trail, or, for some who made a contribution to Senator Clinton, at an exercise bike workout session with former president Bill Clinton.[15] At the end of each financial reporting period, the candidates sent out urgent appeals encouraging supporters to make a donation before the filing deadline in an effort to make their fund-raising numbers look as good as possible. And if able, they dipped into their own pockets or borrowed funds in an effort to stay in the chase.

Overall, by the end of the primaries, the candidates had taken in more than $1.2 billion (Table 5.1). Most of this sum, representing about three out of every four dollars received during the primaries, was raised by the top two candidates in each party, Democrats Obama and Clinton, and Republicans McCain and Mitt Romney.

Table 5.1 Summary of Presidential Campaign Financing (as of August 31, 2008)

Candidate	Receipts	Disbursement	Individual	PAC	Candidate	Other	Public Funding
			Sources of Funding				
DEMOCRATS							
Obama, Barack	453.9	376.5	426.8	0	0	27.1	0
Clinton, Hillary	220.1	211.6	194.1	1.3	13.2	11.5	0
Edwards, John	49.6	43.5	35.1	0	0	1.6	12.9
Richardson, Bill	22.2	22.1	21.8	0.3	0	0.1	0
Dodd, Christopher	15.1	15.1	8.9	0.7	0	4.6	0.9
Biden, Joseph	11.9	11.1	7.8	0.2	0	1.9	2.0
Kucinich, Dennis	5.5	5.3	4.4	0	0	0	1.1
Gravel, Mike	0.5	0.6	0.5	0	0	0	0
Subtotal	*778.8*	*685.8*	*699.4*	*2.5*	*13.2*	*46.8*	*16.9*
REPUBLICANS							
McCain, John	210.6	177.8	184.3	1.3	0	25.0	0
Romney, Mitt	105.2	105.1	59.8	0.4	44.7	0.3	0
Giuliani, Rudolph	58.7	58.6	55	0.4	0.8	2.5	0
Paul, Ron	34.5	30.4	34.3	0	0	0.2	0
Thompson, Fred	23.5	23.2	23.2	0.2	0	0.1	0
Huckabee, Mike	16.1	16.1	16	0.1	0	0	0
Tancredo, Thomas	8.2	8.2	4	0	0	2.1	2.1
Brownback, Samuel	4.2	4.2	3.5	0	0	0.7	0
Hunter, Duncan	2.8	2.8	2.3	0	0	0	0.5
Thompson, Tommy	1.2	1.2	1	0	0.2	0	0
Cox, John	1.1	1.1	0	0	1.1	0	0
Gilmore, James	0.3	0.4	0.3	0	0	0	0
Subtotal	*466.4*	*429.1*	*383.7*	*2.4*	*46.8*	*30.9*	*2.6*
Total	1245.2	1114.9	1083.1	4.9	60.0	77.7	19.5

Note: Based on data reported by the Federal Election Commission. Figures in millions of dollars. Figures may reflect minor variances due to rounding.

Obama outpaced all others by a substantial margin. During the entire primary period, he raised $454 million, including more than $40 million in general election money that had been raised from individuals who had already given the $2,300 maximum contribution in the primaries and had made another contribution for use in the general election. His $414 million in primary receipts was almost $200 million more than the $220 million amassed by Clinton, who in turn topped all other candidates, including the Republican nominee, McCain. Obama and Clinton established themselves as the fund-raising leaders early in the race and never relinquished this position. Obama emerged as Clinton's principal challenger when he raised $25.7 million in contributions in the first quarter of 2007, basically matching the sum that Clinton received in first quarter contributions, an unexpected outcome. From then on, Obama led the fund-raising race, finishing 2007 with a total of $99.6 million, as compared to Clinton's $98.7 million, which included the $10 million Clinton had transferred from her Senate committee at the start of the campaign. Thereafter, Obama surged ahead, out-raising Clinton by more than $70 million during the hard-fought primary period from January 1 to May 31, 2008. In this period, Obama raised an additional $186 million in primary money from all sources, bringing his total at the end of May to $286 million (not including almost $10 million in prospective general election contributions that he had received by this time), as compared to an additional $116 million for Clinton, which brought her total at the end of May to $214 million (not including almost $24 million in prospective general election contributions). Obama then raised another $130 million of primary money during the summer months leading up to the convention.

Republican fund-raising throughout the election cycle paled in comparison to the amounts generated by the top Democrats. At the end of 2007, Mitt Romney led the Republican pack, with total receipts of $90 million, but this sum included $35.4 million in personal loans that he had made to his campaign. Former New York City mayor Rudolph Giuliani, who was number two in Republican fund-raising at the end of 2007 with a total of $56 million, raised as much from individual donors ($52.5 million) as Romney did.[16] McCain, who had a strong start in the first quarter of 2007 ($14.8 million), saw his fund-raising prospects ebb throughout the preelection year, and he finished 2007 with a total of $40 million and very little money in the bank. McCain had to secure $4 million of bank loans and drastically cut back his campaign just to gather the resources needed to compete in New Hampshire.[17] But his faltering campaign was revived by his critical New Hampshire victory, and he went on to capture the nomination. Thus most of the $211 million he raised during the primary was received after he had in effect become the party's standard-bearer. Of his $211 million total, $132 million (62 percent) came in after March 31, once donors began to turn their attention to the general election race.

Small Contributions

The key element of Obama's fund-raising strength was his campaign's success in attracting small donations of less than $200. No previous presidential contender had ever raised as much money through small contributions as Obama did, which made his small donor fund-raising the preeminent campaign finance story of the 2008 election. According to an analysis conducted by the nonpartisan Campaign Finance Institute, Obama had garnered more than $217 million in small contributions of $200 or less by the end of August 2008, a sum that exceeded the amounts raised from such contributions by all other candidates in both parties combined.[18] He alone was responsible for more than half of the $410 million of primary money that came from small contributions. In comparison, McCain raised $62 million from small contributions, while Clinton took in $52 million. No other candidate approached these sums. Small contributions constituted 53 percent of Obama's total primary money, as compared to 31 percent of McCain's funds or Clinton's funds. In terms of small contributions, Obama was in a league of his own.

Obama's success was a function of the remarkable productivity of his online fund-raising. From the very start of his campaign, Obama made online fund-raising and volunteer recruitment an integral component of his political operation. Nine days before launching his candidacy in February 2007, Obama retained the services of Blue State Digital, a market research firm specializing in new media that was founded by four former members of Howard Dean's 2004 presidential campaign.[19] Chris Hughes, one of the cofounders of Facebook, also supported Obama and took a sabbatical from that company to join the campaign's staff. Led by these Internet-savvy entrepreneurs, the Obama campaign built a state-of-the-art website that featured a social networking hub, My.BarackObama.com, which became known as MyBO. Their goal was to use this hub to build an "online relationship" with supporters that would encourage them to contribute to the campaign, undertake volunteer activities, and mobilize others to vote.[20]

MyBO set a new standard for using the Internet to recruit and engage a vast network of financial supporters. In addition to providing standard web-based fund-raising tools, such as a "donate" click button that facilitated online credit card contributions, MyBO offered a variety of ways to participate in campaign fund-raising efforts. To spur such giving, the campaign emphasized the construction of email solicitation lists, which was accomplished by capturing the addresses of website visitors, encouraging supporters to sign up to receive email alerts or text messages, asking individuals to register online if they wanted to attend campaign events, and collecting email addresses from those who attended campaign rallies. The campaign spent significant sums on Internet advertisements to expand their presence on websites and search engines to drive traffic to MyBO, and used paraphernalia sales, special limited edition memorabilia offers, and other gimmicks to generate initial donations of $5 or $10 or $30 to expand the pool of donors who could then be solicited again for an additional contribution.[21] By the end of the election, the campaign had built an email list of 13 million addresses, and sent out more than 7,000 different messages, many of which were targeted to donors of specific amounts (for example, different messages were crafted for those who might give small contributions or those who might give larger sums of $1,000 or more).[22]

MyBO also promoted interaction between supporters and the campaign to enhance donor participation. Individuals who made a contribution were often asked to participate in a matching program that asked them to make another contribution that would be matched by another donor. Supporters also could sign up for a "recurring gift" program that would allow them to make donations of as little as $25 on some regular basis via credit card.[23] Users could also establish their own fund-raising page or affinity group to encourage their friends or contacts to make a donation, and then watch their personal "fund-raising thermometer" climb as those individuals gave in response to their requests. In these ways, MyBO gave donors a personal role in the campaign's fund-raising efforts and promoted the creation of a corps of thousands of individuals who were willing to solicit their own networks for campaign dollars.[24] This device was so successful that the campaign set up a grassroots finance committee that helped train supporters in how to collect donations from their friends, relatives, or coworkers, essentially assisting them in how to become "microbundlers."

Obama's online fund-raising began to pay off in the fourth quarter of 2007 and grew exponentially. In the three months before the start of the election year, Obama received $22.2 million from individual donors, including $10.4 million from small individual contributions. This was almost three times the $3.7 million that Clinton received in small contributions during this period. Following his victory in Iowa, Obama's online fund-raising surged. In January alone, he raised $32 million, including $28 million that was contributed online, with 90 percent of this amount coming from individuals who gave $100 or less, and 40 percent from those who gave $25 or less.[25] This one-month online total exceeded the $27 million that Howard Dean had received through the Internet during his entire 2004 campaign.[26]

In February, building on the momentum generated by a number of significant victories on Super Tuesday, Obama raised an astounding $55 million. This one month total was greater than the aggregate amount raised by any previous candidate during the entire period from the start of a presidential candidacy through the end of February, with the exception of Bush in 2004. As in January, most of Obama's total came from small contributions, with 90 percent of online donations consisting of gifts in amounts of $100 or less and more than 50 percent in amounts of $25 or less.[27] Obama raised this sum without participating in any traditional fund-raising events, a feat he was able to accomplish due to the size of his fund-raising base.[28] By the end of February, Obama had already attracted more than 1 million donors. To put this in some perspective, President Bush did not pass the million-donor mark in 2004 until May of that year.[29]

Obama's online fund-raising success provided him with a number of strategic advantages. First, it allowed him to raise money efficiently and at a relatively low cost. His campaign could solicit thousands of proven or potential donors with a simple email transmission, which is much less expensive than direct mail or other mass solicitation techniques. And many of those who gave did so without an initial solicitation; they simply decided to give to Obama, went to the website, and took a few minutes to make a donation. This offered the opportunity to raise large amounts quickly. For example, after his victory in Iowa, he collected $2.8 million online; in the two days after his loss in New Hampshire, $4.4 million; and in the two days after Super Tuesday, $7.6 million.[30] It also allowed him to spend less time attending fund-raisers or calling potential donors, which made more time available to campaign and meet with prospective voters.

Second, Obama's army of small contributors gave him a large pool of donors who could give repeated contributions. Because the vast majority of Obama's contributors gave small amounts, they could give again and again without approaching the maximum contribution limit. And thousands of them did give repeatedly. According to an analysis of Obama's primary campaign receipts conducted by the Campaign Finance Institute, of the 403,000 individuals who donated at least an *aggregate* of $200 or more and thus had their names disclosed in the filings reported to the Federal Election Commission, at least 212,000 were repeat donors who began by making an undisclosed small contribution of less than $200. About 93,000 of these repeat donors gave a total of $400 or less; 106,000 gave more than $400 but less than $1,000; and 13,000 gave $1,000 or more.[31] These repeat donors ended up giving about $100 million to the campaign. They proved to be a vital component of Obama's fund-raising effort and helped to keep his campaign coffers filled throughout the long, grueling Democratic nomination contest.

Third and most importantly, Obama's online fund-raising provided him with the capacity to outspend Senator Clinton at crucial points in the nomination contest. He had the resources needed to build organizations in every state, which put him in a position to compete for delegates nationwide. He was therefore able to stretch the playing field in the crucial early stages of the race, especially on Super Tuesday, when he was able to mount aggressive campaigns in more states than Clinton. Obama's capacity to finance a truly national campaign strained Clinton's resources, since she lacked the money needed to match Obama state by state. Obama was therefore able to accumulate the delegates needed to establish a lead after the first month of primary contests, which he never relinquished in his victorious march to the nomination.

The practical advantage Obama attained as a result of his financial strength was perhaps most evident with regard to television advertising. According to broadcast advertising data gathered by the private firm TNS Media Intelligence/CMAG as analyzed by the University of Wisconsin Advertising Project, Obama spent $74.8 million on television advertising from the beginning of the campaign through to the end of May, as compared to Clinton's $46 million total.[32] (McCain spent only $11.1 million on television in this period.) Prior to the February 5 Super Tuesday voting, Obama and Clinton were relatively equal, with Obama spending $18.2 million on television and Clinton, $16.7 million. In Super Tuesday states, Obama held an advantage, airing ads in sixteen states at a cost of $14.2 million, while Clinton advertised in thirteen states for a total of $11.2 million. Furthermore, Obama outspent Clinton in eight of the twelve states where both contenders were on the air (only Obama purchased ad time in Colorado, Georgia, Kansas, and Minnesota—all states he won—and he did not purchase time in Idaho, where Clinton did but still lost).

After February 5, Obama's fund-raising surge led to a much greater advantage. In the remaining February contests held after Super Tuesday, Obama achieved a 4 to 1 margin in most states, as he allocated $4.4 million to television versus Clinton's $1.2 million. From the beginning of March through the end of May, a period that included a number of battlegrounds, such as Ohio, Texas, Pennsylvania, Indiana, and North Carolina, where Clinton needed victories to try to catch Obama in the delegate race, Obama maintained control of the airwaves, outspending Clinton in every state, while disbursing a total of $41.6 million to Clinton's $19.7 million. Although this ability to purchase more advertising time did not always lead to victory, it helped Obama maximize his vote potential and kept financial pressure on Clinton, who eventually had to lend a total of $13 million to her campaign in order to remain competitive.

Like Obama, Clinton did raise substantial sums of money online, but she could not match her opponent's success. For the most part, she based her fund-raising effort on the more traditional model of presidential campaign finance, concentrating on the solicitation of large contributions of $1,000 or more in an attempt to raise large sums quickly from her well-established base of supporters. Consequently, by the end of 2007, only 14 percent of her total receipts came from small contributions, as compared to 32 percent of Obama's. After witnessing Obama's fund-raising success in January, she began to place more emphasis on online giving. In all, 35 percent of the $14 million she raised in January came from small contributions.[33] In February, her online donations rose after her campaign revealed that the senator had loaned $5 million to the campaign to help finance her efforts in the Super Tuesday states. Of her $36 million February total, $30 million came from online donors, including donations from almost 200,000 new contributors. More than half of this total came from those who gave less than $200.[34]

By March, Clinton was regularly touting her website and urging her supporters to make a contribution online.[35] Her victories in crucial general election states helped to spur such donations. For example, within twenty-four hours of her victory in Pennsylvania's April 22 primary, more than 100,000 supporters gave a total of $10 million, which represented her best fund-raising day of the campaign.[36] But even this was not enough to match Obama's torrid pace. By the end of the campaign, Clinton had raised $52 million from small contributions, which was a notable sum, but less than a quarter of the amount Obama raised from such donors.

On the Republican side, McCain also received a notable amount from small contributions, which totaled $62 million by the time the nominating convention was over. But his campaign never experienced the kind of surge or sustained giving that proved to be so critical in the Democratic race. In fact, about a third of the money McCain generated from small contributions ($19.3 million) was not received until the weeks in August leading up to the convention, well after the general election campaigning had begun and Obama had decided to forgo general election public funding.[37] While McCain had a website that made available the standard fund-raising tools, his campaign wasn't able to capitalize on social networks or new technologies in the ways that Obama or Clinton did.

McCain was not unique in this regard. Among the Republicans, only the insurgent challenger Ron Paul, whose libertarian ideology struck a chord with Republican conservatives, succeeded in raising substantial sums through small donations made primarily by online supporters. In all, Paul received a total of $21.6 million from small contributions, which was double the amount received by any of the other Republican challengers.

Why McCain—and Republicans more generally—failed to connect online is difficult to explain. McCain may have suffered from his reputation as a maverick and his positions on issues that failed to conform to the views of conservatives and right-wing evangelicals, who have traditionally formed the base of Republican small donors. Another factor may have been the demographics of his constituency, which was not centered among younger voters, as was the case with Obama. Whatever the reason, McCain never became an online phenomenon, although he did raise a significant amount of money from small donors by relying on more traditional, more expensive direct mail fund-raising.

Large Contributions

Small donor fund-raising was the focus of much of the public attention given to campaign finance in 2008, but most of the candidates adhered to the patterns of the past and raised most of their money through large contributions of $1,000 or more. Given the importance placed on early fund-raising in media appraisals of a candidate's viability, presidential aspirants have a strong incentive to raise as much money as quickly as possible in the year before the election. Conventional wisdom dictated that the best way to pursue this strategic objective, especially in the earliest stage of a race when most of the candidates are not well known and the public is not yet focused on the race, is to concentrate on large donations, particularly contributions of the $2,300 maximum. Candidates also seek large contributions because it is the most efficient way to maximize the financial potential of their core supporters, who typically have given to their past campaigns for other offices.

With the exception of Obama, all of the major contenders for the nomination raised the major share of their campaign funds from individuals who gave large contributions. Overall, the Republicans and Democrats amassed more than $473 million in primary funds from contributions of $1,000 or more, including $272 million from maximum donations of $2,300.[38] With respect to large contributions, the Democrats fared better than the Republicans, raising $249 million in primary funds from large donations, as compared to $224 million for the Republicans. Among Republicans, McCain led the way with $110 million from large contributions, which represented 54 percent of his total receipts from individuals. Of this amount, $67 million came from those who contributed the $2,300 maximum. Giuliani received close to $45 million, which constituted 82 percent of his receipts from individuals, while Romney's large donors gave $44 million, or 74 percent of his total individual receipts.

As in the case of small donations, Obama was also the fund-raising leader among the Democrats with respect to large contributions. In all, Obama garnered $119 million in primary funds from large contributions, including almost $60 million from donors who gave the maximum $2,300 gift. No other Democrat came close to this total. The scope of Obama's fund-raising success was therefore a result of his ability to raise large sums from individuals across the financial spectrum. Even though large donations made up only 29 percent of his total individual contributions, which was by far the lowest percentage from this source for any nominee in recent elections, the scale of his campaign fund-raising was so vast that this low percentage represented a substantial sum of money. Only Bush in 2004 raised more from large contributions.[39]

Obama realized a $31 million advantage over Clinton solely from large contributions. Clinton received 52 percent of her total funds from individuals in contributions of $1,000 or more, for a total of $88 million. Even more, one out of every three dollars she took in from individuals, or $54 million, came from donations of the maximum amount. Other Democratic contenders—John Edwards, Bill Richardson, Joseph Biden, and Christopher Dodd—also received a majority of their individual donations from those who gave $1,000 or more.

Most of these large contributions were solicited with the assistance of "bundlers," the name given to individuals who serve as volunteer fund-raisers for a campaign and gather large dollar checks on behalf of a candidate. These individuals "bundle" checks they have received from donors—often for the maximum amount—and deliver them or direct them to the campaign. This is usually done by selling tickets to fund-raising dinners, sponsoring fund-raising events, or simply soliciting checks from established fund-raising networks, business contacts, or associates in a firm or company.

The participation of bundlers in presidential fund-raising efforts is not a new development. Since the early 1980s, candidates have relied on such individuals, often naming their top fund-raisers as members of their "finance committee," "business council," or a group given some other title. But their role became more prominent in recent elections due to Bush's reliance on bundlers and the voluntary public disclosure of the names of his "Rangers" and "Pioneers," the nomenclature given to those who raised at least $100,000 or $200,000 for his campaign.

In 2008 the top contenders relied on bundlers to help them gather the large sums of money that they were seeking. Early in the election cycle, the candidates actively recruited individuals who had fund-raising experience and had proven to be effective bundlers in the past. To encourage them in their efforts, the campaign recognized those who met certain target levels—$50,000, $100,000, $500,000, or more—and listed them as part of a campaign group. For example, Clinton had her "Hillraisers" and Giuliani had his "All-America Team." The names of these individuals were often publicly disclosed by a campaign, which helped to create a psychology that encouraged them to try to gain status by achieving higher fund-raising goals.

The bundlers whose names were disclosed by campaigns in 2008 were primarily involved in securities and investments, real estate, lobbying, law firms, or the entertainment industry.[40] An analysis of the disclosures made by the Obama and McCain campaigns as of August 2008 that was conducted by the nonpartisan Center for Responsive Politics determined that Obama had recruited at least 509 bundlers who had raised a minimum of $63 million, while McCain had recruited 534 bundlers who brought in at least $75 million.[41] The top bundlers each raised at least $500,000, a level met by 47 of Obama's supporters and 65 of McCain's. However, the center's dollar estimates were based on the fund-raising threshold associated with each individual listed (e.g., $100,000 or $200,000). Consequently, these totals represent conservative or minimum sums. A more reasonable estimate may be as much as a third higher, bringing the total for Obama's supporters to more than $80 million and McCain's to $100 million. Although not included in the study, Clinton also recruited a significant number of bundlers. In all, 311 individuals qualified as "Hillraisers" by each raising at least $100,000 for her campaign. These bundlers thus brought in a minimum of $31 million, and, more realistically, much more. Thus bundlers helped raise anywhere from $169 million to more than $200 million for the top three candidates.

General Election Fund-raising

Obama's decision to opt out of public financing in the general election gave him a substantial financial advantage over McCain in the fall campaign. In all, Obama's general election contributions totaled $331 million, more than four times the amount that would have been provided by public funding. Because he was not taking the public grant, he could also spend his leftover primary funds, which totaled about $35 million, on general election campaigning. With these funds included, Obama's general election funding totaled $366 million, a remarkable sum for what was essentially a twelve-week campaign. It was a war chest that McCain, even with the help of the Republican Party, found impossible to match.

Obama

When Obama announced his decision to turn down public funding in June, it was already a foregone conclusion that he would be able to raise

more than the $84 million that public funding would provide, given
the amount he had raised in the primaries. But how much more was
uncertain, and he would have to raise significantly more than $84 mil-
lion if he wanted to match his opposition. In the general election,
Obama would have to compete financially with not only McCain but
also the Republican National Committee (RNC), which could spend
more than $19 million in coordination with McCain under the provi-
sions of federal "coordinated spending" rules, as well as an unlimited
amount of money in "independent expenditures" that could not be coordinated with McCain or his staff. The party could also spend unlimited amounts of money on generic voter registration and mobilization
efforts that did not specifically mention McCain but helped him indirectly by registering and turning out Republican voters. This meant
that, even with public funding limits, McCain and his party were likely
to spend $200 million or more on the general election. Similarly, the
Democratic National Committee (DNC) could provide assistance to
Obama, but the committee was trailing the RNC by a substantial margin in fund-raising, and was unlikely to match the RNC's spending. (At
the end of August, the DNC had a cash balance of less than $18 million
available to spend, as compared to $76 million for the RNC.) Thus to be
financially competitive, Obama would have to raise two to three times
more than the $84 million sum.

This was a feasible goal, given the breadth of the financial base that
Obama had developed during the primaries. Every primary donor
could be asked to make another donation for the general election, which
meant that even those who had given the $2,300 maximum in the pri-
mary could give another $2,300. If Obama could raise only half of the
amount that his campaign had received by the end of May, he would be
well on the way to achieving this lofty financial target. In addition,
Obama could continue to recruit new donors, expanding his base of
support even further, and thus bring in new money from those who
had not made a contribution earlier in the election cycle.

Obama's fund-raising in the months leading up to the general election demonstrated that he had made the right strategic choice. Throughout the late summer and fall campaign, his donor base continued to
grow exponentially. The investments made in MyBO and the encour-

agement given to supporters to solicit donations from their personal networks created a fund-raising infrastructure that produced unprecedented sums of money. By the end of August, Obama had already amassed $77 million in cash that could be used in the general election, a sum almost equivalent to the amount he could have received from public funding.

Thereafter, his fund-raising skyrocketed. In the crucial month of September, he raised $150 million, including $100 million in online donations.[42] This astonishing monthly total virtually ensured that he would have the funding required to meet his campaign budget and match the combined sums likely to be spent by McCain and the RNC. It also gave him the resources needed to maintain aggressive campaign operations not only in the traditional presidential battleground states, but also in a number of states that generally voted Republican in presidential elections, including Virginia, Indiana, North Carolina, and Georgia, where the Democrats felt they had a chance of winning.

Even more, the influx of cash allowed his staff to expand many of its planned operations. Over the course of September and the first week of October, the campaign added $25 million to its direct mail budget, as well as tens of millions of dollars to its media and field budgets.[43] At this time the campaign also decided that it had the money to finance a thirty-minute primetime television advertisement to be broadcast on national networks the Wednesday before Election Day. This was the first half-hour ad broadcast nationally by a presidential candidate since 1992, when billionaire Ross Perot had aired such an ad as part of his independent candidacy for the presidency. The Obama ad appeared on CBS, NBC, Fox, and Spanish-language network Univision, as well as MSNBC, BET, and TV One. It drew an estimated audience of 33 million viewers and cost the campaign more than $3 million.[44]

In October, the money was "just raining down," according to Obama's chief of staff, Jim Messina.[45] In the first two weeks of October alone, the campaign took in an additional $36 million, and by the time the election was over, $79 million more had come in. In all, Obama received donations from more than 3 million supporters. These donors had made 6.5 million contributions online, including 6 million gifts made in increments of $100 or less.[46] In addition, 70,000 people had established MyBO fund-raising pages, which produced $30 million for the campaign.[47]

Obama's superior resources allowed him to dominate the campaign both on the ground and over the air. By August, Obama had at least 336 campaign offices nationwide, while McCain had only 101.[48] Yet Obama continued to expand his organization. By the beginning of October, he had built extensive ground operations in all of the key Electoral College states, including forty offices in Missouri, forty in Michigan, twenty in Virginia, eighteen in Ohio, and eighteen in Pennsylvania.[49] He held a comparable advertising advantage, outspending McCain by margins of 3 or 4 to 1 in some of the battleground states. According to the Nielsen Company, during the "general election period," defined as the period from June to November 2008, Obama placed significantly more spot television ads than McCain, buying 419,667 spots, as compared to McCain's 269,992.[50] In short, with private contributions alone, he was able to finance a campaign that McCain couldn't match under the restrictions of public funding.

McCain

McCain did not have a poorly funded campaign. Like other presidential nominees in the past, he raised private funds to supplement the $84 million of public money that he received. These private contributions, which were also subject to the individual contribution limit of $2,300, were used to pay the legal and administrative costs incurred in the general election to comply with the requirements of federal law. Known as GELAC funds (general election legal, accounting, and compliance funds), they could be used to defray a variety of expenses, including up to 10 percent of a campaign's payroll expenses and overhead costs. Through the end of the election year, McCain had spent $20 million from his campaign's GELAC account. When this money is added to the public grant, the total amount spent by his campaign was $104 million.

Furthermore, like Bush and Kerry in 2004, McCain received substantial party support. Under federal law, a national party committee is allowed to spend a limited amount of money in coordination with its presidential nominee. In making these "coordinated" expenditures, the party committee may consult with the candidate or members of the campaign staff to determine how this money should be spent. In 2008 each national party committee was allowed to disburse up to $19.5 million on such coordinated expenditures. The RNC spent this amount in support of McCain.

In addition, a party committee can provide direct support to a candidate in other ways. A party can spend an unlimited amount of money expressly advocating the election or defeat of a presidential candidate, so long as these expenditures are not coordinated with a candidate; that is, they must be made independent of a candidate or his campaign. In 2008 the RNC spent $53 million independently in support of McCain, with essentially this entire sum spent on negative ads against Obama. When the party's coordinated and independent expenditures are added to the amount spent by McCain, the total spent in support of the Republican ticket rises to more than $176 million.

Parties can also support a presidential nominee by sharing the costs of hybrid ads, which include a generic party message that supports the party or its candidates as a whole, in addition to statements promoting the presidential candidate. These ads, which were first used in 2004, allow a candidate to share the costs of advertising with the party in a way that does not require the costs of such ads to be allocated against the coordinated spending limit. The practice became a matter of controversy in 2004, when the RNC first used this approach to finance more than $45 million in advertising. The Democrats soon followed suit, spending $23 million in this way.[51] After the election, the Federal Election Commission did not find this practice to be in violation of federal law.[52] Accordingly, in 2008, the McCain campaign broadcast some hybrid ads that were jointly funded by the party committees, but the amounts spent on such ads were not disclosed and cannot be discerned from party spending reports.

Finally, the party committees can also supplement the public funds of a presidential candidate by spending money in ways that can indirectly assist a candidate. In this regard, the principal method is to spend money on generic Republican voter identification and turnout programs designed to get Republicans out to vote. In 2008 the RNC and state party organizations spent tens of millions of dollars on such efforts, but the exact amounts are not known.

Thus, as in 2004, public funding made up only a part of the Republican presidential campaign budget. What was different in 2008 was the way in which much of this money was collected. The candidates and their parties both made extensive use of joint fund-raising committees as a means of raising money for their campaigns and their parties.

Joint fund-raising committees are established by a candidate and a national party and/or state party committee that undertakes fund-raising activities designed to benefit all of the participants. Such committees have been used by parties and federal candidates in the past, but their role has never been as prominent in presidential campaigns as was the case in 2008. Beginning in April of 2008, McCain began to work with the RNC and state parties to establish such committees. These committees offered the advantage of allowing the participants to solicit large sums from well-heeled donors.

For example, under the provisions of the Bipartisan Campaign Reform Act, better known as "McCain-Feingold," the aggregate amount any individual could give in a federal election cycle to candidates, parties, and PACs was increased from $25,000 per year to $95,000 per two-year election cycle. With adjustments for inflation, this two-year aggregate limit rose to $108,200 for the 2008 election cycle. In addition, the law increased the amount an individual was allowed to give to a candidate or party committee. So, with the adjustments contained in the law, an individual could give up to $2,300 per election to a candidate, up to $28,500 per year to a national party committee, and up to $65,500 in total to all party committees or PACs. Thus, at a joint fund-raising event, an individual could give $2,300 to a candidate's primary campaign and/or general election campaign (or GELAC fund in the case of McCain), $28,500 to the RNC, and $10,000 to a state party committee. An individual who gave to more than one party committee could give as much as $65,500 in all. This made it possible for one individual to give $33,100 ($2,300 plus $2,300 plus $28,500) and as much as $70,100 at one fund-raising event if the donor could give the maximum party amount ($2,300 plus $2,300 plus $65,500). In this way, McCain and his party could raise large sums quickly and efficiently for use in the general election.

As noted in Table 5.2, both sides raised significant amounts of money through the use of joint fund-raising committees. The Republicans were the first to make use of such committees, establishing McCain Victory 2008, McCain Victory Committee, and following the convention, McCain-Palin Victory 2008 as their principal committees. They also formed a number of committees with specific state parties. In all, these committees took in a total of $172 million. Most of this money was then transferred to the RNC, which received $119 million from these committees, including $69.8 million from McCain-Palin Victory 2008. McCain received almost $32 million, including $20.3 million in funds for his primary committee and $11.6 million in compliance funds for use in the general election. The remaining sum, about $21 million, was transferred to state parties and was probably used for general election voter mobilization efforts.

Table 5.2 Joint Fund-raising Activity

Republican Joint Fund-raising Committee	Total Amount Raised	McCain 2008	McCain Compliance	RNC	State Parties
McCain Victory Committee	11,182,940	991,842	-	10,191,098	-
McCain Victory 2008	66,066,653	15,378,785	8,405,244	33,349,059	8,933,565
McCain Victory Ohio	3,597,748	1,454,453	550,457	612,451	980,387
McCain Victory Florida	2,326,750	296,333	217,905	1,077,076	735,436
McCain Victory California	8,039,104	1,997,425	1,284,100	2,159,499	2,598,079
McCain Victory Kentucky	558,694	198,337	-	-	360,357
McCain-Palin Victory 2008	74,987,455	-	1,088,245	69,769,466	4,129,744
McCain-Palin Victory California	3,871,179	-	23,707	915,823	2,931,649
McCain-Palin Victory Michigan	-	-	-	-	-
McCain-Palin Victory Ohio	1,418,627	-	-	1,152,948	265,678
Grand Total	172,049,150	20,317,174	11,569,658	119,227,421	20,934,897

Democratic Joint Fund-raising Committee	Total Amount Raised	Obama for America	DNC	Democratic Nominee Account	State Parties
Committee for Change	19,027,052	-	-	-	19,027,052
Obama Victory Fund	175,050,000	86,950,000	88,100,000	-	-
Democratic White House Victory Fund	9,598,779	-	9,450,000	148,779	-
Grand Total	203,675,831	86,950,000	97,550,000	148,779	19,027,052

Once the Republicans began to use these joint committees, the Democrats also adopted this approach. Three committees were eventually established, with most of the fund-raising done through the Obama Victory Fund, a committee jointly established by the Obama campaign and the DNC. In all, the Democrats raised almost $204 million through these joint efforts, or about $31 million more than the total achieved by the Republicans. These efforts proved to be particularly lucrative for Obama, who received $87 million from these committees, or 42 percent of the total proceeds and $55 million more than McCain received. The largest share went to the DNC, which received $97.6 million, while state parties made $19 million.

These joint committees helped McCain and the Republicans raise funds that were sorely needed for the general election. But even in this case, a fund-raising tactic devised by the Republicans to tap into the largesse of the wealthiest donors proved to be of greater benefit to Obama and the Democrats. With respect to fund-raising in 2008, Obama had greater success than any other contender, no matter what type of fund-raising was involved.

Looking Ahead

The 2008 election was characterized by an intensive and unending chase for campaign dollars, spurring candidates to use any means available to try to raise money. Yet the outcomes offered seemingly contradictory lessons regarding the importance of money in presidential campaigns. The Democratic nomination contest followed the patterns of the past. The candidates who raised the most money early emerged as the clear front-runners and were confirmed as the leaders in the race once the actual voting began, leading to a highly competitive spending race. Obama, the candidate who had the most money, was able to wage a better funded, more extensive campaign, and ended up winning the nomination. He then outspent his general election opponent by a substantial margin and won the presidency.

The outcome in the Republican contest told a different story. The best funded candidates faltered, and two candidates with relatively little money available to spend, Mike Huckabee and John McCain, won the Iowa and New Hampshire contests respectively, and emerged as the top contenders for the nomination. McCain, even though he was outspent by some of his opponents, found a way to the nomination, despite having to depend on bank loans and manage a sparse budget throughout the early primary season.

What the primaries revealed is that money can help establish a candidate's viability and front-runner status early in the race, and can play a crucial role in helping a candidate survive the rigors of the front-loaded presidential selection process. They also demonstrated that candidates who can attract the most popular support are the ones who are best positioned to sustain their fund-raising efforts and continue to compete. But a candidate with major weaknesses cannot resolve these flaws by simply spending money. And those who are strapped for cash can triumph over rivals with bigger bank accounts if they can tap into a reservoir of public support.

Future candidates, however, are unlikely to fix their attention on the mixed message concerning the importance of money. Instead, they are likely to focus on Obama and the new model of fund-raising that he established. Presidential hopefuls and political professionals will seek to emulate Obama's success and attempt to harness the power of the Internet as Obama did. Whether others can be as successful as Obama remains to be seen. The 2008 experience suggests that technology alone doesn't guarantee financial success. Obama benefited from a number of factors that may be hard to replicate. He was an inspiring and charismatic candidate, seeking to make history as the first African American nominee of a major party, and as the first African American president. He was running as a candidate representing change, in an election defined by an electorate anxious for change. And he was embraced by a new generation of online activists and young voters who fervently participated in his campaign in ways that were not possible only a few years ago.

Although future candidates may not be able to develop fund-raising operations of a scope comparable to Obama's, they will certainly adopt and seek to refine the approaches and tactics used by the candidates in 2008. Like Obama, they will integrate online electioneering into their campaign plans from the start, and emphasize online fund-raising in the search for campaign dollars. They will work to improve the interactive tools and techniques needed to capitalize on social networks, and generate new means of involving supporters in their fund-raising efforts. Fund-raising is therefore likely to become increasingly decentralized, but there will still be a role for bundlers and joint fund-raising committees, since 2008 proved their value as means of aggregating large sums quickly.

There will be little role, however, for public funding. The experience in 2008 ensures that public funding will not be a meaningful source of money in primary elections, and in general elections it will, in all likelihood, be relegated to an alternative of last resort. Obama demonstrated that it is possible to finance a general election without public funds, and he gained a major strategic advantage over McCain by doing so. Future candidates will not want to suffer McCain's fate. As a result, they will only choose public funding if private funding is not a viable option. Moreover, in 2012, Obama will be expected to opt out again, which will intensify the pressure on challengers to forgo public funds. Already, some pundits are anticipating that Obama will become the first billion dollar *candidate*.[53] If this prediction proves to be true, those who enter the money race will once again be chasing Obama.

Acknowledgment

The author thanks Lokesh Todi and Molly Corbett of Colby College for their assistance with the research and data on which this chapter is based.

Notes

1 Chris Cillizza and Jeffrey H. Birnbaum, "Predictions from FEC Chief," *Washington Post*, December 3, 2006; Anthony Corrado, "The Race for the White House," *National Voter*, June 2007, 8–10; "Fix Federal Aid for Presidential Races," *Christian Science Monitor*, January 26, 2007; and "A Billion Dollar Election Warning," *New York Times*, February 4, 2007.

2 In the 2004 primary and general elections, George Bush raised a total of $356.2 million from all sources, while John Kerry received a total of $318.1 million.

3 In the 2008 election cycle, the Republican and Democratic National Committees raised a combined $687.7 million.

4 For the 2004 figure, see Federal Election Commission (FEC), "Presidential Campaign Activity Summarized," press release, February 3, 2005, www.fec.gov/press/press2005/20050203pressum/20050203pressum.html (accessed February 1, 2009). For 2000, see John C. Green and Nathan S. Bigelow, "The 2000 Presidential Nominations," and Anthony Corrado, "Financing the 2000 Presidential General Election," in *Financing the 2000 Election*, ed. David B. Magleby (Washington, D.C.: Brookings Institution, 2002), 54, 89.

5 Eliza Newlin Carney, "The Death of Public Financing," *National Journal*, June 16, 2007, 34.

6 Carney, "Death of Public Financing," 34.

7 Anthony Corrado, "Financing the 2000 Elections," in *The Election of 2000*, ed. Gerald M. Pomper et al. (New York: Chatham House, 2001), 105.

8 John C. Green, "Financing the 2004 Presidential Nomination Campaigns," in *Financing the 2004 Election*, ed. David B. Magleby et al. (Washington, D.C.: Brookings Institution, 2006), 115.

9 Green, "Financing," 115.

10 Campaign Finance Institute, "Funds Doubled, Small Donations Quadrupled ... " press release, October 4, 2004, www.cfinst.org/pr/prRelease.aspx?ReleaseID=10 (accessed February 7, 2009).

11 Jeff Zeleny and Patrick Healy, "Obama Shows His Strength in a Fund-Raising Feat on Par with Clinton," *New York Times*, April 5, 2007; Zeleny and Healy, "Fix Federal Aid for Presidential Races," *Christian Science Monitor*, January 26, 2007.

12 Campaign Finance Institute, "Big, $1,000+ Donations Supply 79% of Presidential Candidates Early Money," press release, April 16, 2007, www.cfinst.org/pr/prRelease.aspx?ReleaseID=136 (accessed February 9, 2009).

13 Campaign Finance Institute, "Presidential Fund-raising in 2007 Doubles 2003," press release, February 11, 2008, www.cfinst.org/pr/prRelease.aspx?ReleaseID=179 (accessed February 9, 2009).

14 Russ Buettner and Marc Santora, "In '08 Campaign, Money Chase Circles the Globe," *New York Times*, September 22, 2007; Helen Kirwan-Taylor, "How Are They Leaning in Notting Hill?" *New York Times*, April 13, 2008.

15 For some examples, see Carney, "Death of Public Financing," 38.

16 Campaign Finance Institute, "Big, $1,000+ Donations."

17 Matthew Mosk, "McCain Got Loan by Pledging to Seek Federal Funds," *Washington Post*, February 16, 2008.

18 Campaign Finance Institute, "After Holding Financial Advantage in Primaries, Obama Likely to Achieve Only Parity with McCain in General Election," press release, September 25, 2008, www.cfinst.org/pr/prRelease.aspx?ReleaseID=205 (accessed February 9, 2009). All of the figures in this paragraph are from this source.

19 Tom Lowry, "Obama's Secret Digital Weapon," *Business Week*, June 24, 2008.

20 Matthew Mosk, "Obama Rewriting Rules for Raising Campaign Money Online," *Washington Post*, March 28, 2008.

21 Mosk, "Obama Rewriting Rules."

22 Jose Antonio Vargas, "Obama Raised Half a Billion Online," *washingtonpost.com*, November 20, 2008, http://voices.washingtonpost.com/the-trail/2008/11/20/obama_raised_half_a_billion_on.html.

23 Christopher Cooper and John Emshwiller, "Fund Race: Obama Outflanks 'Hill-raisers,'" *Wall Street Journal*, May 8, 2008.

24 Joshua Green, "The Amazing Money Machine, *The Atlantic*, June 2008, 60.

25 Michael Luo, "Small Donations Add Up for Obama," *New York Times*, February 20, 2008.

26 Jose Antonio Vargas, "Campaigns Experimenting Online to See What Works," *Washington Post*, February 3, 2008.

27 Jeff Zeleny and Katharine Q. Seelye, "More Money Is Pouring in for Clinton and Obama," *New York Times*, March 7, 2008.

28 Zeleny and Seelye, "More Money."

29 Paul Farhi, "In April, Kerry's Fund-raising Nearly Doubled Bush's; President Has Spent $130 Million in Race," *Washington Post*, May 21, 2004.

30 Luo, "Small Donations Add Up"; Kristin Jensen and Jonathan D. Salant, "Obama Entered February with Cash Edge of Millions over Clinton," *Bloomberg.com,* February 21, 2008, www.bloomberg.com/apps/news?pid=newsarchive&sid=aDV7PERUwoTc (accessed April 5, 2009).

31 Campaign Finance Institute, "Reality Check: Obama Received About the Same Percentage from Small Donors in 2008 as Bush in 2004," press release, November 24, 2008, www.cfinst.org.pr/prRelease.aspx?ReleaseID=216; Kate Naseef, "Obama Raised Same Percentage of Funds from Small Donors As Bush, Study Says," *BNA Money & Politics Report*, November 25, 2008.

32 TNS Media Intelligence/CMAG and Wisconsin Advertising Project, "Nearly $200 Million Spent on Presidential Campaign TV Ads to Date," press release, June 2, 2008, http://wiscadproject.wisc.edu/wiscads_pressrelease_060208.pdf (accessed February 12, 2009). All figures cited in this paragraph are taken from this source.

33 Mary Jacoby, "Obama Raised Twice As Much As Clinton in March," *Wall Street Journal*, April 4, 2008, A4.

34 Jacoby, "Obama Raised"; Associated Press, "Clinton Raises $35 Million in 1 Month," February 28, 2008.

35 Michael Luo, "Clinton, Emphasizing Web Presence, Sees Rise in Online Donations," *New York Times*, March 22, 2008.

36 Fredreka Schouten, "Small Amounts Add Up for Candidates," *USA Today*, May 2, 2008.

37 Campaign Finance Institute, "After Holding Advantage in Primaries," Table 1.

38 "After Holding Advantage in Primaries," Table 2. The figures on large contributions that follow are all based on this source.

39 In 2004, Bush raised $157 million from individual donations of $1,000 or more.

40 Center for Responsive Politics, "John McCain: Bundlers," www.opensecrets.org/pres08/bundlers.php?id=N00006424, and "Barack Obama: Bundlers," www.opensecrets.org/pres08/bundlers.php?id=N000009638.

41 "John McCain: Bundlers."

42 Vargas, "Obama Raised a Half a Billion Online."

43 Ryan Lizza, "Battle Plans: How Obama Won," *New Yorker*, November 17, 2008, 52.

44 Lizza, "Battle Plans"; Kristin Jensen and Julianna Goldman, "Obama's Prime-time Ad Demonstrates Money Advantage Over McCain," *Bloomberg.com,* October 30, 2008, www.bloomberg.com/apps/news?pid=newsarchive&sid=aiKGAaw6tylw (accessed April 5, 2009).

45 Lizza, "Battle Plans," 52.

46 Vargas, "Obama Raised a Half a Billion."

47 Vargas, "Obama Raised a Half a Billion."

48 http://fivethirtyeight.com/2008/08/obama-leads-better-than-31-in-field.html (accessed February 13, 2009).

49 Karen Ball, "Can Obama's Grass-Roots Army Win Missouri?" *Time*, October 6, 2008.

50 www.swamppolitics.com/news/politics/blog/2008/11/barack_obamas_localtv_ad_campa.html (accessed February 14, 2009).

51 Anthony Corrado, "Financing the 2004 Presidential General Election," in *Financing the 2004 Election*, ed. David B. Magleby et al. (Washington, D.C.: Brookings Institution, 2006), 143.

52 Kenneth P. Doyle, "FEC Audit Orders No Bush Repayment; Dems Say Limit Breached by $42 Million," *Bureau of National Affairs Money & Politics Report*, March 23, 2007.

53 Shailagh Murray and Matthew Mosk, "Under Obama, Web Would Be the Way," *Washington Post*, November 10, 2008.

6

The Selling of the President in a Converged Media Age

Leonard Steinhorn

In 2004, far removed from the flip-flop charges and Swift Boat ads of that year's presidential campaign, Toyota was rolling out a new automobile brand that would augur the future of American politics in far more ways than anything Karl Rove would do to get his candidate reelected. To most observers, Toyota was at the top of its game, challenging the American automotive giants for worldwide preeminence. Its formula seemed to be working. But to Toyota the warning signs were clear: the median age of Toyota owners was well over fifty, and according to its market research, young people saw the brand as old-fashioned, stale, and something only their parents would drive. To capture this new generation, the company would have to reinvent itself. So what Toyota did was create an entirely new style and brand, the Scion, which would be targeted to younger drivers and trendsetters not merely through the hip and boxy design of its signature cars but through a new and unconventional approach to marketing.

Toyota understood that the old mass marketing approach was failing to reach younger consumers, that in a multimedia world broadcast advertising was no longer the magic wand that turned curiosity into sales, that the car itself mattered less to young people than the association conferred by a cool brand. Yes, Toyota ran television and billboard ads and placed some nice glossies in magazines. But traditional ads would play a supporting role to a larger strategic focus on viral marketing built on multiple online, media, and social networking platforms designed to attract this new generation of drivers. To roll out the campaign, custom-built Scions in bright "solar yellow" and "hot lava orange" colors were conspicuously parked outside trendy clubs and concerts with attractive models circulating nearby, drawing in early adopter young people who would "discover" the brand and then pass on the news to their friends. Scion cultivated indie music and art magazines, promoted edgy websites, sponsored snowboarding games and avant-garde media, and pursued such guerrilla marketing tactics as slapping posters all over city walls in defiance of local laws. "Young buyers must discover things on their own, Scion's creed holds, finding products in the marketplace the same way they discover nightclubs that are too hip to have signs on the door," wrote the *New York Times*.[1]

In 2004, while Facebook was still a little known site for college students and YouTube had yet to be conceived, Scion had already figured out the core principles behind marketing in the new media world: establish a unique and iconic brand, broaden the concept of advertising by using every possible media platform to create an emotional bond with your audience, and let people sell your brand through their own social networks. And it worked: Scion quickly emerged as the new hot car, and in the first two years of sales, its median buyer was thirty-one years old, youngest in the automobile industry. Four years later, Barack Obama would apply these same principles to his winning presidential campaign, and in the process he would transform political marketing for years to come.

The King Is Dead.
Long Live the King!

So much has been written about the massive power and outsized role of televised campaign advertising these last few decades that any objective reader might think that everything else in politics is merely secondary and routine. That's not to say there haven't been good reasons to anoint the thirty-second spot king of the political hill in recent years. After all, ours was a culture dominated by television, which from the 1950s onward had become the primary medium for news, comfort, and entertainment. Phrases such as "electronic hearth" and "glued to the tube" were not merely glib commentary but rather a reflection of the fact that Americans were spending a good chunk of their days—almost four hours—sitting in front of the TV and consuming its images. Scholars have ably documented the relationship between the rise of television and the decline of political party participation, and they also have shown how campaign advertising filled the political void, creating "capital-intensive, choreographed media spectacles" that channel focus group–tested messages to voters and insinuate themselves not merely into our living rooms but into our emotional association with candidates.[2] As Neil Postman observed in *Amusing Ourselves to Death*, his 1985 landmark book on our mass media culture, "In America, the fundamental metaphor for political discourse is the television commercial."[3]

In a political kingdom where advertising reigns ubiquitous and supreme, it's quite natural to assume that ads are so decisive and powerful that they determine elections. So we read how Americans in 1964 were swayed by the legendary Daisy ad, which ran only once on nationwide TV but evoked such larger-than-life fears of nuclear war that voters turned away from Senator Barry Goldwater and delivered a landslide to President Lyndon Johnson. Or how the 1988 election was determined by the double helix of race and crime that was coded into the notorious Willie Horton ad. Or how Ronald Reagan's gauzy Morning in America spot bathed voters in such small-town patriotic warmth that they couldn't but reelect him in 1984.

Such analyses are surely tempting, and they reflect the salience and visibility of advertising in our contemporary media and political culture. But they attribute way too much power to the spot and not enough to the larger branding strategy of which the advertising campaign was merely an expression and component part. In other words, our fixation with political advertising, as understandable as it may be, has led us to confuse the dazzling and sexy tactics that grab our attention with the overall behind-the-scenes communication strategy that makes these tactics work. In glorifying the ad du jour, we lose sight of the fact that political campaigns—even before television—have always been about using every possible media vehicle to create an iconic image of your own candidate and an unflattering impression of your opponent.

Television didn't exist in 1840 when patrician William Henry Harrison rebranded himself as a man of the people, a humble frontiersman who drank hard cider and hailed from log cabin roots, images that were reinforced in the banners, bunting, posters, and cabin-shaped whiskey bottles that advertised his winning campaign. Nor did television have anything to do with the hope and confidence Franklin Roosevelt instilled and his ability to portray his presidency as a voice of the people, leading an entire hardscrabble generation to identify politically and emotionally with the New Deal. John Kennedy may have been the first real television president, but his campaign ads were fairly mundane and had little to do with his winning image as a torch bearer for a new generation anxious to break from a stale, musty, and stifling past. Richard Nixon may have run ads associating his opponent with Vietnam and civil unrest, but the real lesson from that campaign, as documented by Joe McGinniss in his groundbreaking book on the 1968 election, *The Selling of the President*, was Nixon's effort to rebrand himself as a broad-minded and visionary leader, a unifier, a man of peace and reason, a new Nixon completely unlike the untrustworthy old.

Thus it wasn't the Daisy ad's nuclear mushroom that made voters nervous about Barry Goldwater, but rather the larger frame created by the Johnson campaign that in such uncertain times, both at home and abroad, Goldwater was too volatile, extreme, and narrow-minded to be president. Nor was Willie Horton the reason why voters never gravitated to Dukakis but rather the perception, shaped throughout the election by his opponent George H. W. Bush, that Dukakis was a remote, standoffish elitist detached from mainstream America, and that Democrats remained a party stuck in the permissive, antiwar, indulgent 1960s. And as appealing as the Morning in America ad was, it only manifested a Reagan brand that his White House had been cultivating for years, one steeped in the symbols, values, and perceived authenticity of an erst-while America that many voters either yearned to restore or never wanted to give up.

Despite all the attention paid to campaign advertising, the truth is that television ads alone will not win an election. But an effective branding campaign—one that turns every media tool into an advertising vehicle—will. Media come and go and morph over the years, and what may be the dominant medium today may end up sharing the stage with others tomorrow. Political campaigns have always been integrated marketing campaigns, ones that use every possible vehicle and channel to reach the emotional sweet spot of voters. Years ago torchlight parades, banners, buttons, pamphlets, and songs connected voters with candidates, and in recent decades television ads submerged all other media in reaching the public, making it seem as if ad buys alone would enable a candidate to prevail. But today, with media converging and transforming almost daily, with a newly dominant visual medium—YouTube—barely a few years old, with online interactivity changing our very experience with politics, news, information, and media, the old ways that seemed so magical a few years ago no longer apply. Toyota figured it out with its Scion brand; Barack Obama understood it as he launched his long-shot presidential campaign.

Perhaps the greatest irony of the Obama candidacy is that he spent nearly twice as much on television advertising as John McCain did during the general election and Hillary Clinton did in key primary states, yet his improbable candidacy may not have overcome the odds had his branding relied solely on the thirty-second spot. Like Scion, he figured out that traditional TV advertising, while necessary, is not sufficient in a converged media era for building a brand and creating an icon. Like Scion, he recognized not only the extent to which our culture has changed but also the powerful ways that new media have transformed the relationship between people and their brands. Obama was doing what successful presidential candidates before him had done—creating and nourishing his brand—but he was the first to understand how our new and more diverse media environment has so thoroughly changed the strategic calculus for getting elected.

The Audacity of Change

"The shift to new media," writes the British technology and politics expert Anthony Painter, "is a cultural rather than a technological one," as cyber-savvy denizens of today increasingly define their personalities and lives in relation to their mobile and interactive new media world.[4] As more and more Americans go online for their news and entertainment, and as they increasingly do it on portable devices that give them instantaneous access to information and spin as well as the opportunity to create their own virtual response, campaigns must decode and understand this new media culture or risk fraying the electronic threads that they hope will bind them to potential voters.

According to the Pew Internet and American Life Project, which has done extensive research into our online habits and trends, about 75 percent of all baby boomers, 80 percent of the Generation X cohort, and 90 percent of under-thirty Americans are active online. And while the type of activity varies according to life stage, education, and other demographic factors, the very nature of the Internet creates an interactive culture that didn't much exist when television ruled our media environment. If old media communicated through a monologue, new media engage us not only in a dialogue but in a large, organic, dynamic discussion with multiple friends and peers, often all at once. This participatory Internet culture, according to Pew researchers Mary Madden and Susannah Fox, replaces "the authoritative heft of traditional institutions with the surging wisdom of crowds." For young people, social networking sites such as Facebook and MySpace serve this interactive need, but their urge to communicate and engage is no different from those who rely primarily on email. As Madden and Fox observe, "the beating heart of the Internet has always been its ability to leverage our social connections."[5]

This emerging new media behemoth thrust itself into the 2008 presidential campaign in unprecedented ways, according to a Pew study conducted just as the presidential primary season ended. Even before the nation focused on the general election, nearly half of all Americans, 46 percent, used the Internet, email, or mobile phone text messaging to get news about the campaign and to share political thoughts with others.

Thirty-five percent watched online videos related to the election (three times the number that did in 2004), and one in six Americans read a candidate's position paper online. Of the vast majority of adults under thirty who participate in social networking sites, half used them to get or exchange information about the candidates and campaign; among eighteen- to twenty-nine-year-old Internet users, one in eight posted their own political commentary or writing; and among Obama voters, two-thirds had gone online to get political news and information. That the online magnet draws voters into the process is evident from the 28 percent of wired Americans who said that their online activity made them feel more personally connected to the campaign and the 22 percent who said they would not have been as involved in the campaign were it not for the Internet.[6] Presumably these numbers would be even higher had Pew conducted them after the November election, particularly given Obama's aggressive effort in the summer and fall to accumulate cell numbers, email addresses, and social networking links. But whatever the actual statistics, they clearly document the enormous and growing synergy between political campaigns and our interactive online culture.

Currently about 75 percent of American households are online, compared to only 61 percent that have cable television. Internet users between the ages of eighteen and sixty-five spend more than one-sixth of their weekly media consumption in front of the computer (and this doesn't include their time reading, writing, and responding to email). Add to this metric the fact that about 85 percent of Americans have cell phones, which is the next frontier for online activity. With wired younger cohorts replacing their less technologically literate elders, the potential for nearly universal online participation is clear. Five decades ago we began to understand how the primacy of television was reshaping our civic culture, turning visual imagery into the new language of politics. Now we must once again figure out how these new media are transforming and influencing the way we engage the political process.

Perhaps the biggest mistake would be to categorize the Internet as simply another information medium with its own particular bells and whistles but not all that different from newspapers or TV, much the way observers of early television thought of it as radio with pictures.

True to the McLuhan notion that the medium is the message, the very qualities of the online experience are rewriting the rules of how we receive information, what we expect from it, how we process it, and what we do with it. Equally mistaken is the notion that new media are simply a more sophisticated one-way channel for content creators and message disseminators to infuse their target audience with a particular message or desire. Call that the old TV advertising model of communication, in which passive citizens absorb whatever the brand maestros serve them. Now it may be true that some brands use the Internet quite successfully to pull their publics into their message orbit. But the larger point is that those publics want, expect, and demand a voice in the brand or image with which they are willing to associate, and they are also ready to shout at the top of their virtual lungs if the brand meets or exceeds their expectations—or if it disappoints.

In the old days, when content producers had all the power and delivered it to us via our living room screen, we had few checks and balances beyond our remote controls and wallets. But online media have empowered us and given us a voice. They have created not merely an interactive culture but a centrifugal one: through links and content sharing and content production as well, we now have the opportunity to spin off ideas, commentary, rumors, humor, visuals, videos, and anything else that captures our imagination to all others in our electronic universe, which then gets spread virally throughout the online world. Thus we all become both thought leaders and information consumers among our circle of peers and contacts, and as thought leaders we become quite attuned to the quality, authenticity, originality, and cool factor of what we send to others. So slick and hype are out (we don't want our friends and contacts to think we're ciphers and stooges for someone else's message), as is anything that seems like a traditional sales pitch. But we're more than happy to serve as ambassadors for what we perceive to be genuine and unique. Yogi Berra once said of a restaurant that "nobody goes there anymore—it's too crowded," and what he meant is that the trendsetters had ventured out to find a new cool haunt that they could "discover" and then share with their friends. Remember the Scion creed— that people want to find things out on their own, that they want to be the ones to discover the hot club that's too hip to have a sign on the door. That's how we approach what we find on the Internet.

So in the new media culture we imagine ourselves as cool hunters and cool consumers in a cool community of peers, which may explain why we remain so connected all the time—we don't want to be left behind—as well as why we so quickly share content with those we know—we want our turn as an influential in the virtual communities we inhabit. According to one study, the typical consumer today sees about 30,000 ad messages per week but acts on only four; our response to recommendations from friends we trust is far more obliging: for every three recommendations our friends send us, we accept and act on one of them.[7] We also seek out online sites with any form of social content, including wikis that allow all of us to contribute and edit content as well as sites with user-generated product reviews such as Trip Adviser and Amazon.com, which appear to provide a sense of raw authenticity unfiltered by a marketing campaign. It's not that large-scale ad campaigns don't work anymore, but rather that ads are increasingly most useful in piquing our interest, which we then pursue interactively online, and it's that interactive experience that then leads to our emotional connection with the product or idea. Whereas television is a mass medium, the equivalent of a speech to a large audience, the Internet is an intimate medium that draws us into a virtual town square of perceived friends, colleagues, and neighbors.

The result is an American culture increasingly shaped by these new media values. It's a culture that wants to be in the know, one that sees information and insight coming not from some distant source or authority figure but from a social network of friends and peers, one that gives people a sense of ownership over a brand or an idea because they either discovered it for their social network, helped disseminate it to others, or heard about it from someone they trust. Knowledge, in effect, becomes part of one's social experience. In this culture, authenticity (or the perception thereof) trumps hype, relationship building trumps the sales pitch, personalized interactions trump mass appeals, friends trump ads, and multiple media platforms trump the old reliance on television. Americans in the new media era may be sitting at their computer desks or navigating their laptops or texting via cell phone, but to them they're active participants in their world rather than passive recipients of mass media infotainment.

This nonhierarchical, participatory, almost rambunctious new media culture arrived, perhaps not coincidentally, with the emergence of a new majority worldview born in the baby boomer 1960s and adopted by their echo boom kids. No longer are we living in the old Silent Majority America where everyone knew their place, where sturdy men and supportive women lived in a prototypical 1950s ethos that to them defined the true American narrative. Today we increasingly value innovation and change over loyalty and custom, expressiveness and personal freedom over stoicism and traditional values, inclusion and pluralism over hierarchy and insularity, transparency and creativity over authority and work rules. Americans may still be religious, but they don't feel obligated to obey church authorities, they respect many pathways to truth, and they often say they're more spiritual than devout. Look at boomers, their younger siblings, and their kids—the same cohorts that have most embraced the new media culture—and they tend to be more open on issues of race, gender equality, sexual orientation, religious choice, and individual freedom, with today's youth generation the least hierarchical and most inclusive and socially liberal in our history.[8]

What has masked the political impact of these changes in culture and media is that the oldest, most technologically challenged and socially conservative cohorts vote in numbers much higher than their percentage in the population, meaning that in election after election they have had a disproportionate say in who gets elected and how campaigns communicate to us. So if candidates pour their resources into reaching a cohort far less amenable to new media and contemporary cultural values, elections will tend to reflect a wave of the past rather than a wave of the future. For years even the best journalists have mistaken these election results for cultural trends, not realizing that all too often they're looking not through the windshield but in the rearview mirror. Witness, for example, the media frenzy over the "moral values" voter after the 2004 election, a result not of any political or cultural trend but of the fact that voters sixty and older that year represented about 25 percent of the electorate even though they comprised only 17 percent of the total population.

The perception that our political culture has been static since, say, the 1980s has led many politicians and pundits to proclaim that the "the real America," as 2008 Republican vice presidential candidate Sarah Palin called it, is embodied by the proverbial Joe Sixpack or blue-collar Reagan Democrat who works in the factory all day and then relaxes at home for hours in front of the TV—personified by John McCain's Joe the Plumber in 2008. This is the Silent Majority template that Richard Nixon created, one shaped by a generalized resentment toward the cultural and racial upheavals that grew out of the 1960s. For many years it was quite a powerful political force, especially since it spoke the cultural language of the World War II and postwar Silent generations, which as they got older voted in numbers disproportionate to their share of the population, particularly in comparison to the upstart boomers who saw the world differently but had yet to throw their electoral weight around. So to win elections, all a campaign had to do was run ads that tapped into cultural issues and air them for the beer drinking majority sitting in front of their television sets in places like Macomb County, Michigan, known as the archetypal home of the Reagan Democrats.

Barack Obama, however, took a calculated risk that our political culture has moved on, that the once dominant political cohorts are being replaced by new and rather large generations that either have no stake in the culture wars of old or simply accept that Americans have changed and have no interest in revisiting the battles of years gone by. Obama guessed—correctly as we now know—that the center of gravity in politics has shifted toward younger-thinking Americans who are much more comfortable not only with contemporary values and cultural change but with a new media approach to processing information and civic participation.

It's not that Obama himself has transformed our politics. Rather, he recognized far earlier than most other politicians the tectonic shifts under way in our culture. Indeed the evidence was there for all to see long before the 2008 election cycle began. On a wide variety of cultural issues, surveys over the years have shown declining support for traditional social values and growing respect for pluralism and different lifestyles, with independent voters, the big prize in every election, about as liberal as most Democrats in their social views. Even young evangelicals have been drifting away from a singular focus on cultural issues. On the most divisive contemporary social issue still in play, gay marriage, the trend has been toward an equality that would have been unimaginable two decades ago. Consider the 2006 Wisconsin referendum on gay marriage: 71 percent of voters sixty-five and older opposed gay marriage, whereas 60 percent of under-thirty voters supported it (note that these older voters constituted 28 percent of the electorate that year versus only 17 percent for the younger cohort, meaning that the older group had a disproportionate say in the outcome). The paradigm shift in our media habits has been equally compelling. By the middle of 2008, Americans were conducting 5 to 8 billion Google searches per month, Facebook and MySpace combined for more than 100 million users in the United States, the typical MySpace user was spending about thirty minutes on the site and viewing about fifty-five pages per visit, and the average American cell phone user was sending and receiving about 350 text messages a month, compared to making and receiving only two hundred phone calls. Nor did the mass medium of television escape this personalization of media. The audience for broadcast shows and news has steadily declined, replaced in part by niche cable media, and Americans were watching television less according to the network schedule and more on their own time, using TiVo and DVR devices not only to record programs but to skip the ads.

With these media, technological, and cultural changes well in place, the members of a new silent majority were waiting for a politician to give them voice—for a leader who spoke their language, trusted their media, embraced their interactivity, understood their worldview, and symbolized their diversity. It's worthwhile noting that John McCain chose to make a 1960s radical, William Ayers, the centerpiece of his attack on Barack Obama, figuring that the old cultural tensions would once again work their magic, and that an independent group supporting McCain spent a considerable sum on a TV ad campaign in Macomb County, Michigan—Reagan Democrat country—questioning Obama's association with his fiery minister, Jeremiah Wright. Neither tactic worked, and McCain lost Michigan in a landslide, 57.3 to 40.9 percent. The new political culture had arrived, and there was no turning back.

The Converged Media Candidate, 2008

John McCain began the 2008 campaign with a formidable brand identity, making him the one Republican that Democrats most feared in the general election. Here was a man of honor, a war hero, someone who served and sacrificed and seemed to stand for the old sturdy virtues that made America great—a narrative that would appeal to the older generations, the ones who voted in disproportionate numbers and leaned culturally conservative. Yet the McCain brand also appealed to younger voters—a maverick and man of integrity willing to stand up to entrenched powers as well as to the ideological leaders of his own political party. By bridging the traditionalist elders with the more contemporary and audacious younger cohorts, McCain offered the GOP a fighting chance to keep the White House despite the deep unpopularity of the Bush administration.

For Barack Obama, his brand was built around his compelling life story as well as an inchoate yearning among Americans to move beyond the cynicism and bitterness of recent politics and to instill a new hope and idealism on behalf of political change. Obama's unique biography exemplified a form of redemption for America, a visible symbol of how our country could move beyond the old conflicts and bind different people together in a diverse and varied nation. But his brand didn't rest on symbolism alone. Americans for years had told pollsters that they wanted to make a difference but thought that anything they tried wouldn't matter, that politicians wouldn't listen to them no matter what they said or did. What Obama promised was empowerment, the opportunity to have an impact, the chance to participate in a community of idealists larger than ourselves. His brand would effectively become our brand as well. It was a message that spoke powerfully to the new media generation.

Both Obama and McCain offered appealing brands that in their own particular ways fit the times and engaged the voters. We know, of course, that the headline news of 2008 is how Obama's brand soared while McCain's collapsed, but the real question is why, and that has much to do with how Obama created a comprehensive integrated communication campaign unlike anything seen before in politics, one built

on the principles of our new media culture, one that embraced supporters not merely as voters but as agents of change. Unlike the persuasive
advertising and mass communication campaigns of old, the ones that
relied almost exclusively on thirty-second TV spots, everything Obama
did—including his advertising—was geared toward building relationships between supporters and his campaign and each other, toward establishing the bonds of trust and interactivity and networking that are
at the core of new media. Everything about the campaign was designed
to reinforce the brand, so someone who set up an Obama Facebook
page or forwarded an Obama text message, for example, felt empowered
as a participant in the Obama effort to change America. The medium
became the message, and the message became the medium.

Senator McCain dabbled in online and search engine advertising,
but for the most part ran a traditional campaign that never kept pace
because it was almost purely image based and not rooted in the social
relationships so essential to building an emotional connection in this
new media era. Thus his brand suffered when his advertising or decisions
seemed to contradict his image, as when one of his ads made the false
and seemingly outrageous accusation that Obama supported comprehensive sex education for kindergartners, a claim so far-fetched that it
made voters question McCain's honor and integrity, the qualities that
were the bedrock of his appeal. Compare that to when Obama broke his
promise to take federal funding for the general election. Obama never
suffered much for it because his campaign's social network had built
strong personal bonds of engagement and trust with supporters, thus
enabling his candidacy to withstand this breach of faith.

So the real story of 2008—why this election serves as an object lesson for future campaigns—is how Obama created his integrated communication campaign and turned every media tool, new and old, into
an instrument to nourish his brand and emotionally connect it with the
American public. Obama's campaign did not merely communicate to
voters, but rather wove a web of communication allowing supporters
and potential supporters to interact with each other and with the campaign and with the media and with anyone in their online universe
vaguely interested in politics and the election. The old one-way or even
two-way communication models ceased to apply here—think instead of

an organic network that has nodes of activity everywhere. Persuasion counted less than participation and emotional engagement, which to Obama was the key to raising money, motivating volunteers, and ultimately winning votes.

Consider the vast social network the campaign generated. Obama first invited people into his online neighborhood and made them feel welcome without giving them a sense that all he wanted was their personal data for some sales pitch later on. Unlike the McCain site, people visiting Obama's online home did not need to sign up first or give their email address and zip code to check out volunteer options or other forms of participation. This made the initial contact seem far more authentic and far less slick, key traits of the new media culture. Indeed the site literally encouraged a unique personal relationship with each visitor by making it easy to set up a personal my.barackobama.com account (known as MyBO) with its own blog, fund-raising page, and tools to access local voters, print out fliers, find events, and join neighborhood groups. Facebook and MySpace have millions of users, but each one sees his or her profile as unique and distinctive, which is exactly the feel the Obama campaign wanted to create—individual identity within a community context.

It should surprise no one that a key Obama hire was a Facebook co-founder, and a sprawling Internet team of ninety online workers ultimately created the most formidable grassroots campaign in political history, with 13 million on its email list, 3 million online donors, 1.5 million who signed up online to volunteer, thousands of individualized membership groups, and satellite sites that included 3 million Facebook and 2 million MySpace friends as well as more than 100,000 who followed the short bursts of campaign text on Twitter.[9] Add to that the campaign's mobile phone outreach enticing upward of 3 million Americans to share their cell numbers with the promise that they would be the first to receive breaking campaign news, such as the vice presidential selection, and also providing them with cell phone applications including wallpaper downloads, streaming video, Obama ringtones, tools to organize call lists for all contacts in battleground states, and even directions to the nearest brick and mortar campaign office. In effect, the Obama campaign's social networking swirl created millions of online and mobile advertising messages that pervaded almost every sector of electronic life every hour of every day. Those empowered, hundreds of thousands of them, would then serve as online advocates promoting Obama at every opportunity, such as voting for pro-Obama articles on sites such as Digg.com, which would then catapult the piece to the top of Google searches, and serving as rapid responders who would send out facts to rebut accusations made by the McCain campaign. At bottom is a deep and powerful psychological insight: by empowering supporters to make their own contacts and write their own blogs and send online content and associate constantly with the campaign, it became an election not just about Obama but about us.

Of course every social networking community needs content, and Obama's team provided that as well. Each Obama appearance and speech was treated as a content-sharing opportunity, which explains why his campaign hired a fairly large production staff to create sophisticated video for the web and all other visual media. Obama's YouTube channel posted more than 1,800 videos and registered nearly 20 million views throughout the campaign, and if you happened not to be online, you could catch the same content on the DISH satellite network's all-Obama channel or see a teaser video on DirecTV.

But once again the genius of this campaign was not in what it created but in what it empowered and emboldened others to create. Supporters put together thousands of home brewed videos that they shared with their personal network, and some of the high-profile online video productions reached audiences greater than many news and entertainment shows on TV. For example, the musician Will.I.Am's powerful rendering of Obama's post-New Hampshire primary "Yes We Can" speech, featuring such celebrities as Scarlett Johannson, Kareem Abdul Jabbar, John Legend, and about fifteen others singing Obama's words, generated more than 4 million YouTube views in one week and more than 15 million by the time of the November election. Comedian Sarah Silverman's online video appeal to Jewish voters, "The Great Schlep," captured more than 7 million hits and led nearly 13,000 Obama supporters to sign up online and commit to visiting relatives in Florida who were on the fence in the election. Obama encouraged the same ingenuity with his sunrise logo, creating a website, Logobama, that allowed individuals and constituencies to adopt and customize the logo as a way to show their personal association with the campaign. Some supporters placed their own photo inside the O, gay groups turned the flag stripes into rainbow colors, and environmental groups shaded it green. All told, an estimated 35,000 logo versions served as graphic ads promoting Obama. Yes, there may have been some user-generated content that crossed the line or muddled the message, but the Obama team, knowing that they couldn't control what people created, made a virtue out of a necessity and communicated to supporters that they trusted them as custodians of the message, which further reinforced the sense of ownership people felt toward the campaign.

And what about the actual ads themselves? As with the rest of his campaign, Obama broadened the definition of advertising, diversified the types of ads he showed, multiplied the number of media platforms that aired his spots, created synergy between his traditional ads and other media outreach tools, and shifted the focus away from persuading voters to relationship building, to creating a community of supporters who would interact with his message and ads. It's not that Obama broke through with any new techniques. Both he and McCain relied on traditional thirty-second spots; they both advertised on network shows and cable channels geared to motivating their base and likely voters; they both targeted online ads to users based on demographics, keyword searches, and articles they downloaded; and they both created phantom web-only ads that were a bit more edgy and meant to drive the cable news narrative of the day.

But as one blogger noted in differentiating the Obama and McCain online advertising strategy, "McCain's approach to Internet marketing appears to be that of placing paid advertising while Obama and his supporters have utilized the far more progressive social networking approach which they have supplemented with paid advertising."[10] To be sure, Obama's huge financial advantage enabled him to run more ads, experiment with two-minute spots, and air a thirty-minute infomercial that blanketed the airwaves six days before the election. Obama tried to use the longer-form techniques to communicate that he wasn't just another candidate running slick and deceptive ads. But there was always a social networking subtext to what he did. His thirty-minute infomercial became a social event for supporters to gather in living rooms or union halls around the country. His online ads directed users to Obama's website, volunteer effort, fund-raising page, and text messaging program; supporters were encouraged to share ad links peer-to-peer through their Facebook and MySpace pages; grassroots bloggers were urged to embed the ads on their sites.

If one advertising initiative exemplified Obama's approach most vividly, it was his placement of ads in a wide variety of video games, from Guitar Hero to the Burnout Paradise and NASCAR 09 racing games to basketball and hockey sports games; the ads would appear on virtual billboards or other signs inside the games. A large proportion of gamers are male teens, many of whom are too young to vote, so it would be logical to conclude that Obama was targeting them as future advocates and supporters. But that's only part of the story. The gaming culture is highly social, not only when people play together but on game-related discussion boards and websites. According to a Pew Internet and American Life study of teenage gaming culture, those who take part in the socially interactive side of gaming—particularly the web discussions and other online activities—tend to be more engaged in civic and political life overall.[11] By associating himself with these games and communicating a cool message that he was one of them, Obama connected with an already existing social network that would be favorably inclined to generate buzz about his candidacy. And it would permeate one of the most difficult demographics to reach, younger men. This was advertising and branding and social networking and new media all rolled into one, with a dash of the Scion creed that people not only want to be in the know and associated with the next cool thing but want to spread their discovery to all their friends.

By the time he won the presidential election, the Barack Obama brand had become a worldwide wonder. He had become an icon, someone who seemed to embody our most personal aspirations and hopes, a larger-than-life figure who exceeded the powers and abilities of any mere mortal. T-shirts, MTV videos, X-box games, pop-up Internet ads, viral videos, popular songs, magazine covers, contemporary art, commercial posters—few were the media platforms and cultural venues that didn't feature his image or name. "President-elect Obama has achieved a level of popularity that does not translate to the way we've perceived other candidates, but rather to the way we see brand names like Ford, Visa and even Oprah," observed a writer for the online *Huffington Post* shortly after the election.[12] No traditional advertising campaign could have created this phenomenon. Obama established a brand, symbolized it with a message and logo, synchronized it with our cultural moment, and created a communications strategy built on the mystic cords of social networking and the dynamic synergy of new media. He never veered from his plan, and his steadiness helped solidify the growing personal bond his supporters felt toward him. "Contrary to rumors you may have heard," Obama quipped during the campaign, "I wasn't born in a manger." And indeed he was ribbed throughout the election for his perceived celebrity status. But he created far more than celebrity. Obama had purposefully formed a campaign that turned his candidacy into a cause that would become emotionally meaningful to millions of supporters, and his election became theirs. History has shown that connecting with people is far more powerful than persuading them, and it would be hard to imagine future campaigns not trying to replicate the Obama model.

Notes

1 Phil Patton, "As Authentic as 'The Matrix' or Menudo," *New York Times*, July 25, 2004.

2 See Shanto Iyengar and Adam F. Simon, "New Perspectives and Evidence on Political Communication and Campaign Effects," *Annual Review of Psychology* 51 (February 2000): 149–169.

3 Neil Postman, *Amusing Ourselves to Death: Public Discourse in the Age of Show Business* (New York: Viking, 1985), 126.

4 Anthony Painter, "The Contagious Campaign (Part One)," in *Viral Politics: Communication in the New Media Era*, ed. Anthony Painter and Ben Wardle (London: Politico's Publishing, 2001), 4, 41.

5 Mary Madden and Susannah Fox, "Riding the Waves of 'Web 2.0': More Than a Buzzword, But Still Not Easily Defined," Pew Internet and American Life Project, October 5, 2006, www.pewinternet.org/pdfs/PIP_Web_2.0.pdf. See also Sydney Jones and Susannah Fox, "Generations Online in 2009," a Pew Internet Project data memo, January 28, 2009, www.pewinternet.org/pdfs/PIP_Generations_2009.pdf.

6 Aaron Smith and Lee Rainie, "The Internet and the 2008 Election," Pew Internet and American Life Project. June 15, 2008, www.pewinternet.org/pdfs/PIP_2008_election.pdf.

7 Eric Reyes, "Discover Your Base of Influencers—and Put Them to Work," BNET, www.bnet.com/2403-13237_23-245719.html.

8 For a full analysis of the cultural changes our country has undergone, see my book on baby boomers: Leonard Steinhorn, *The Greater Generation: In Defense of the Baby Boom Legacy* (New York: St. Martin's, 2006). See also Steinhorn, "Scrooge's Nightmare," *Salon.com*, November 25, 2004; Steinhorn, "Blue-Collar Fault Line Is Not to Blame," *Politico*, May 5, 2008.

9 For a good overview of Obama's online campaign, see Jose Antonio Vargas, "Politics Is No Longer Local. It's Viral," *Washington Post*, December 28, 2008.

10 Zane Waltz, "Obama Wins TKO of McCain by Internet," posted on *Associated Content.com*, July 6, 2008.

11 Amanda Lenhart et al., "Teens, Video Games, and Civics: Teens' Gaming Experiences Are Diverse and Include Significant Social Interaction and Civic Engagement," Pew Internet and American Life Project, September 16, 2008, www.pewinternet.org/pdfs/PIP_Teens_Games_and_Civics_Report_FINAL.pdf.

12 Danny Groner, "Leading the New Political Evolution in Advertising," *Huffington Post*, November 17, 2008.

7

How the Media Covered the 2008 Election: The Role of Earned Media

Dotty Lynch

We aim to supply news.
—Ivy Ledbetter Lee, public relations maestro, 1906

"Earned media" is a public relations term that refers to positive news media coverage of an event, issue, or person, initiated by a campaign. According to Texas Politics "one of the most efficient and cost-effective ways to reach a large audience is through earned media. Earned media is positive news coverage that you actively work to get. By creating newsworthy stories or events and offering the stories to news outlets in your area, you can generate effective media coverage that targets specific audiences with your specific message."[1]

In this chapter we will look at the history of earned media and its evolution in political communications theory. We will then examine the news environment of 2008 which formed the backdrop for presidential campaign communications. Finally we will examine how attempts at earning positive media, controlling the message, and setting the news agenda were executed; how successful they were; and what lessons candidates and political professionals can learn for the future.

The History of Earned Media

The concept has been a staple of public relations since antiquity. Examples of communicating information to positively influence opinions and behavior can be seen as far back as 1800 BCE in Iraq, where farm bulletins were produced on how to sow crops. Art was designed to deify kings; the walls of Pompeii were inscribed with election appeals. Julius Caesar's *Commentaries*, the reports he sent back to Rome about his epic campaign, are considered great examples of propaganda. In the seventeenth century the Catholic Church created the Congregatio de Propaganda to put out information to spread the faith.[2] Using "third party validators" is a common practice in public relations campaigns today.

In the United States the drive to gain popular support occupied much of the fight between Alexander Hamilton and Thomas Jefferson. Around that time there were numerous examples of what we think of as modern public relations techniques designed to mold public opinion and frame debate. Symbols, slogans, and staged events like the Liberty Tree, "No Taxation Without Representation," and the Boston Tea Party helped establish an image to gain public approval. Getting your story out first, a public relations commandment, is exemplified in the pamphlet about the Boston Massacre and the engraving of Paul Revere that rallied colonists to the cause.

Historian Allan Nevins has called the *Federalist Papers* "history's finest public relations job" and Andrew Jackson's kitchen cabinet, headed by Amos Kendall, was filled with public relations geniuses. (Almost all of them were former newspapermen who knew how to engage the press.) Around the turn of the twentieth century public relations and press agentry took hold in America in general and in political campaigns in particular. In the late 1800s P. T. Barnum beat the drum and created a desire for the circus. In 1896 the William McKinley campaign created a publicity bureau, which disseminated press releases and cartoons to the news media and posters and pamphlets to voters. The Republicans spent $3.5 million on that campaign and at least $500,000 on publicity and press bureau activities.

The granddaddy of American public relations, Ivy Ledbetter Lee, changed the Rockefeller family image from mean corporate millionaires to philanthropic giants. He described his prime function as a publicist. "We aim to supply news," he proclaimed in connection with the anthracite coal strike. Henry Ford used "free media" successfully to build credibility for his cars. Ford viewed good publicity as a necessary complement to paid ads. He put Fords into racing events, formed clubs of Ford owners, and rocked the industry by announcing $5 pay for an eight-hour day as a way to build support for his cars. Paid advertisements came into their own in the1920s. Ford also used opinion surveys; in 1912 he asked Model T owners why they had bought the cars.

Survey research became an important part of public relations when George Gallup discovered sampling in the late 1920s. Gallup joined Young and Rubicon as the advertising industry's first marketing director in the 1930s and conducted polls to measure the opinions and behavior of the public and provide guidance on how campaigns were working. Gallup's methodology and success spawned a proliferation of survey and marketing research, which became a staple of strategic communication plans.

Franklin Roosevelt's mentor, Louis Howe, is credited with steering FDR's moves in the public arena using radio to communicate directly with the public and sell his New Deal. Howe died in 1936, but New Dealers carried on his legacy in using communications media to build public support for economic programs and paving the way for the American entrance into World War II. The war produced a new understanding of public relations and propaganda techniques, which modern campaigns have built on steadily as technology has developed. The advent of television in the 1950s and the Internet in the 1990s has created new channels for communications and an escalation of costs and new techniques.

Earned or Free?

In political circles the term "earned media" didn't receive currency until the late 1980s. Campaign communications (other than paid advertising) intended to generate good publicity for the candidate in the news media were known as free media and included press releases, relationships with reporters, news advisories, press conferences, conference calls, books, speeches, endorsements, interviews, debates, visuals, op-ed pieces, and even stunts. Having up-to-date press lists, knowing which reporters are covering a story, identifying coverage decision makers, and cultivating relationships with reporters and editors are part of the communications professional's toolbox.[3]

Toward the end of the 1980s, campaign consultants, who prided themselves as maestros of media manipulation, insisted that this task was not free. Kind of like Ronald Reagan proclaiming "I paid for this microphone," political media consultants wanted the world to know it was their good work that was responsible for good press and there was nothing free about it! (Campaigns, of course, were well aware of this since they paid the consultants' bills.)

The term "earned media" applied to campaigns in news coverage seems to have appeared first in a *Newsweek* article about sound bites in 1988. "Satellite hookups and cable TV, which furnish saturation coverage of the campaigns, have made the search for the perfect line a near obsession. Campaigns spend—and often waste—thousands of dollars boiling down all of the issues into broad themes that can be used in both 'paid media' (political TV ads) and 'earned media' (which recently replaced 'free media' as the favored euphemism for news)."[4]

Positive news coverage is crucial to successful campaigns since news reports have more credibility than paid advertising, even amid skepticism toward the press and the use of direct online communication. One of the first hurdles campaigns face is letting voters know who their candidates are and getting an audience to pay attention to their messages. It is mainly the news media who will carry that information to voters in either a positive or negative light. Getting the candidate covered and conveying the message you want to transmit takes great skill and some luck.

A memo from the Kansas Democratic Party to local campaigns in 2004 is a good example of the calculation behind earned media strategies and the attitude of campaigns toward the press: "Realistically, how much of your campaign will the press be interested in? . . . There is a reason this is called earned media and not free media. You do not pay for the media to cover your campaign but you will have to earn it. You cannot expect the press to cover your campaign just because you are running for office. That is why you have to have a plan for how you will earn media coverage."[5]

These strategists thought that the word "earned" made campaign coverage more acceptable to reporters and editors than the word "free," although many reporters bristle at both terms since they believe they are more than just a conveyor belt for campaign publicity.

Framing and Delivering the Message

There are three basic components to earned media: the messenger, the message, and the receiver and conveyor of the message through the news media to the public. Campaigns spend time and money on public opinion research to determine which messages will move voters. A multitude of facts must be transmitted to the public about a candidate, and strategies are devised on how to get the most salient messages to the voter through multiple channels, including the news media.

The concepts of framing the argument and setting the agenda are dominant among modern campaign media consultants. University of California linguistics professor George Lakoff, who translated framing theory into political applications, has been a guru of former Democratic National Committee chair and presidential candidate Howard Dean. Lakoff has participated in numerous Democratic Party strategy sessions during the past five years. His book *Don't Think of an Elephant* was studied religiously by Democrats on Capitol Hill who were desperate to come up with a winning message after years of Republican dominance in the House of Representatives. Some of his work was in reaction to that of Frank Luntz, the Republican campaign consultant, who has gained great currency with his memos on the power of using certain words in political dialogue. Luntz's idea of "fourteen words never to use" was instrumental in selling Newt Gingrich's Contract with America. (The words government, privatization, and outsourcing were to be replaced by Washington, personalization, and overregulation.) Lakoff suggested that Democrats needed to choose better language if they were to compete with Republicans and choose issues that had positive cultural connotations.[6]

Both Lakoff and Luntz drew on the groundbreaking work of anthropologist Erving Goffman in the 1970s on how individuals make sense of events by organizing and filtering them through their predispositions. Effective communicators are those who are able to shape judgments by using existing cultural meanings to describe events.[7]

Lakoff and Luntz have their detractors among campaign professionals, but the concepts of framing the message, using and avoiding specific value-laden words, and setting the agenda are staples among practitioners of "earned media."

The News Media

The news media spend a lot of time trying to get access to political operatives, listening to and reading their spin, and begging to be "fed" while at the same time resenting attempts at manipulation. There is a dance that goes on between the media and political operatives, and the 2008 campaign was no different. If anything there was more dancing, more attempts at "earning" media, and greater use of new technologies to get it and to report on it. And there were more reporters checking more facts and begging, resisting, and decrying at the same time.

News Values

In their landmark book, *The Interplay of Influence*, Kathleen Hall Jamieson and Karlyn Kohrs Campbell detail the relationships among news, politics, advertising, and the Internet and emphasize the two-way communication between the media and society. Not only does the media influence and persuade the public but individuals, groups, institutions, and politicians influence the media.

They also describe the elements of hard news that the media uses to determine which events get covered: drama, conflict, violence, personal (over process), actions or events, things that are novel, deviant, or extraordinary, and issues and events that are linked to other issues that are already in the media. It is against this set of news values that political communications are assessed, and successful campaign practitioners know them instinctively. Good news, celebrity news, and exclusives will also get coverage if news executives and reporters believe they are important or will boost audience ratings.[8]

News norms are changing, and in 2008 campaigns had to adjust to a different media landscape. Opinion journalism flourished on cable and online, stories became shorter and their shelf lives even shorter, and the 24/7 news cycle and the widespread use and speed of the Internet meant a constantly changing and sensationalist news environment. Boomlets from Obama's "putting lipstick on a pig" to Clinton's gaffe about the RFK assassination screeched around the media for a day and then gave way to the next hot item.

Converged Media

The Pew Research Center headline in December 2008, "The Internet Replaces Newspapers as Major Source of News," confirmed a trend that most campaign professionals already knew. Forty percent of adults said the Internet was one of their top two news sources, while only 35 percent said it was newspapers. Television was still dominant, with 70 percent saying it was a major source, but among eighteen- to twenty-nine-year-olds, TV was tied with the Internet at 59 percent.[9]

The change for politicians and reporters who entered the fray during the past thirty years has been dramatic. A CBS News/*New York Times* poll conducted in January 2009 shows the overall trend toward television and the Internet and away from print.

Table 7.1 Changes Over 30 Years: Where Do You Get Your News?

	CBS News/New York Times Poll 2009	LA Times Poll 1979
Television	60%	41%
Newspapers	14	42
Internet	13	n/a
Radio	7	11
Magazines	1	2
Talking to people	4	3

Note: CBS News/*New York Times* Poll conducted by telephone, January 11–15, 2009, 1,112 adults, +/–3%; Los Angeles Times Poll conducted by telephone, December 1979.

Source: CBS News/*New York Times* Poll, "American Public Opinion: Today vs. 30 Years Ago," *Sunday Morning*, February 1, 2009, www.cbsnews.com/htdocs/pdf/SunMo_poll_0209.pdf.

Campaign News

The change in the way people receive their political information over the past thirty years went into warp speed in the past four years and caused some major readjustments in the news media and political campaigns. The use of the Internet for campaign news jumped 23 percent from 2004, although twice as many still picked television, especially cable TV, as their primary source of news.

But political coverage on TV also took a new form. According to the Pew study nearly half cite cable news compared to only 24 percent who say the networks.[10]

The study also highlighted the partisan, opinionated nature that often dominates cable programs and audiences, which forces campaigns to pick their shots and choose their audiences in an attempt to define the agenda and control the message.

Table 7.2 TV News Sources in the 2008 Campaign

TV News Sources in the 2008 Campaign	
October 2008*	Oct* %
Cable Net	**46**
CNN	25
Fox	21
MSNBC	10
Network TV	24
Local TV	13
Other	1
Don't know	1

Note: Based on total population; multiple responses allowed. TV viewers may name more than one cable news source: however the *Cable Net* percentage counts cable viewers only once.

* Based on combined surveys conducted Oct 17–20 and Oct 24–27, 2008

Source: Pew Center for the People and the Press, "Internet Now Major Source of Campaign News," *News Interest Index*, October 31, 2008, http://people-press.org/report/467/internet-campaign-news.

Period of Adjustment and the Clickocracy

Jose Antonio Vargas, who covers politics and the Internet for the Washington Post.com, has coined the word "clickocracy" for the democratization of politics, which was spawned by the web in 2008.[11] For many campaigns this was a difficult transition. Vargas quotes Micah Sifry, cofounder of Tech President, a bipartisan blog that tracks how candidates are campaigning online. Sifry says that every campaign experienced tension over how to use the Internet, although the Obama campaign led the way. "Again and again, we've seen how well they've married online enthusiasm with on-the-ground mobilization." Sifry claimed that Obama's Internet team made an early mistake in seeking control of a MySpace page that was independently created by an Obama supporter, and the campaign has conceded that eventually it did best by letting a thousand flowers bloom on their own. Vargas reports that "lapse, however, is nothing compared with the wariness that many Republican candidates have about the Web" and cites Michael Turk, who led President Bush's online strategy in 2004 and recently worked as a consultant for Fred Thompson, as saying many Republicans still think of the web as "an expensive brochure, like a slick direct mail." McCain's website, for instance, "is definitely an extension of the broadcast, send-receive model," he says. "The overwhelming majority of space on his home page is all about McCain, and not about how real people can get involved." But the candidate's campaign has made some improvements. "They've opened up comments on the site," Turk observes.

Mindy Finn, who headed Mitt Romney's online strategy, has talked about the issue of control, which is central to hierarchical organizations that want everyone in lockstep on message. "For campaigns, losing control also means letting candidates show more of their real personalities. A candidate is not going to be 'on' all the time, unless he or she is a really good actor. A candidate has to be himself or herself. In this new online era, everyone's watching, and if you're not being yourself, chances are you'll slip. And someone, somewhere, will blog about it, or upload it on YouTube."

Vargas points to the video of Romney talking about his support of abortion rights and gay rights, which appeared on a YouTube mash-up and "went viral" as a major example of this phenomenon. Speaking of viral, one of the more interesting and undercovered uses of viral media was the Huckabee campaign in Iowa, which used a network of fundamentalist Christian churches and Bible study groups to spread the word about Huckabee. The church communities mobilized their members and Huckabee zoomed to the top of the Iowa caucuses below the radar of most national media.[12] But most campaigns were forced onto the Internet as a fund-raising tool and accepted the other elements of the clickocracy because they came with the territory.

More Coverage Earlier Than Ever

The Pew Center for Excellence in Journalism, which monitored campaign coverage, reviewed 25,000 news stories in print, TV, online, and radio in 2007 and 2008.

In the first five months of 2007, there was unprecedented coverage of what used to be called the invisible primary phase of the campaign. The Pew Excellence in Journalism News Index project tabulated 5,051 newspaper and TV stories about the top tier candidates in the first half of 2007. Figures on the amount of time network news devotes to campaigns prepared by the Tyndall Group shows that the amount of time in just the first half of 2007 outpaced the total amount of time spent in the annual preelection presidential years for the last four campaign cycles.[13]

Table 7.3 Off-Year Broadcast TV Minutes of (ABC, NBC, CBS) Campaign Coverage

Year	Minutes
2007 January–July	340
2003 January–December	167
1995 January–December	294
1991 January–December	146

Source: The Tyndall Report, 2007. Unpublished data provided to the author from Andrew Tyndall, http://tyndallreport.com.

Pew also reported that just five of the seventeen major party candidates (Obama, Clinton, McCain, Romney, and Giuliani) received over half of the stories, although not all of that attention was positive.

Table 7.4　Tone of Coverage from January 1 to May 31, 2007

	Percentage of All Stories	
	Positive	*Negative*
Hillary Clinton	26.9	37.8
Barack Obama	46.7	15.8
John McCain	12.4	47.9
Rudy Giuliani	27.8	37.0

Source: Pew Research Center's Project for Excellence in Journalism, "The Invisible Primary: Invisible No Longer," *Excellence in Journalism News Index*, October 29, 2007, www.journalism.org/node/8200.

Hillary Clinton received the most attention, but the coverage, especially on talk radio, was more negative than positive. Of the top four candidates, only Barack Obama's early coverage was net positive.

Chickens and Eggs

Clearly candidates were struggling to earn good press, which is crucial in presidential elections. Most campaign professionals believe that coverage by the news media is far more important than paid advertising, although millions of dollars are spent on ads. Candidates need to be covered in order to become known, to frame the debate, to control the agenda, and to raise money. The chicken and egg relationship between news coverage and fund-raising was evident in the 2008 campaign. Decisions on which candidates the news media would take seriously depended largely on two sets of numbers: those in polls and those in dollars. Name recognition and money dictated coverage, and, conversely, coverage had a huge bearing on name recognition and fund-raising.

Declining news budgets and the huge field of candidates forced the news executives to make choices and candidates struggled to make it into the first tier, which would guarantee them news coverage and enhance their ability to raise money.

Earned Media: What Worked and What Didn't

The Rollout

The ultimate rollout in political campaigns is the announcement of a candidacy. It is the one thing that is almost certain to get covered, even in local campaigns, and successful campaigns pay a lot of attention to packing in their best messages and visuals in events surrounding the announcement. In 2008, twenty major party candidates ran for president, but the content, form, and coverage of their announcements varied widely.

The two top-tier Democratic candidates Hillary Clinton and Barack Obama differed in the form their announcements took. Barack Obama "preannounced" in January and made a formal announcement on a Saturday in February on the steps of the State House in Springfield, Illinois, in a nationally televised event evoking Abraham Lincoln, also a short-term state legislator from Illinois. Hillary Clinton, the universally known front-runner, used a surprise Internet announcement on Saturday, January 20, 2007, two years to the date before the next presidential Inauguration, to evoke the presidential mantle. Obama had online tie-ins (his preannouncement a month earlier was done on his website), but it was Clinton, the establishment candidate, who emphasized her "new media" side albeit in a very conventional, controlled, warm and cozy living room setting. Obama, a master of the big event and big speech, tipped the media off in advance and produced a theatrical, professional, dramatic event designed to compensate for his youth and inexperience. He associated himself with Lincoln, the president who freed slaves, hoping to spark discussion of a postracial American, which his campaign wanted to put in motion.

John McCain waited until April 2007 to "kick off" his campaign although he had preannounced on the David Letterman Show in February and had been campaigning actively since 2006. His formal announcement (which was labeled by many as a "re-launch") was at a big outdoor rally in Portsmouth, New Hampshire, in which he tied together two positive elements: his victory over George W. Bush in the Granite State in 2000 and his naval background. Then McCain took the announcement show on the road to the early primary states to spread the word to the local press.

John Edwards, the number three Democrat, had spent a lot of time since the 2004 election stressing his commitment to end poverty. The son of a South Carolina millworker, a millionaire trial lawyer who lived in North Carolina, Edwards chose to announce in New Orleans, the site of Hurricane Katrina, in late December 2006 rather than in one of his home states. Edwards was hoping to capitalize on a slow news period between Christmas and New Years and get press. However, former president Gerald Ford died and Saddam Hussein was executed during the same week, relegating Edwards's announcement to a minor story in an uncharacteristically busy news week.[14]

Mitt Romney, who spent $50 million of his own money and had the cream of the GOP media-consulting crop at his disposal, did the traditional announcement with all the bells and whistles. He launched some early paid TV and web ads detailing all the good parts of his biography. Like John Edwards, he passed up his two home states, deciding that Utah was too Republican and Mormon and Massachusetts was too Democratic and blue, and scheduled his announcement for the swing state of Michigan, where he was born and where both his parents had been governor. He spoke at the Henry Ford Museum in Dearborn and emphasized his roots in American business enterprise. The media, however, focused on video (presumably dug up by an opposing camp) showing his less than conservative stances on social issues when he ran for office against Ted Kennedy in Massachusetts. Much of Romney's early goal was to make it into the first tier along with McCain and Giuliani. He achieved that with his substantial cash on hand and an arsenal of high-priced campaign consultants who vouched for his ability to go the distance. He made the early cut as far as the mainstream press was concerned, and national reporters were assigned to cover his campaign in 2007.

The Russert Primary

Two Washington insiders, Senator Joe Biden and Senator Chris Dodd, and outsider Mike Huckabee chose insider forums. Biden appeared on Tim Russert's *Meet the Press* on January 7 to tell the world (or mainly a handful of political elites who already knew it) that he was a candidate. Dodd chose the *Imus in the Morning* radio show for his first words, although he traveled to his home statehouse in Connecticut for a more traditional backdrop two days later. Huckabee received a segment of *Meet the Press* in January 2007, ensuring his announcement automatic coverage. But the questions focused heavily on things he did not want to have emphasized—raising taxes in Arkansas and paroling a convicted rapist in Arkansas. He followed up this appearance with a web video, but it took Huckabee, who had surprisingly strong relationships with the national media, a long time to get back on his own message after this interview.

New Mexico Governor Bill Richardson took the Sunday show route to preannounce on ABC's *This Week with George Stephanopoulos* in January. After considerable campaigning in early primary states, he made his formal announcement in Los Angeles near Pasadena, where his mother had traveled from Mexico to make sure her son would be born on U.S. soil (and thus be qualified to run for president someday). Since Clinton and Obama were "earning" huge amounts of publicity stressing their nontraditional backgrounds, Richardson sought to underscore his Latino roots as well as his strong résumé in national politics and policy. Some of the coverage, however, was skeptical of his California connection.

"I didn't spend much time here; in fact, it was about eight hours, because I went right back," Richardson said. "Now there's a California primary so I'm trying to improve on those roots." His remarks were candid but did not convey the message the campaign hoped to have covered.[15]

Stars That Failed to Twinkle

Two Republican candidates who were touted by the media as "stars," Rudy Giuliani and Fred Thompson, had huge internal campaign debates over how and when to announce. Giuliani never did. He just started campaigning. Thompson postponed his announcement several times and when he finally took a page out of the McCain and Schwarzenegger playbooks and went on late night TV to do it, was widely panned as too boring and too late.

Thompson campaign manager Bill Lacy has said[16] that the politician turned actor suffered from his real-life personality, which never lit up the screen the way his character, Arthur Branch, did on *Law and Order*. Thompson continued a string of boring public appearances that were well attended and covered by the media, with the thrust being how dreadful they were. The *New York Times* ran a picture of Thompson speaking while a supporter did not even try to stifle a huge yawn to describe the Thompson campaign. This didn't do much to counteract the press narrative that Thompson lacked "fire in the belly."

As for Giuliani, he did an interview on CNN's *Larry King Live* in February 2007 that seemingly served as his announcement. This MSNBC account of his "announcement" sums up his problem:

> It was difficult to determine whether the CNN appearance qualified as an official announcement of his candidacy. During a news conference Saturday after a speech in Sacramento, Calif., Giuliani was asked, "Are you in this for good?" "Yes, I am committed," he said. "This is something I believe I can bring something to, from the experiences that I've had." When asked a follow-up question about when he would make a formal announcement, he responded, "Well, formally announce? I don't know. If you go back to my speech, I think I may have. I'm not sure." He then alluded to making an announcement in multiple locations "so we get more attention" but provided no details.[17]

Books

Books by and about the candidates have become part of the rollout package. They allow candidates to introduce themselves in their own terms and explain any skeletons in their closets. Barack Obama's books, *Dreams of My Father* and *The Audacity of Hope*, shaped what the media and the interested public knew about him, even before he began his presidential campaign, and large portions appeared in early news profiles. His admission of "doing a little blow" in his high school years was discussed and cast as ancient history before anyone could uncover it and make it into a scandal.

Hillary Clinton's memoirs of her White House years, *Living History*, allowed her to put the health care debacle in perspective, and *It Takes a Village* helped shape her image as a public official with a long track record on children's issues. John McCain had several books in his arsenal, but Robert Timberlake's *The Nightingale's Song* about McCain's years in Vietnam validated his history as a POW. Mike Huckabee came on the national scene with a book about tackling obesity, *Quit Digging Your Own Grave with a Knife and Fork*, which he used to get positive feature stories about his own struggle with obesity. He then parlayed it to craft an image of someone who related to the millions of overweight and obese Americans and as a candidate who wanted to tackle the issue of health care.

Lessons: Controlling the Message: Surprise (Clinton) can work to prevent reporters from covering your announcement with a lot of questions regarding issues you don't want to emphasize. Well-executed events with appropriate symbolism (Obama and Romney) can earn positive media that will publicize your theme and frame your campaign message in a credible forum.

Using the free platforms available, especially the Sunday talk show, is a risk. While they guarantee attention they may also generate negative information that dominates your positive themes and message.

Publishing your autobiography can help shape a positive image, but stretching the biographical details may get noticed, as in the case of Bill Richardson and to some extent Mitt Romney. Planned, well-executed announcements often work but they give your opposition and the press time to get negative information in the initial story.

Debates

After the announcements, primary debates were the next surefire hit for campaign coverage and were especially important to second- and third-tier candidates who wanted to be taken seriously. Events that feature multiple candidates are likely to attract reporters who then can cover several campaigns at a time and write about conflict, something that always makes news. Debates can also level the playing field by putting the second and third tier on the same stage with the top bracket. At the beginning of the season some in the top tier sought to limit the number of times they had to debate and stand next to their lower-tier competitors, many of whom hoped to "break out of the pack" during one of these forums. But after the first few debates the top candidates realized they didn't have much to worry about. The lower-tier candidates were given fewer questions and less airtime during the debates, and the TV and print coverage went almost exclusively to the top tier.

Breaking Out Is Hard to Do

"George, I've been standing here for the last forty-five minutes praying to God you were going to call on me." This was Dennis Kucinich's answer to a question posed by George Stephanopoulos asking each candidate's view of a personal God. Kucinich spent a lot of the tiny amount of airtime he got at the forum complaining about the tiny amount of air time he was getting.[18]

While the audience size for these debates was bigger than ever before, most voters relied on the coverage of these events rather than watching them live. And if lower-tier candidate Chris Dodd of Connecticut was hoping that his appearance in early debates would be covered in his (close to) hometown paper, he was sorely disappointed. In a big *New York Times* story on the April 2007 South Carolina debate, the five-term incumbent senator made his first appearance in the twenty-third paragraph: "Senator Christopher J. Dodd of Connecticut also took part in the debate," the *Times* reported.[19]

Debates theoretically offer the less well-funded candidates opportunities to get coverage, but reporters can only handle so many candidates and story lines at a time. It is also difficult for campaigns to control their message since the questions are random. John Edwards, for example, wanted to talk about poverty but found himself getting the "gay marriage" question in a string of forums. Former Wisconsin governor Tommy Thompson's campaign was hoping that the media coverage of the debates would catapult him forward, but in an early debate at the Reagan Library, Thompson made a gaffe saying he thought employers should have the right to fire gay employees. He received some flak for that but his explanation got him even more publicity and not the kind his campaign hoped to earn. Thompson said a dead hearing aide battery and an urgent need to go to the bathroom were why he blew the question.

In 1988 subgroups of candidates tried to break out of the pack to get exposure. In July 1987, Democratic congressman Dick Gephardt and Republican congressman Jack Kemp held an unusual bipartisan debate in Iowa and managed to get exposure that way. There were some forums in 2008 where both sides showed up; the liberal Machinists union endorsed Huckabee because he was the only Republican who came to their forum. In February 2008, a debate was hosted and aired by MTV and My Space, *Closing Arguments: A Presidential Super Dialogue*, in which Republicans Huckabee and Ron Paul and Democrats Clinton and Obama all appeared although not at the same time. But for the most part in 2007–2008 debates were single-party events and the second and third tiers pretty much stayed where they were after multiple attempts to use the forums to break out.

The Top Tier

For the top Democratic candidates, Clinton and Obama, these forums went on until the Obama camp realized that this format was no longer working for him. Clinton had stumbled in an October 2007 debate over a question from Tim Russert on driver's licenses for illegal immigrants, and her campaign started to lose steam and the aura of inevitability. But in an ABC debate the weekend before the New Hampshire primary the Clinton campaign believed she had "found her voice" and that the debates were helping to keep her campaign alive. Following another ABC debate in April 2008, Obama halted his participation in further forums. Reporters George Stephanopoulos and Charlie Gibson turned the tables on Obama in that forum and hammered him with questions ranging from Jeremiah Wright and Bill Ayers to the issue of wearing the American flag lapel pin. Obama supporters bombarded ABC with complaints about moderators asking gotcha questions. However, over 10 million viewers watched Obama deal with issues that were clearly "off message" and that was the last debate of the primary season.

The Republican debates began a week later than the Democratic debates in May 2007 and ended on January 30, three months before the final Democratic debate. They had twenty-one compared to twenty-six for the Democrats and began and ended at the Reagan Presidential Library. McCain did no head-to-head debates since Romney, Huckabee, and Paul were all in the final debate with him; Obama and Clinton had six. One of the more memorable sessions was the YouTube debate in 2007. Republicans were initially wary of a venue where questions could come from melting snowmen and lesbian couples. "I think the presidency ought to be held at a higher level than having to answer questions from a snowman," Mitt Romney told the *Manchester Union Leader*. But Republicans eventually concluded that passing up YouTube would be a mistake. Tech-savvy conservatives created a website (Save TheDebate.com) to persuade party elders that ignoring YouTube was not a smart move in the 2008 environment.

The forum was relatively uneventful except for some controversy over the final question from a gay retired brigadier general with ties to Hillary Clinton's campaign. The Save the Debate folks complained that CNN had not acted in the spirit of YouTube to remove filters and had instead introduced too many news editorial filters into the process.

General Election Debates

During the summer of 2008, the Obama campaign was spinning reporters with the idea that the general election debates in 2008 would do for Barack Obama what they had done for Ronald Reagan in 1980. They would give voters who wanted change the assurance that the new guy was competent and steadfast as well as a change from the status quo. The McCain campaign countered that it would demonstrate McCain's superior knowledge of foreign policy and show a contrast between a steady hand and a mere celebrity.

As the economy worsened, so too did McCain's standing in the polls. McCain tried a Hail Mary play for earned media by announcing that he was suspending his campaign to go back to Washington to deal with the economy and might even skip the first debate. Many in the Obama camp believe that day, September 24, was the day McCain lost the election.[20] The McCain campaign says it had a small comeback at the end of October but concedes that McCain's bold move and his debate performances did not turn the election in his favor. Polls conducted immediately after the debates showed Obama winning all three and emerging as the candidate voters believed would best deal with the economic crisis.

Lessons: Debates are opportunities for the lesser known and challenger candidates to get coverage and attention. But large playing fields and random questions can dilute the impact an unknown candidate has and can even perpetuate the low-tier image. A small mistake can be fatal, as it was for Tommy Thompson, and even a minor moment of confusion can be costly, as it was for Clinton.

Front-runners try to avoid these forums for the obvious reasons but must not seem to be hiding. George W. Bush lost considerable support in New Hampshire in 1999 when he skipped the first debate in Dartmouth.

While debates can help coverage, it is not certain that they will get candidates a clear shot at good earned media.

If you throw a Hail Mary pass, it better be successful. McCain's high-profile debate strategy was a dud in part because he had no political plan to execute it.[21]

Controlling the Message

Controlling the Message: The Primaries

Despite the problems the Obama campaign faced when press scrutiny became harsher and he starting losing primaries, a study by the Pew Research Center's Project for Excellence in Journalism and the Joan Shorenstein Center on Press, Politics, and Public Policy at Harvard University concluded that Obama had done the best job of controlling the message.[22]

The dominant personal narratives for Obama were ones he tried hardest to project, a sign that he largely succeeded in controlling his media message, particularly early on. The most common of all was the notion that he represents hope and change. This was followed by the idea that he is a charismatic leader and powerful communicator. Obama has also succeeded in getting substantial coverage that refutes one of his greatest possible vulnerabilities, the idea that his appeal is too narrow or limited to blacks and elites. These three impressions permeated the coverage of his candidacy.[23]

Interestingly, the study found that Clinton was almost as successful as Obama in getting out her big message, that she was ready to lead the country from "day one." However, the report noted "the public seemed to have developed opinions about her that ran counter to the media coverage, perhaps based on a pre-existing negative disposition to her that unfolded over the course of the campaign." The Clinton campaign and its supporters have blamed sexism and a media double standard for many of those negative assessments. The Pew study, however, asserts that her media coverage was mostly positive and focused on the messages she wanted out.

The Pew study counts numbers of stories and their tone but not the intensity of tone and it doesn't make a distinction between stories that set the agenda and those that are just standard reporting. The Clinton campaign felt it was not able to control the agenda, and the general consensus is that Obama did get better press, especially in the early days of the campaign. Being new and being a winner tends to generate positive coverage. She, of course, was not new to the press, and it took Clinton until the later primaries to recover from the early losses. Although her campaign constantly tried to generate fresh biographical pieces (an ad parodying the *Sopranos* with Hillary and Bill in a diner, for example), the media generally saw her as yesterday's news with a lot of "baggage."

McCain's coverage was more negative than positive during the primary season, in part, perhaps, because he was seen to be losing ground in 2007. In addition, Pew finds that the master narrative about McCain was he was not a true conservative. "More than five in 10 of all the assertions studied about McCain conveyed that idea, about six times as many as the number of assertions rebutting it. This was clearly not the message McCain was trying to convey during the primaries and his choice of Palin had a lot to do with trying to motivate the GOP base which were concerned about his conservative bona fides."[24]

Controlling the Message: The Conventions

The so-called political dinosaurs, the national political conventions, have actually morphed from being major decision-making bodies into the number one earned media events of presidential campaigns. Over 1,500 credentialed media covered each convention and convention stories dominated the news holes. Campaigns view conventions as their biggest opportunities to earn media and tell their stories. In 2004, the Democrats went so far as to ban negative speeches denying their partisans the "red meat" they love during the convention so they could show John Kerry as a Vietnam vet "reporting for duty." In Denver, the Obama campaign was frustrated by the attention the media gave to Hillary Clinton and her supporters despite their attempt to focus attention on the Obamas and the general election. Looking at the breakdown of stories that week, Clinton was the number two single story covered followed by the McCain choice of Sarah Palin. The Obamas combined did manage to dominate the week.

McCain's choice of Sarah Palin announced on the Friday following the big Obama speech in INVESCO Field was designed to turn to media's attention away from the Democrat, and by and large it was successful. Conflict and surprise always trump happy talk. However, for the Republicans an act of God, called Hurricane Gustav, rained on their free media parade and knocked out the first night of their convention. Nonetheless, for the first time since spring, McCain went ahead of Obama in the polls and received more press attention than Obama.

Like Obama, McCain also was upstaged by a lady and although Sarah Palin produced a short-term boost for McCain in the polls, by mid-September her positive effect had started to wane.[25]

Lessons: Even though networks don't carry the conventions "wall-to-wall," conventions still attract wide audiences and are opportunities to get out positive messages.

Table 7.5 Campaign Story Lines of the Week, August 25 to September 1, 2008

	Total Percentage of Campaign Newshole
Democratic convention	25.0%
Hillary/supporters at the convention	12.3
Sarah Palin named VP	12.2
Convention speech by Obama	9.6
Obama as historic nominee	6.2
Biden named VP	5.8
Michelle Obama's role	4.6
Total number of campaign stories:	*744*

Source: Pew Research Center's Project for Excellence in Journalism, "Denver and Palin Fuel Biggest Campaign Week Yet," *PEJ Campaign Coverage Index*, September 2, 2008, www.journalism.org/node/12612.

Table 7.6 Campaign Story Lines of the Week, September 1 to September 7, 2008

	Total Percentage of Campaign Newshole
Sarah Palin named McCain's VP	27.6%
Republican convention	15.2
Convention speech by McCain	13.4
Palin family scandals	9.7
Gustav's effect on the Republican Convention	7.1
Palin's public record	6.2
Total number of campaign stories:	*567*

Source: Pew Research Center's Project for Excellence in Journalism, "The Palin Phenomenon Drives Campaign Coverage," *PEJ Campaign Coverage Index*, September 8, 2008, www.journalism.org/node/12693.

Surprise and conflict will trump the predictable and puffery.
Hurricanes and natural disasters will trump conventions.
Convention horserace bounces are often short-lived.

Controlling the Message:
The General Election

A later Pew study of the general election coverage suggests again that
Obama was cast in a more favorable light by the media than was Mc-
Cain although the coverage of Obama was not overwhelmingly positive.
"For Obama during this period, just over a third of the stories were
clearly positive in tone (36 percent), while a similar number (35 percent) were neutral or mixed. A smaller number (29 percent) were negative. For McCain, by comparison, nearly six in ten of the stories studied
were decidedly negative in nature (57 percent), while fewer than two in
ten (14 percent) were positive."[26]

McCain was able to overcome the disparity in the amount of coverage, and by the end of August their coverage was equal. Before the conventions Obama received 50 percent more coverage than McCain. Was
it media bias against Republicans, smart strategic moves by the Obama
campaign, or just the way the cookie crumbles? That question will be
debated for years, but clearly Obama and the media were in sync.

The Pew study found that the coverage of Sarah Palin had an "up
and down trajectory" and that in the end her coverage was more negative than positive (39 percent negative, 28 percent positive, 33 percent
neutral). Her coverage, however, was more positive than McCain's, which
became extremely negative with his reaction to the economic crisis and
his attacks on Obama's character. Only 5 percent of Palin's coverage
was about her personal life. Joe Biden got very little national coverage
and except for his debate performance, which was assessed positively, almost all the coverage he received was about gaffes. However, by the end
of the primaries his positive ratings were much higher than Palin's.

The study also found that the economy was not the only topic
covered, though it was the top issue. Horserace coverage dominated
the general election with 53 percent of the news hole reporting on
strategy, tactics, and polling, compared to 20 percent on policy. As the

reporting focused on politics, Obama's coverage became much more positive.

Drudge, Huffington Post, and the Role of Blogs in Setting the News Agenda

In their book *The Way to Win: Taking the White House in 2008*, reporters John Harris and Mark Halperin include a chapter, "Matt Drudge Rules Our World," in which they cite the ways the Drudge Report caught the eye of the political universe and drove news decisions.[27] Many on the left complained about the analysis, believing they gave too much credit to a report with right-wing ties,[28] but like it or not, the Drudge Report was even more influential in setting news agendas in 2008 than it was in 2004.

Chris Cillizza in the washingtonpost.com's The Fix has done a lot of reporting on "Drudge-ology." Regardless of the reason given for Drudge's power, "everyone The Fix spoke to agreed that there is no single tool more powerful in the modern media for breaking a story or turning up the volume on a little-noticed comment." Kevin Madden, press secretary for Mitt Romney, said Drudge's site serves as a "national political assignment editor of sorts for those covering the campaign trail." Katie Levinson, former communications director for Rudy Giuliani, echoed Madden's sentiment: "The Drudge Report has become the must-read for TV anchors and radio personalities before they go on air, for bookers sorting out what's 'newsy' in a non-stop news cycle, and for political candidates looking to avoid getting blindsided by the press."[29]

At the Harvard Conference in December 2008 national reporters ranging from CNN's John King to *The Washington Post's* Dan Balz spoke about the calls in the middle of the night from their news desks wanting to check out a story headlining on Drudge or another blog and wondering why these top reporters hadn't flagged it.[30] In the past the major print newspapers set the news agenda and campaigns would rush out at 10:00 P.M. when the papers came off the presses to check the front-page headlines. By 2008 it fell to the 24/7 websites, and Drudge often became the defining source.

Drudge's power as a clearinghouse in the cluttered news environment and his ability to shape the news made it essential for Democratic operatives as well as Republican ones to play ball with him. Leaking him stories of big successes in fund-raising, endorsements, polls, or crowds, or steering him to bad stories or pictures about an opponent was a way to get the story noticed by hundreds of media organizations and set the day's agenda of stories on cable, the web, and radio news. Hillary Clinton's campaign had an "emissary" to Drudge and for a while Drudge was especially kind to Clinton. However, the relationship went sour and by the end of the primary campaign the Clinton camp had put Drudge on its enemies list.

Phil Singer, Clinton's former deputy communications director, unloaded on Drudge at *National Journal* and Google's 21st Century Campaign symposium. He said Drudge "bastardized" the media, spurring reporting that was "incomplete, inaccurate," and sometimes "false."

> I think the significance of Drudge has less to do with right-wing versus left-wing. The significance of Drudge is that he does like to break news. In so doing, he creates a prisoner's dilemma of sorts between news organizations. If he teases the *New York Times* front page for the next day, that is going to send all the *New York Times'* competitors into a tizzy to see if they can a) chase it down, b) if they can chase it down, break it. And that sometimes leads to rushed journalism . . . or sometimes [journalism that is] incomplete, inaccurate, perhaps not as detailed as it should be, lacking a certain nuance. And you get perhaps a false report or a skewed report that contributes to the zeitgeist.[31]

Obama media guru David Axelrod, while not admitting outright that he worked with Drudge, conceded that Drudge and other major blogs were a reality of modern campaigning who must be dealt with.[32]

Bittersweet

The *Huffington Post* strove to match Drudge's influence from the left and had some success in being a "must read" for campaign operatives and reporters. It was also a way for the Obama campaign to send messages to supporters and the press. Despite the Obama support from Huffington one of its "citizen journalists" in its Off the Bus project broke one of the most damaging stories of the campaign about Obama.

Mayhill Fowler attended a fund-raiser in San Francisco that was barred to the press and recorded Obama talking about citizens of Pennsylvania:

> You go into some of these small towns in Pennsylvania, and like a lot of small towns in the Midwest, the jobs have been gone now for 25 years and nothing's replaced them. And they fell through the Clinton Administration, and the Bush Administration, and each successive administration has said that somehow these communities are gonna regenerate and they have not. And it's not surprising then they get bitter, they cling to guns or religion or antipathy to people who aren't like them or anti-immigrant sentiment or anti-trade sentiment as a way to explain their frustrations.[33]

Fowler, an Obama supporter, realized that these comments could damage Obama and held back reporting them for several days but ultimately decided that they should be published.

Lessons: Drudge remained an important force in setting news agendas and campaigns had to deal with him proactively to get their messages (positive and negative) into the media.

Like it or not, the squeaky wheel gets attention and ideologues and aggregators replaced the mainstream as agenda setters in the 24/7 world.

Old media or new, no news person or blogger is ever a friend. Drudge switched gears from Clinton to Obama to McCain in a flash.

In the age of tiny cell phones and audio recorders nothing is really "closed press."

Endorsements

Voters tell pollsters that they rarely follow endorsements and that they make up their own minds when they vote. But campaigns spend enormous amounts of time courting editorial writers, especially in the early primary states. The Biden campaign, for example, kept its hopes up early on because he consistently got good vibrations from editorial writers in Iowa who liked his foreign policy credentials. It hoped that an endorsement from the *Des Moines Register*, for example, would validate him and propel him from the bottom tier. The McCain campaign made heavy use of endorsements in paid ads and made even heavier use of the "dis-endorsement" of Mitt Romney from his hometown newspaper, the *Boston Globe.*

Celebrity endorsements are also dismissed by voters as nonfactors, but Obama's early endorsement by Oprah Winfrey drew considerable media attention to Obama. Oprah sent a message to women and African Americans that Obama, not Hillary Clinton, was her candidate. At the time in 2007, many African Americans were supporting Clinton because of her track record on their issues and because they weren't sure Obama could win. Oprah "broke ranks" with one of her sisters saying that she wasn't negative about Hillary but just liked Obama better.

For the Obama campaign, however, the really significant endorsement came on January 28, 2008. At American University in Washington, D.C., Senator Ted Kennedy and Caroline Kennedy endorsed Obama at a big, noisy rally and passed the mantle of JFK's "new generation of leadership" to Obama. The endorsement was a shock to Hillary Clinton, who had received campaign contributions from Caroline Kennedy and assumed her colleague from Massachusetts would stay neutral. Clinton campaign aides were heartsick over this development and calculated that it was worth millions of dollars in free media.[34]

Kennedy delivered the Obama message loud and clear. "We, too, want a president who appeals to the hopes of those who still believe in the American dream and those around the world who still believe in the American ideal and who can lift our spirits and make us believe again. I've found that candidate and I think you have, too." The event was carried live on cable and portions were rebroadcast on the nightly news shows, much to the delight of team Obama.

There was a consensus among all campaign managers attending a debriefing at Harvard in December that that was the key endorsement of the primary campaign and rivaled only by the endorsement of Obama by Republican Colin Powell in the general election for its powerful impact.[35]

Interviews

News Shows

News organizations love interviews. They create news, show the organization has clout with the big players, and they are cheap compared to enterprise stories or entertainment shows. Campaigns have a menu of choices to fit their strategies—cable, morning TV, local news either live or via satellite, evening news live or pretape, Sunday morning talk shows, and more and more often in 2008, entertainment and comedy shows. Cable TV needs 24/7 programming and on a given day scores of guests come through their studios. Newspaper reporters work hard to get candidates and campaign aides to sit down to do lengthy interviews for profiles. Broadcast networks, though not what they used to be, have morning shows that draw millions of viewers. *Good Morning America*, *The Today Show*, and *The Early Show* are vehicles for candidates and their aides to begin the day's spin-orama. Cable shows like MSNBC's *Morning Joe* often draw opinion leaders, and campaigns routinely send surrogates and even the candidate to make sure their spin is in the mix.

In 2008, *60 Minutes* was still one of the highest rated news shows and as a result scored interviews with just about any candidate it wanted. Virtually every major candidate appeared, but it was Barack Obama who made the best use of the Sunday evening TV platform. And after the election CBS was making equal use of the access it had to Obama. CBS made a DVD entitled *Obama: ALL Access* that it publicized on its website sharing with viewers its "extraordinary access to the Senator, the candidate, and the president-elect." Not to be outdone, CNN, NBC, and ABC were also offering DVDs of the inauguration and other parts of the momentous occasion.

As a caution, campaigns in 2008 learned that not all airtime is necessarily good airtime. Exhibit A: the Sarah Palin debacle with Katie Couric. Palin's campaign made a calculation that Palin needed to do a few controlled interviews to demonstrate her credibility for office and chose two network evening news anchors, ABC's Charlie Gibson and CBS's Katie Couric. The campaign was so sure Palin would show well with Couric that it agreed to a series of interviews to be shown night after night on the *CBS Evening News*. The interviews did not turn out well and Palin says she wanted to stop them in midstream, but the campaign thought that would look worse than continuing what turned out to be a train wreck. While the evening news shows ratings continued to decline, the interviews received millions of hits on YouTube. Palin's ratings went down as did John McCain's.

Comedy and Entertainment Shows

Political candidates and even presidents have been dabbling in entertainment TV for a while. In the 1950s the Kennedys appeared on Jack Paar's late night show and in 1972 Richard Nixon made an appearance on *Laugh-In* with Sammy Davis Jr. In the late spring of 1992 Bill Clinton had just about clinched the Democratic Party nomination but he was running third in the polls behind incumbent George Bush and the new kid on the block, the rich quirky Ross Perot. Perot had received glowing media coverage, including a profile on *60 Minutes.* To pump some fresh air in the campaign, the Clinton brain trust unveiled something it called the Manhattan Project, which included ways to show Clinton in a new light. He appeared on Arsenio Hall's show playing his saxophone—a very nontraditional venue. And, lo and behold, the campaign started to turn around. Early in his presidency Clinton's foray into new media hit a snag when he decided to go on MTV and answer an interviewer's odd question about whether he wore boxers or briefs.

The quest to get positive exposure in big nontraditional audiences in the midst of a crowded field of candidates made the late night comedy scene a part of the 2008 campaigns' toolbox of earned media possibilities. As already noted, several candidates actually made their announcements (or preannouncements) on the Letterman and Leno shows. *The View* and the *Ellen DeGeneres Show* also became must-dos to capture the daytime female audiences, especially after Oprah gave her heart and her air time to Obama.

Candidates also dipped their toes into the slightly riskier domain of Comedy Central. John McCain, who prided himself as a master of establishment media types, got into some scuffles with the liberal Jon Stewart but kept coming back for more, hoping that his ability to counter old age jokes would open minds among young people.

But the biggest surprise of the year was *Saturday Night Live*'s revived relevance. SNL has a rich history of stinging political parody from Chevy Chase's bumbling Gerald Ford to Dana Carvey's goofy George H. W. Bush, but had lost ground to the edgier shows on Comedy Central in recent years. But in 2008 they nailed it. Their skit during the primaries showing the press grilling Hilary Clinton while fawning all over Barack Obama has been documented by Pew as precipitating harsher scrutiny of Obama.[36]

Tina Fey's Sarah Palin captivated the news media in the general election. Her portrayal of Palin's debate performance and lack of grasp on foreign policy issues coincided with the downturn in the number of voters who believed Palin was qualified to be president. Both Palin and John McCain went on SNL in October to try to control the damage, but Fey's Palin will go in the history books.[37]

Lessons: Interviews and nontraditional forums are an inexpensive way to get your candidates known and your message out, but you need to be selective about the forum and prepared for curve balls.

Ghost Ads

A device that has been used in the last twenty years, using paid ads to generate earned media coverage, hit a peak in 2008. In earlier years campaigns would make sensational ads, hold a press conference to unveil them, rush copies to TV stations, and then often make small actual media buys with little cash behind them, counting on the news media to carry the message. In 2008 the advent of the web and YouTube allowed campaigns to make ads that were never on TV at all and show them on the web. They often implied that these were running "somewhere" though in fact many were never broadcast and never intended to be broadcast. Some of these "ghost ads" were made to influence voters, but many were made to influence the media alone. In some cases the ads were so entertaining, so sensational, or made such a good strategic point that TV news put them on the air.[38]

The McCain campaign used these ads as a type of "video press release" during the Democratic convention to try to get some of their anti-Obama messages into the media commentary. On days that

Democrats were talking about national security issues the McCain campaign released an ad called "Tiny," which accused Obama of downplaying the importance of Iran, a country he once described as "tiny." The ad ran only ten times but reminded pundits of the Obama quote and raised the specter of his inexperience in a dangerous world. The McCain campaign was the master of these ghost ads, but the Obama campaign did a bit of vaporizing as well. An ad accusing McCain of being out of touch because he owned seven houses had a minuscule run on the air. An ad during the primaries following the Clinton 3:00 A.M. telephone ad that used the same imagery but said Obama had better judgment on the Iraq War, was never run for real. That ad appeared only on cable news shows providing them with an irresistible visual to illustrate the Obama-Clinton back-and-forth.[39]

Many of the ads the campaigns spent huge amounts of money on were actually positive bios and issue related and received little attention from the news media. But one paid ad that ran over 12,000 times generated huge news coverage. The "Celebrity" ad, which compared Barack Obama to Paris Hilton, was launched by the McCain camp to deflect the media blitz of the big enthusiastic crowds on Obama's international trip in the summer of 2008. It was one of the most successful examples of paid ads generating news coverage. And, according to the Obama campaign manager David Plouffe, the ad and the reaction to it caused them to scale back Obama's big rallies for several weeks. "It got much more in our heads than it resonated with voters," said Obama pollster Joel Benenson. "It wasn't doing any damage in our polling." Plouffe said tamping down the rallies "was a huge mistake because they had helped us organizationally" and director of scheduling Alyssa Mastromonaco explained, "Because there was such enthusiasm for Barack, toning down the crowd and limiting the number of people that were coming wasn't helpful to our organizational field efforts. Our state staff was furious."[40]

Lessons: Ghost ads worked well to get the chattering classes chattering and, despite criticism by media watchdogs, were effective in getting a message out.

Ads, ghost and real, can impact internal strategic decisions, even if they don't sway voters directly.

Stunts

The 2008 presidential race included the predictable stunts that are in the toolbox of minor presidential candidates and local candidates who do not receive press coverage on a daily basis. Candidates debate empty chairs, giant animals (usually chickens) are sent to rallies to make a visual point, candidate press availabilities are invaded by the other side, and so on. Major candidates are wary of stunts, since they can boomerang. Barack Obama's decision to go bowling and Hillary Clinton's shots-drinking were heavily lampooned. When coverage is guaranteed, the game is to control the message, and Obama's big international trip in the summer of 2008, going to foreign places where he would draw the huge adoring crowds, sometimes had a stunt-like feel. John McCain's decision to suspend his campaign and possibly skip the first debate falls in the same category. His decision to tout "Joe the Plumber" as a living example of Democratic programs gone awry spun out into a stunt-like moment. As Joe started to enjoy the limelight, reporters found several things in his background that took the play away from McCain's message to the possibility that this was another example of inept vetting by the McCain campaign, something McCain did not want in light of Sarah Palin.

Lessons: Stunts are risky and even when they generate news stories, they can backfire. High-profile candidates need to proceed with caution when pulling stunts.

What Comes Next?

The 2008 campaign was historic in many ways as barriers were torn down across the political and media landscapes. Campaign coverage and interest were at all-time highs, and technology ratcheted up the amount of information available to the public and the speed with which it was communicated. Both the news media and political campaigns spent a lot of time trying to determine how to deal with the technological changes and the candidates. Successful news organizations were those that found the best ways to use and harness technology to reach voters in meaningful ways.

Many of the "tricks of the trade" in earned media are the same ones that have worked for years and even centuries, although many had to be adapted. Clearly some campaigns and some reporters and news organizations adapted better than others. Reporters and practitioners will spend a lot of time assessing the 2008 campaign to determine which fundamental principles still apply and which have to be relegated to the archives. If change continues at this pace, one wonders if in the 2012 presidential campaign YouTube will look charmingly quaint, whether half hour nightly network news broadcasts and papers on newsprint will even exist, and whether all news and campaign functions will be interactive. It is clear that going back to the old ways is not an option, but it would be valuable to assess which of the new technologies are helps or hindrances to democracy and how much a factor they were in the historic dimensions of the 2008 campaign.

Acknowledgment

Patrick Jakopchek was an invaluable contributor to this chapter.

Notes

1 "Talking Politics: Free Media Versus Earned Media," http://texaspolitics.laits .utexas.edu (accessed February 4, 2009).

2 Scott M. Cutlip and Allen H. Center, *Effective Public Relations* (Englewood Cliffs, NJ: Prentice-Hall, 1978), chap. 4. Much of the history of public relations is taken from this volume, one of the bibles of the PR industry.

3 Jason Salzman, *Making the News* (Boulder: Westview, 2003), chaps. 5, 13.

4 Jonathan Alter and Howard Fineman, "The Search for the Perfect Sound-Bite," *Newsweek*, January 18, 1988, 22.

5 "Your Campaign Plan: Earned Media," www.ksdp.org/?q=node/view/51 (accessed February 4, 2009).

6 Matt Bai, "The Framing Wars," *New York Times*, July 17, 2005, 38.

7 Matthew C. Nisbet, "What Is Framing?" http://scienceblogs.com/framing -science/about.php (accessed February 4, 2009).

8 Kathleen Hall Jamieson and Karlyn Kohrs Campbell, *The Interplay of Influence: News, Advertising, Politics, and the Mass Media* (Belmont, CA: Wadsworth, 2006).

9 Pew Research Center for the People and the Press, "Internet Overtakes Newspapers as News Outlet," *Pew Research Center Publications*, December 23, 2008, http:// pewresearch.org/pubs/1066/internet-overtakes-newspapers-as-news-source. The Pew

Foundation has supported high-quality research for years, which has enhanced the quality of media analysis enormously. Many Pew studies are cited in this chapter, conducted by the Pew Research Center for Excellence in Journalism and the Pew Center for People and the Press. The Pew Center on Internet Life was an invaluable resource for its extensive reach in documenting political coverage across media platforms.

10 Pew Research Center for the People and the Press, "Internet Now Major Source of Campaign News," *News Interest Index*, October 31, 2008, http://people-press.org/report/467/internet-campaign-news.

11 Juan Antonio Vargas, "Campaign USA: With the Internet Comes a New Political 'Clickocracy,'" *Washington Post*, April 1, 2008, C01.

12 Zephyr Teachout, "Mike Huckabee Is Running the Best Web Campaign," *Personal Democracy Forum: TechPresident*. November 25, 2007, www.techpresident.com/blog/entry/13845/mike_huckabee_is_running_the_best_web_campaign.

13 Dotty Lynch, "How the Media Shapes Elections," *America Magazine*, October 22, 2007, www.americamagazine.org/content/article.cfm?article_id=10297.

14 Matt Lewis, "Bad Timing/Web Goof Spoils Edwards' Big Day," *Matt Lewis & the News*, December 28, 2006, www.mattlewis.org/blogger/2006/12/ford-website-spoil-edwards-announcement.html.

15 Scott Martelle, "Richardson Officially Enters Race," *Los Angeles Times*, May 22, 2007, A17.

16 Institute of Politics, John F. Kennedy School of Government, Harvard University, *Campaign for President: The Managers Look at 2008* (Lanham, MD: Rowman & Littlefield, 2009), chap. 1, "The Decision to Run," 11. Since 1972 the John F. Kennedy Institute of Politics at Harvard University has held a conference with major presidential campaign decision makers following every election. The Campaign for President: The Managers Look at 2008 conference in Cambridge, December 11–12, 2008, provided helpful insights into campaign decisions that greatly enhanced this chapter.

17 "Giuliani Confirms He's Running in 2008," MSNBC.com, February 15, 2007, www.msnbc.msn.com/id/17158406.

18 Lynch, *How the Media Shapes Elections*.

19 Adam Nagourney and Jeff Zeleny. 2007. "In Mostly Sedate Debate, Democrats Show More Unity Than Strife," *New York Times*, April 26, 2007, 24.

20 *Campaign for President*, chap. 5, "The General Election," 202.

21 *Campaign for President*, chap. 5, "The General Election," 198–199.

22 Pew Research Center's Project for Excellence in Journalism, "Character and the Primaries of 2008," Journalism.org, May 29, 2008, www.journalism.org/node/11266.

23 "Character and the Primaries."

24 "Character and the Primaries."

25 Margie Omero, "The Palin Effect—Its Rise & Fall," Pollster.com, October 8, 2008, www.pollster.com/blogs/omero_the_palin_effectits_rise.php.

26 Pew Research Center's Project for Excellence in Journalism, "Winning the Media Campaign." Journalism.org. October 22. 2008, www.journalism.org/node/13307.

27 Mark Halperin and John Harris, *The Way to Win: Taking the White House in 2008* (New York: Random House, 2006), 52–64.

28 Greg Sargent, "Overstating Drudge's Influence for Fun and Profit," Talking PointsMemo.com, September 17, 2008, http://tpmelectioncentral.talkingpointsmemo.com/2008/09/overstating_drudges_influence.php.

29 Chris Cillizza, "Drudge-ology 101: McCain, Obama, and Media Bias," Washington Post.com, September 17, 2008, http://voices.washingtonpost.com/thefix/2008/09/drudge ology_101_.

30 *Campaign for President*, chap. 3, "The Internet and Presidential Politics," 105.

31 Sam Stein, "Ex-Clinton Spokesman: Drudge Bastardizes the Press," *Huffington Post*, June 11, 2008, www.huffingtonpost.com/2008/06/11/ex-clinton-spokesman -drud_n_106584.html.

32 *Campaign for President*, chap. 3, "The Internet and Presidential Politics," 107–108.

33 Mayhill Fowler, "Obama: No Surprise That Hard-Pressed Pennsylvanians Turn Bitter," *Huffington Post*, April 11, 2008, www.huffingtonpost.com/mayhill-fowler/obama -no-surprise-that-ha_b_96188.html.

34 *Campaign for President*, chap. 4, "The Democratic Primaries," 138.

35 *Campaign for President*, chap. 5, "The General Election," 203.

36 Pew Research Center's Project for Excellence in Journalism, "Press Takes a Harder Look at Obama—and Itself," March 2008, www.journalism.org/node/10004.

37 Eric Deggans, "Politics, 'SNL' Style," *St. Petersburg Times*, October 9, 2008, 2B.

38 Stephen Dinan, "Negative Ads Everywhere, Nowhere; Public Rarely Sees the Harsher Ones," *Washington Times*, September 20, 2008, 52–64.

39 Paul Farhi, "The Ads That Aren't: Candidates Let Media Spread the Message," *Washington Post*, September 11, 2008, C01.

40 *Campaign for President*, chap. 5, "The General Election," 177–178.

8

Fieldwork in Contemporary Election Campaigns

Paul S. Herrnson

Fieldwork has traditionally been a major element of American election campaigns. Discussions of fieldwork conjure up images of armies of campaign workers knocking on doors first to register voters and then to bring them to the polls. They also bring to mind a conception of politics dominated by urban political machines and corrupt party bosses. At the turn of the twentieth century, often labeled the golden age of politics, a well-heeled team of fieldworkers who could assess constituents' needs and deliver their votes was a critical foundation for any political organization's or candidate's power (Sorauf 1980). Currently, candidates and parties need more than a crack field staff to successfully compete in electoral politics. Nonetheless, fieldwork remains an important campaign activity.

Campaign fieldwork does not capture as much attention in the press as do public opinion polls, television commercials, fund-raising events, and other contemporary election activities. Yet voter identification, registration, targeting, literature drops, and get-out-the-vote drives remain central components of modern elections. For many bottom of the ticket elections, such as races for city council, the state legislature, and even a few House seats, fieldwork remains the major activity of the campaign. This is especially true in primaries and midterm or odd-year elections; lacking the excitement provided by a presidential contest, such elections require campaigns to undertake extra efforts to encourage citizens to vote. Finally, fieldwork is one of the few areas of campaigning in which political parties, interest groups, and volunteers continue to play an important role beyond making contributions and spending money.

Although some of the techniques used to conduct fieldwork have changed, the goals of these activities remain essentially the same as they were during the golden age: to identify, communicate with, and mobilize campaign supporters. It should come as little surprise that well-run campaigns today integrate their field operation into the rest of their organization and activities. This chapter focuses mainly on three aspects of campaign fieldwork: voter identification and targeting, campaign communications, and voter mobilization. First, I summarize how these activities are performed. Then, I discuss the impact that fieldwork has on election outcomes. And finally, I consider the implications that fieldwork has for political parties and volunteerism in contemporary election campaigns.

Voter Identification and Targeting

One of the first activities conducted by a campaign organization is voter research. Candidates and their campaign staffs must determine which groups of voters are inclined to support them, support their opponent, or are undecided. Voters have traditionally been categorized on the basis of geography, religion, ethnicity, race, income, education, profession, and party identification (Campbell, Converse, Miller, and Stokes 1960). More recent classifications are based on combinations of age, ideology, and lifestyle. Some of these include voters who are described using terms like "yuppie," "soccer mom," and "generation X-er." In cases where issues form the core of a voter's political identity or are the primary motivation for an individual's political involvement, the issue itself may be used to define the group, as is the case with pro-choice or pro-life voters.

Once voters have been classified into groups—likely supporters, unlikely supporters, or undecideds—campaign strategists seek to determine the intensity of each group's support. Strategists use historical data to speculate whether particular groups of voters are likely to vote in the first place. The question raised for those who are identified as likely voters or potential voters is whether they will cast their ballots for a particular candidate (or party) no matter what, or if their support is "soft" and in need of some reinforcement. If the latter is true, what can be done to solidify the bloc's support? Sometimes a group's loyalty is contingent on a show of support for the group's position on a specific issue. Strong support for Israel, for example, is generally considered useful in shoring up the "Jewish vote." Similarly, a vocal stance on civil rights is usually helpful in attracting the votes of blacks, and running on "family values" helps many candidates win the support from conservative Christian voters.

In addition to group loyalties, campaigners also consider group size and turnout level when designing their targeting strategies (Axelrod 1972). It makes more sense for candidates to allocate scarce campaign resources in the direction of large groups that vote in relatively large numbers and might need some encouragement to turn up at the polls than to direct those resources toward small groups that have low levels of voter turnout. Building a winning coalition requires candidates and their campaign staffs to perform a balancing act. Campaigners must consider the size, turnout, and loyalty of different segments of the population when deciding which groups will be targeted. Once the target audiences are determined, the next step is to use demographic, geographic, and polling information to create a campaign plan that determines where voter mobilization activities will be conducted, the content of the candidate's message, and where and by what means that message will be communicated to voters. In recent years, some candidates, political parties, and interest groups have supplemented these traditional sources of voter information with marketing data regarding homeownership, consumer habits, and lifestyle issues.

During the golden age, party fieldworkers were largely responsible for gathering voter information, identifying the target audience, and then implementing the campaign plan. At the lowest level of the party organization, precinct captains kept in touch with voters living in their neighborhoods and collected information about the size, probable turnout, and loyalty of different voting blocs. They assessed the kinds of appeals (most were patronage based) that could be used to win support and formulated a plan for communicating those appeals to voters. Their fieldwork formed the foundation for the campaign plan. A summary of the information the precinct captains collected was communicated to ward leaders, who used it to formulate their own campaign plan. Ward leaders used the information to allocate money, patronage jobs, and other resources among precinct leaders and to set a broader campaign strategy. Following this, the ward leaders transmitted their campaign plans and a summary of the information they had collected from the precinct captains to city or county party leaders. These individuals, in turn, formulated their own campaign strategies and passed along the information they had received to the state party, where leaders used it to develop strategies for statewide races. Finally, the information made its way to the national level, where national party leaders used it to create a national campaign strategy.

Although presidential, most statewide, congressional, and many local campaigns now develop their targeting plans using geodemographic research, public opinion polls, and marketing data, field staff continue to play an important role in many campaigns. Local candidates, their supporters, and, in some areas, party workers continue to knock on doors, make telephone calls, and send emails to try to learn whether citizens intend to vote, whom they support, and whether they have any specific questions or concerns they would like the candidate to address. Some of the more sophisticated campaign websites collect data about website visitors. Campaigns may use computers and personal organizers to collect and record voter information and spreadsheets or statistical packages to analyze it, but the information they collect and how they use it have remained relatively unchanged.

Campaign Communications

Getting out the message is a central part of any campaign. A campaign that doesn't define itself risks being defined by its opponents. Allowing others to define one's campaign, like Michael Dukakis in 1988 and President George H. W. Bush in 1992, is a recipe for disaster. A more recent example is John Kerry's 2004 presidential campaign, in which a group called Swift Boat Veterans for the Truth aired a small number of ads distorting Kerry's military record. The reverberations these ads generated after they were rebroadcast in the nightly news and discussed in other media undermined core aspects of Kerry's image and message, including his potential for strong leadership and commitment to and lifetime of public service.

Modern technology has provided campaigns with a wide variety of tools for communicating with the electorate. Broadcast and cable television, radio, videotape, the Internet, DVDs, text messages, websites, and the airplane have supplemented the handbills, buttons, railways, and other campaign techniques of yesteryear. Nevertheless, the basic goals and strategies of campaign communications remain the same: to introduce a candidate to voters, give them a reason to support that candidate, discourage them from supporting the candidate's opponent, get the candidate's supporters excited enough about the election to cast a ballot on election day, and, occasionally, demoralize an opponent's supporters so they will be less inclined to participate in the election. Although most of the communications for presidential, statewide, and many congressional campaigns are created by political consultants cut from the cloth of Madison Avenue public relations experts, fieldwork plays an important role in the two-way flow of communications between candidates and voters in virtually all elections. Personal contact with voters can be an important source of information about issues and a means for candidates to demonstrate to voters and news correspondents that they are in touch with people's wants and needs. Candidate–citizen interactions in the field allow for spontaneous learning and expressions of concern. Well-attended rallies generate free media coverage and are generally interpreted by the media as evidence of a strong grassroots organization and an indicator of widespread public support.

Candidates frequently weave the conversations they have with individuals they meet along the campaign trail into anecdotes that help them humanize the impact that economic trends, social conditions, and government policies have on ordinary people. Incumbents use anecdotes to highlight the positive impact their programs have had on students, business entrepreneurs, and the like. Challengers use anecdotes about unemployed factory workers, farmers who have lost their land, homeless children, and other needy groups in order to dramatize the failure of policies that were enacted or implemented by incumbents and to indicate how their proposals would directly improve people's lives. Candidates for open seats often use anecdotes to try to establish their compassion for the plight of the less fortunate or to laud the selfless efforts or aspirations of others. Their connection to the party in power usually tempers their message. In his acceptance speech at the 2008 Republican National Convention, GOP nominee John McCain (2008) used anecdotes of those he met along the campaign trail to demonstrate empathy for some of America's less fortunate, when he stated:

> I fight for Americans. I fight for you. I fight for Bill and Sue Nebe from Farmington Hills, Michigan, who lost their real estate investments in the bad housing market. Bill got a temporary job after he was out of work for seven months. Sue works three jobs to help pay the bills . . . I fight for the family of Matthew Stanley of Wolfboro, New Hampshire, who died serving our country in Iraq. I wear his bracelet and think of him every day. I intend to honor their sacrifice by making sure the country their son loved so well and never returned to remains safe from its enemies.

Democratic nominee Barack Obama (2008) used his acceptance speech to show his concern for less fortunate Americans and to place blame for their hardships on the Republican Party. His speech at the Democratic National Convention discussed the hardships faced by military families whose loved ones leave for repeated tours of duty, workers who were losing jobs that had moved overseas, and others who had not fared well during the years of GOP domination of the federal government. He was able to shore up these connections by referencing family members. One of his most powerful statements referenced his mother:

> In the face of that young student, who sleeps just three hours before working the night shift, I think about my mom, who raised my sister and me on her own while she worked and earned her degree, who

once turned to food stamps, but was still able to send us to the best schools in the country with the help of student loans and scholarships.

Unlike McCain, Obama was in a position to blame these shortcomings on the current Republican administration and to suggest that by electing another Republican to the White House Americans would be likely to experience more of the same. Incumbents, challengers, contestants for open seats, and candidates for all levels of office make use of information gathered by field operatives and from face-to-face meetings with citizens in their campaign communications.

Field activities also are used to generate free media coverage. Even presidential campaigns, which make extensive use of paid television and radio advertisements, rely on field events to attract the media. In 2008 Democratic Obama attracted such large crowds and media coverage that the Republican operatives sought to discredit him as a candidate that had little more to offer than celebrity status. However, the outpouring of support for GOP vice presidential nominee Sarah Palin encouraged them to hold more rallies in larger venues in order to increase their share of media attention. Both parties' standard bearers used bus tours to generate free media coverage, reminiscent of the cross-country tour John McCain staged during the 2000 primary season in a bus dubbed the Straight Talk Express.

Field activities are the major form of communications in most state and local campaigns and in some campaigns for Congress. Coffee klatches, town hall meetings, visits to shopping centers, and door-to-door canvassing by a candidate or surrogate campaigners are routinely used to introduce the candidate or publicize the campaign's major themes and issues. Visits to factories, hospitals, or military bases are designed to attract press coverage. Rallies featuring high-profile party leaders and other celebrities serve a similar purpose. Yard signs, posters, and bumper stickers are used to improve a candidate's level of name recognition. Literature drops, phone banks, and email enable a candidate to directly communicate issue information to voters without having to rely on the media. Because they are labor-intensive, cheap, and often involve volunteers, field activities play a big role in campaigns for state and local offices.

Voter Registration and Get-Out-the-Vote Drives

Voter registration and get-out-the-vote drives are key components of fieldwork. By registering new voters who identify with their candidate's party or are likely to be favorably disposed toward the candidate, campaign fieldworkers can influence the outcome of a close race. Computer technology, voter files, and precinct-level data have made it possible to identify supportive electoral constituencies. As noted above, marketing data allow campaigns to pinpoint individuals and households that can be anticipated to support specific candidates and parties. Address lists, telephone numbers, and the mailing labels that many campaigns use to contact voters are usually furnished by party committees or interest groups or purchased from private vendors. Some party committees, interest groups, and private vendors also compile and distribute email lists. Savvy candidates have begun to collect email addresses from individuals who visit their websites. Providing voter contact information and products that facilitate its collection has become a multimillion-dollar industry.

In some localities, campaign fieldworkers can effectively walk from house to house registering likely supporters. In others, like college campuses, it is more profitable to set up registration tables. Union halls, churches, and civic associations also make good locations for registering easily identifiable groups of voters. Voter registration drives that focus on well-defined populations can be accurately targeted and are profitable for a candidate, party, or interest group. Registration drives that are held at sporting events or fairgrounds, by contrast, tend to be less well targeted and can result in the registration of an opponent's supporters. The motor voter law, which requires departments of motor vehicles and some other state offices to provide citizens with voter registration forms, is by design the least discriminating. Indiscriminately registering voters may be good for democracy, but some partisans complain it can harm a candidate's election prospects.

Registering voters is only half the battle in gaining their votes. The other half is making sure they actually vote. Follow-up is often needed to ensure that some voters exercise their franchise. In most states, a well-run voter registration drive will record whether voters know the location of their polling place, or if they will need a ride, a baby-sitter, an absentee ballot, or some other special assistance in order to get to the polls. In Texas and the thirty other states that allow early voting or provide conveniently located countywide polling stations or mobile voting units, campaigns need to spend more resources encouraging individuals to vote during early voting periods and to keep track of those who have taken advantage of this opportunity to avoid spending money on repeated and unnecessary voter contacts. Similarly, campaigns in Oregon, which holds its elections by mail, and campaigns in states with liberal rules governing absentee voting need to devote resources to ensuring supporters post their ballots on time.

Regardless of a campaign's location, most put extra effort into turning out newly registered voters and those with an inconsistent history of turning up at the polls. These voters may need to be contacted several times to ensure their turnout. In order to facilitate the turnout of these voters, some candidates, party committees, advocacy organizations, and state and county boards of elections post maps of local polling places on their websites or include links to Mapquest or some other website that can provide them with directions.

Get-out-the-vote activities are in many ways analogous to the sprint to the finish line that ends a close marathon. Both take place when the contestants are exhausted and have depleted most of their resources, and both can be decisive in determining the outcome of the race. For the politician, the final sprint takes place in the last few weeks of the campaign. By that time, the campaign has all but completed its fund-raising, finished most of its research and targeting, communicated its message, and has stopped registering new voters. Campaigners principally focus on getting out the vote. Most campaigns use telephone banks, postcards, or foot canvasses to remind their supporters to go to the polls. Extra efforts are made to bring voters who need assistance to the polls.

Fieldwork and Election Outcomes

What effect does fieldwork have on who wins or loses an election? Field coordinators, the vendors of voter lists, and the individuals who volunteer to register and bring voters to the polls will typically report that field-work is critical in separating winning candidates from losers. The tens of millions of dollars per election cycle that national and state party committees spent on their coordinated campaigns during the last de-cade suggest that party leaders also consider fieldwork to be an impor-tant part of campaigning (Herrnson 2008). The extensive efforts of some labor unions, trade associations, pro-business, and other advocacy organizations indicate these groups also recognize the importance of fieldwork. Personal anecdotes and financial reports may be useful for measuring a campaign's field effort, but they are limited in terms of what they tell about the impact of that effort on voters and election outcomes. Systematic research is needed to assess the impact that field activities have on votes.

Studying the impact of field activities on election outcomes is a complex task. Ideally, researchers would collect information about the activities that were conducted in conjunction with a particular election and disentangle the effects of fieldwork from the effects of the other campaign efforts. A study that fully isolates the effects of fieldwork would be extremely difficult, if not impossible, to conduct. Nevertheless, political scientists have rigorously studied campaign fieldwork and found that it does indeed affect election outcomes. Personal canvassing has been found to increase voter turnout and affect the division of the two-party vote (Krassa 1988; Huckfeldt and Sprague 1992; Gerber and Green 2004). This suggests that campaign field activities play a bigger role in swaying voter preferences than in bringing voters to the polls.

Fieldwork, Political Parties, and Campaign Volunteers

In this era of money-driven, professionally run, technologically sophis-ticated campaigns, fieldwork remains an area of campaigning that can draw on the resources of party organizations and the efforts of ordinary citizens. Most field activities are labor-intensive and can be carried out by volunteers. Individuals who are efficacious, active in civic groups, and familiar with their neighborhoods make excellent fieldworkers. The telephone calls they make to turn out the vote are usually received more favorably than the mass-distributed, recorded telephone messages disseminated by vendors. Local party committees, where they are vigorous, can be an excellent source of field assistance and campaign volunteers. The same is true of labor unions and other organizations.

A study of congressional elections conducted in 1984 shows that candidates for the House of Representatives and their campaign staffs found party organizations to be a significant source of assistance in field-related election activities. Thirty-two percent of the campaigns reported that local party committees played a moderately to extremely important role in collecting information about voters, and 40 percent stated that local parties played a moderately to extremely important role in carrying out voter registration and get-out-the-vote drives. State party committees were also a significant source of voter information and provided substantial assistance in voter mobilization (Herrnson 1988).[1] National party organizations, however, were helpful in areas of campaigning requiring technical expertise, in-depth research, or connections with political action committees, political consultants, and other Washington operatives (Herrnson 1988). Political parties were most helpful in recruiting campaign volunteers. Fully 52 percent of the campaigns reported that local party committees were moderately to extremely important in this area. Interest groups were ranked next, with 35 percent of the campaigns ranking them moderately to extremely important. In general, Republican House candidates relied more heavily on their party committees for field assistance than did Democrats, who were able to call on labor unions and other interest groups for campaign assistance. Similar findings were reported for campaigns for the U.S. Senate. The results of a study of the 2002 congressional elections were almost identical, indicating that local party committees continue to play an important role in campaign fieldwork (Herrnson 2008).

Fieldwork is important for reasons beyond the impact that it can have on election outcomes or for the opportunities it provides for parties to assert themselves in the political process. Because campaign fieldwork seeks to enfranchise new voters, ensure the participation of those who have voted before, and is conducted by volunteers, it is good for democracy in the broadest sense. Campaign field activities help increase levels of political participation, efficacy, and support for government by encouraging people to get involved in politics.

The experiences of campaign volunteers are especially telling. Most volunteers have little knowledge and few campaign skills when they get involved in politics. No previous training is required for most field activities. Through canvassing their neighborhoods, erecting yard signs, and bringing voters to the polls, volunteers learn that they can influence politics. They discover that in addition to controlling their own votes they can influence the votes of others through working in a campaign. Some become more deeply involved in politics and eventually run for public office.

Most campaigns for lower level office, and some campaigns for Congress, afford campaign volunteers the opportunity to meet with field coordinators, the campaign manager, and the candidate. Usually the candidate and the professional consultants that work in the campaign will periodically hold short briefings with volunteers to boost morale and motivate them to work harder. These briefings give volunteers a chance to learn how the campaign is progressing, become informed about the relevance of the tasks they are performing, ask questions, and make suggestions.

Although it is uncommon for volunteers' suggestions to be adopted, the exchanges that take place at campaign briefings are useful to both the paid staff and the volunteers. The staff learns about issues that are on the minds of those volunteering for them and other citizens. The volunteers have an opportunity to find out more about how campaigns are run and how government works. Discussions of why only selected issues are presented in the campaign's literature, why certain appeals are targeted to specific demographic groups, and why some events are held only in particular neighborhoods serve as practical lessons in representation and coalition building.

The give-and-take that occurs between campaign staffs and campaign volunteers, and between campaign volunteers and the citizens they contact in the field, can give volunteers a feeling of empowerment and engender loyalty to the political system. Other aspects of contemporary elections, such as television commercials, political action committees, fund-raising events, and mass mailings, do little to increase the ties that common citizens have to the political process. These activities do not allow for the elite–mass interaction that is at the heart of grass-roots politics.

Conclusion

Fieldwork is an important element of campaign politics as shown by the Obama campaign in 2008. Even though contemporary campaigns, particularly those for high office, rely heavily on the electronic media, polls, spin doctors, and other modern electioneering techniques, field activities continue to be important in voter identification and targeting, message development and communications, and voter mobilization. Anecdotal as well as systematic evidence demonstrates that field activities can influence election outcomes. Moreover, fieldwork is an area of campaigning that frequently relies on the efforts of political parties and volunteers. In this sense, fieldwork provides important benefits to the broader political system. The exchanges that occur between fieldworkers, candidates, campaign staffs, and ordinary voters are an important part of the dialogue of democracy.

Notes

1 Candidates and campaign officials were asked to rate party committees, unions, political action committees, and other interest groups as not important, slightly important, moderately important, very important, or extremely important in campaign activities ranging from mass media advertising to voter mobilization. These findings are from survey data collected in the 1984 and 2002 Congressional Campaign Studies. For information about the studies, see Herrnson (1988, 2008).

References

Axelrod, Robert. 1972. "Where the Voters Come From: An Analysis of Presidential Election Coalitions, 1952–1968." *American Political Science Review* 66: 11–20.
Campbell, Agnes, Philip E. Converse, Warren E. Miller, and Donald E. Stokes. 1960, 1964. *The American Voter.* New York: John Wiley and Sons.

Gerber, Alan S., and Donald P. Green. 2004. *Get Out the Vote: How to Increase Voter Turnout*. Washington, D.C.: Brookings Institution.

Herrnson, Paul. 1988. *Party Campaigning in the 1980s*. Cambridge, MA: Harvard University Press.

———. 2008. *Congressional Elections: Campaigning at Home and in Washington*, 5th ed. Washington D.C.: CQ Press.

Huckfeldt, Robert, and John Sprague. 1992. "Political Parties and Electoral Mobilization: Political Structure, Social Structure, and the Party Canvass." *American Political Science Review* 86: 70–86.

Krassa, Michel A. 1988. "Context and the Canvass: The Mechanisms of Interactions." *Political Behavior* 10: 233–246.

McCain, John. 2008. Acceptance speech at the Republican National Convention. Transcript available at http://elections.nytimes.com/2008/president/conventions/videos/transcripts/20080904_MCCAIN_SPEECH.html?scp=1&sq=John%20Mccain%20Acceptance%20Speech&st=cse.

Obama, Barack. 2008. Acceptance speech at the Democratic National Convention. Transcript available at www.nytimes.com/2008/08/28/us/politics/28text-obama.html.

Sorauf, Frank J. 1980. "Political Parties and Political Action Committees: Two Life Cycles." *Arizona Law Review* 20: 455–464.

9

Dimensions of Campaigns in the Age of Digital Networks

Alan Rosenblatt

Electoral campaigns still need to win on message and organization, but a digitally networked polity is an increasingly chaotic environment in which campaigns take place. Not only are there more tools and channels to connect candidates to voters, but those tools and channels are available to the voters, not just the campaigns. To make matters more chaotic, in many ways the voters are better at using these new digitally networked tools and channels than campaigns, even better than political parties, the media, and other for-profit and nonprofit organizations.

A few years ago people were asking when the Internet would win a presidential election. Today we recognize that no one can win the presidency without an Internet strategy. Indeed, it no longer makes sense to talk about Internet strategy in isolation. The use of digital network strategy is integral to every part of a campaign, from field organizing to fund-raising, from branding/messaging to press relations, and from registering people to vote to getting people out to vote.

Campaigns always come down to message and organization, regardless of the technology used. But digitally networked technology, especially the Internet and mobile, offers more ways to package and deliver messages, and more ways to connect and organize volunteers, supporters, and voters than ever before. Touching on every aspect of a campaign, digital networks create economies of scale and the ability to overcome time and distance, both representing significant advances in campaign capacity.

What distinguishes network technologies from earlier campaign tools is that voters have many of the same tools at their disposal as campaigns. And with voters being way ahead of campaigns in their use, this increases the democratizing force/potential of the organically emerging grassroots during a campaign. Additionally, organized grassroots actions by advocacy groups are further cluttering the political marketplace.

Consider how the 2008 Obama presidential campaign allowed the formation and growth of an opposition group on its own social network website, my.BarackObama.com (MyBO); clearly the rules are changing as technology evolves. Indeed, the anti-FISA (Federal Intelligence Surveillance Act) vote group on MyBO swelled quickly to about 25,000 members and continues to apply pressure from within the Obama community, even after inauguration, calling for a reversal of the position he took on the FISA vote when he was in the Senate. And through the campaign, Obama welcomed the dissension on his own web servers, something old-school issue management would never do.

The Dimensions of Digitally Networked Campaigns

Online campaigns can be envisioned in three dimensions (or versions 1.0, 2.0, and 3.0, if you prefer a computer metaphor). At the core, the dimensions are about the strategic flow-direction of communication (Table 9.1). One-dimensional (1-D) campaigns are about broadcasting a one-way campaign message, with tight language control, to voters. 2-D campaigns are about building a transactional or two-way relationship with voters; getting them to register to vote, for example. And 3-D campaigns unleash the masses, with communication flowing to and from the campaign, as well as in any direction between and among voters. And in reality, 3-D campaigns are 3-plus dimensions because digi-

Table 9.1 Strategic Dimensions of a Digital Network Strategy for Campaigns

	Level of Measurement	*Direction of Communication*	*Activity*	*Message Control*
1-D Strategy	Information	One-way	Broadcasting	Tight
2-D Strategy	Action	Two-way	Transacting	Tight or Relaxed
3-D+ Strategy	Community	Three-way+	Networking	Chaotic

tal networks allow for time shifting and overcome distance obstacles in addition to facilitating omni-directional messaging and organizing.

Campaigns that effectively tap into the power of the Internet and mobile networks, fully integrating these new dynamics into campaign strategy, will have a decided edge on opponents. Just as online strategies integrate into, rather than replace, offline strategies, these online dimensions also integrate together. Campaigns will have 1-, 2-, and 3-plus-dimensional characteristics.

Voters' ability to take campaigns into their own hands is the big game changer for politics. Because voters can talk to each other, produce and share their own media content, create local and national counter-campaigns (even from within a candidate's own campaign website), they can take the campaign in directions of their own making. By enabling voters to create mass messages, process large numbers of transactions, and build large social networks, they are able to make impacts on the political process once reserved to well-funded countercampaigns or the occasional mass ground protest.

Two Examples of Voter-Generated Chaos

ParkRidge 47's Think Different

The 2008 Obama campaign faced two moments of voter-generated chaos early on. The first occurred when an anonymous video producer, ParkRidge47, produced and posted a video "mash-up" commercial for

Obama on YouTube.com.[1] The video took the 1984 Apple Macintosh commercial featuring Big Brother on a video screen while a blue-lit audience of citizens watches mesmerized and superimposed a video of Senator Hillary Clinton giving a speech on Big Brother's image and her voice replacing his on the soundtrack. Then a runner enters the room wearing an Obama T-shirt and hurls a hammer at the screen, smashing Clinton's face into a million pieces.

The video made waves through the early Obama campaign, first because it was such a compelling, voter-generated commercial, and second because its creator turned out to be Phillip de Vellis, an employee at the Obama campaign's Internet consulting firm Blue State Digital. De Vellis created the video at home on a Sunday afternoon because he "wanted to express my feelings about the Democratic primary, and because I wanted to show that an individual citizen can affect the process."[2]

The controversy set off by de Vellis cost him his job. But the impact he made hit home, as he quickly landed a senior position at a top Democratic media firm. But the impact of this video went deeper. True, de Vellis was a professional with high-end video editing software, but the Think Different video could have just as easily been made with a $99 piece of software.[3]

In the months that followed, the campaign saw many videos pop up on YouTube that captured the attention of the media and the voters. From the scantily clad Obama girl singing her Barack a love song to the more rotund McCain Girls singing out of tune and with gusto, lots of videos helped shape the public perception of the candidates.[4] Indeed, within the Obama campaign, a decision was made to work with volunteers to help them make videos, in addition to the campaign produced clips.

Joe Anthony's MySpace Page

When Barack Obama was elected senator, Joe Anthony launched a MySpace page in support of the new senator. Anthony made his first foray into political activism after being "blown away" by Obama's 2004 speech at the Democratic National Convention.[5] Anthony had built his

MySpace.com/barackobama friend list up to about 30,000 by the time Obama announced his candidacy. With the announcement, the number of friends on the MySpace page grew fast, getting more than 160,000 friends in short order. Then a power struggle emerged between Anthony and the campaign over control of the page. The campaign offered Anthony a job in Chicago to come run the group from campaign headquarters. Anthony declined the offer and asked for a buyout instead.

Leaving aside the specifics of the negotiating, in the end the Obama campaign wrestled control of the URL from Anthony by appealing to MySpace directly. But Anthony was allowed to keep his community list for his own MySpace page. In the span of a day, Obama's MySpace page went from number one among candidates with 160,000 friends to last, with zero.[6] Despite this setback and the controversy around it regarding the takeover of the page, Obama was able to rebuild his friend list and overtake all opponents within a few weeks. As of the writing of this chapter, Obama's MySpace friends list is still climbing and exceeds a million people.

While neither of these events derailed or guaranteed a win for any campaign, they did create a "must deal with" issue for the campaigns to manage. And while there are always things popping during campaigns that must be dealt with, these examples illustrate a whole new capacity for individual citizens to make a substantial impact on a large audience.

1-D Strategy

Optimists would say these new tools will transform E. E. Schattschneider's underrepresented masses into an organized (even if in a swarm fashion) political force. Already, the multiplication of online communications channels is creating a voter-driven challenge to campaigns seeking to distribute its message. One-way broadcasting is being supplemented, and at times replaced, by narrowcasting: distributing messages to targeted and microtargeted audiences. While many voters still rely on email, many others are moving to other channels like Facebook, MySpace, Twitter, SMS text messaging, or instant messenger for their primary mode of online communication. Others are compartmentalizing

their channels, preferring personal communication through some channels, work communication through others, consumer and political
through others.

Given this proliferation of online channels to reach people, campaigns are already finding new challenges when using network technology to deliver their message. In the early days of online campaigns
(before 2000), setting up a website and building a modest email list was
the extent of online voter outreach. Websites were seen as informational
storefronts and email lists were focused on sending out campaign messages. Indeed, an email list of 5,000 supporters in a congressional district is still incredibly valuable, especially for organizing volunteers. And
a candidate's website is still an essential front office. But disseminating
a message can no longer rely on centralized, limited channels if a campaign wants to reach the majority of voters. Respecting communication
channel preferences is essential for campaigns seeking to develop deeper
relationships with voters.

It is important to note that traffic volume is not the only, or even a
necessary, metric of success for a campaign website. In some cases, it is
less about how many people visit a campaign website and more about
who visits the site. In 1998, for example, NetPolitics Group created a
campaign website called MissedVotes.org for a Democrat running for
an open seat in Ohio. The site simply provided a list of links to the
Ohio state legislature's online roll call record to document the many
votes the Republican candidate missed while serving in the statehouse.
The site had very few visitors, perhaps only dozens. But among those
few were most of the reporters covering the race. Whenever the Democratic candidate claimed the Republican candidate missed a particular
vote, the reporters went to the site to verify it before writing up their
stories. The website was a primary factor in shaping the earned media
for the campaign despite its small immediate audience. The lesson here
is that it is always important to know who your audience is and deliver
content that matters to them.

The optimal 1-D campaign strategy uses all available channels, each
targeted to the appropriate audience, to get the message out. In the early
days of the Internet, there were relatively few channels and only a couple dominant ones: websites and email. Today there are too many chan-

nels to track. In addition to websites and email, people also communicate via social network sites like Facebook.com and MySpace.com; mobile/Internet networks like Twitter.com; social media sites like You Tube.com, Flickr.com, Digg.com, and Eventful.com; and via instant messenger online and SMS text messaging over mobile phones. And it is likely that there will be new channels in time, just as some of these existing channels may die off.

Increasingly, the challenge is to rise above the noise to deliver campaign messages to voters in a respectful way, a way that will be received positively. Voters have preferences for how they wish to interact with campaigns. The receivers increasingly are choosing the channel for getting their messages, whether they are political or personal. If campaigns do not deliver to the right channel for each voter, that message may never be seen or, worse, may be seen as a sign of disrespect because the campaign is not sending it through the preferred channel.

2-D Strategy

An essential element of the online experience is the ability to couple transactional tools to the information being disseminated. Networked communication technology allows us to integrate action tools, like emailing Congress, donating money, registering to vote, or writing letters to editors, not to mention facilitating meaningful feedback, into any piece of content delivered to voters.

Delivering opportunities for online citizens to take action is not only desirable and necessary but is expected by the people. The people, to a large extent, are more adept at using the Internet and mobile networks than campaigns, more even than all public and private institutions. That creates great expectations for campaigns and a sophisticated level of scrutiny. This is especially true now that the Internet has overtaken television as the primary source of political news for eighteen- to twenty-nine-year-olds and of approximately equal use for thirty- to forty-nine-year-olds.[7]

There are several technology vendors specializing in building campaign websites, complete with the 2-D action capabilities. Among them are Blue State Digital, which built President Obama's campaign website;

Democracy in Action, which built dozens of progressive congressional candidate websites; PICnet, which specializes in open source Joomla websites; Complete Campaigns; and many more.

These platforms have much in common. All can be used to build a basic candidate website with essential features: email list sign-up, donation processing, and content pages that present essential candidate- and issue-related information. The best of these ensure that the ability to join the campaign email list, volunteer, or donate money are present on every page of the website.

How campaigns use these websites is a set of strategic decisions that can vary across campaigns. Each page on the site presents information that should encourage voters to want to support the candidate, during the campaign and at the voting polls.

The challenge of every campaign is to present the right combination of information about the candidate that encourages voters to look to the campaign website early and often to stay informed. Where in the pre-Internet days campaigns steered totally clear of giving any coverage to what the other candidate is saying, partly to avoid giving the opponent validation and partly because the bandwidth to deliver information to voters was limited (limited inches of news column space, limited pages of pamphlets and postcards, etc.), in the Internet age, scarce bandwidth is no longer a factor.

With increased bandwidth for presenting more thorough information, campaigns can now present their opponents' views fairly, but framed with their own context and response. The 2-D aspect of the Internet creates a new pressure to present both sides of arguments. In this case the dynamic is twisted a bit. If a campaign does not show both sides, voters can take action by opening up a search engine, like Google or Yahoo, and find the opponent's website. Once voters leave one candidate's site for another, the ability for the first candidate to frame the information is lost. By preempting, or delaying this action by giving information about an opponent on a campaign website helps to ensure that voters process the opponent's campaign message with the first campaign's context.

The key to the second dimension of online campaign strategy is to make sure all campaign messages and content are in some way actionable and that the action is one click away.

3-D Strategy

The greatest source of chaos in the political environment is the enhanced ability granted by the Internet for people to connect with each other in any combination, across time constraints, geographic boundaries, and with the same array of tools available to campaigns. The potential for a Joe Anthony, a Phil de Vellis, or a Joe da Plumber to steal attention from the campaign is ever present. And while many claim to be able to create viral campaigns, the truth is we have little idea what causes one idea to go viral and another to fizzle. The same network strategy employed by two different candidates cannot yield the same result. And like chaos models, changing the starting point of a campaign strategy will change its results.

The 3-D nature of digital networks gives an individual the ability to set off movements, even if small, through the polity. Consider the efforts of Eli Pariser and David Pickering, two college students whose email petition opposing a military response to 9/11 spread like wildfire as it gathered 500,000 signatures in less than one month.[8] Their success helped supercharge MoveOn.org when Pariser took his list and became its executive director. There are many more stories of students launching new advocacy groups from their dorm rooms and of a few friends getting together to start a group online that becomes a prominent voice in a campaign.[9]

In a world where the power of the people is enabled by digital and mobile networks, campaigns have to adjust how they view their supporters. Rather than viewing them as message receptacles and followers to organize, campaigns have to treat supporters as strategic partners.

Regardless of whether or not campaigns treat followers as strategic partners, many of them will implement some strategy to organize their own personal networks. It is important to remember that the 2004 Howard Dean campaign discovered 7,500 voters already organized into monthly meet-ups across the country on MeetUp.com. And like the Dean campaign, all campaigns must monitor these types of developments and develop a strategy for incorporating them into the campaign plan—whether or not they become a formal part of the campaign. And as the 2008 Obama campaign showed, enabling new individual efforts to emerge and flourish is now a permanent part of the campaign playbook.

The Tools of the Trade

Keeping up with the networking tools available to campaigns is a daunting task, to say the least. And the odds of a new one emerging by the time this chapter is published is high. That said, it remains helpful to understand the types of software available and some examples of each.

Grassroots Organizing Tools

The core of any campaign is organizing the voters, especially the most engaged and supportive of them. Many of the online tools available to political campaigns are variations of tool suites developed for the advocacy community in the mid-1990s.

One of the key features of grassroots organizing tools is the ability to match people to their political jurisdiction (state, district, and precinct) by their zip code and/or address. This allows campaigns to collect basic contact information from voters, information relatively easy to collect, and build a contact list that can be microtargeted based on the political culture and configuration of each precinct.

Once voters are matched to their precinct, the campaign can send email alerts with links to take action to anyone on the list. With zip code matching it is possible to automate the process of sending contextualized messages to every voter; messages that refer to specific impacts of an issue or a policy to the area where the recipient lives. This increases the stickiness and persuasiveness of the campaign message. And it increases the likelihood that people will do what the emails asks them to do—give money, volunteer, register to vote, and so on.

The products in this category of software are available from Democracy in Action, Blue State Digital, Capitol Advantage, Convio, Aristotle, Vocus, NGP, SoftEdge, and Grassroots Enterprise. These tools have overlapping functions and serve a majority of the campaign market.

Constituent Relations Management

As campaigns build larger lists of supporters and constituents, they must be able to sort them based on a variety of factors, including demographics, issue opinions, level of influence, and behavior interacting with the campaign. But beyond being able to sort and target communications, it is crucial that campaigns develop meaningful relationships with voters, in terms of providing each side with value and respect.

A constituent relations management system (CRM) allows campaigns to track and cross-reference information about supporters, integrating everything from contact information to attendance at events, to donations, to what emails people open and what web pages they visit. With this information, some aspects of the campaign/constituent relationship can be automated, such as delivering newsletters and web pages that reflect the interests of each person. The manual aspects of the relationship are enhanced, allowing for more meaningful personal communications, such as fund-raising phone calls.

While there are many small open source and proprietary CRM software platforms, the industry leader is Salesforce. Coupled with email management systems like Eloqua, another industry leader, the email relationship and the website relationship can be fully integrated with the backend Salesforce database. Likewise, fund-raising systems also integrate in the back end with the CRM.

Content Management

Campaign websites must be able to evolve over the course of a campaign. The flow of content onto and off of the site can be difficult to manage. Thankfully, content management systems allow campaigns to enter content into a database that publishes the content to the website. CMSs are especially helpful when individual pieces of content are being published to multiple web pages and when many people are responsible for updating the site. It also makes archiving website content easy.

Blue State Digital, Convio, and Kintera are among the proprietary CMSs. Drupal and Joomla are among the open source CMSs.

Email

The partner to CRM is the blast email service. Rather than try to use an end user email client, like Microsoft Outlook or a web email service like Gmail.com, campaigns must use an email service that is designed for mass emails. The email services include keeping your email blasts from being black-listed as spam. If you try to use your office email server to send mass messages, you may quickly find that you are unable to send email to anyone.

Online services like Constant Contact are stand alone and inexpensive options. Many CMS and CRM systems have email blasts built into their service. And there are many email marketing vendors that can provide the email services, as well as strategic advice.

But as with all use of technology, it is about delivering the right message over the right channel. From a strategic perspective, the disintermediation of communication channels has shifted control over the distribution channel from the producer of the message to the consumer of the message. A new approach to email blasting systems, as originally conceived and developed by a company called OwlBee, is to deconstruct email messages into component parts, separating text from image and long versions of text from shortened versions. Then, depending on how subscribers receive the messages, the system assembles the right package for the message—rich media email, text-only email, short text message, and so on.

Social Networking

Social networking affected electoral campaigns for the first time in 2004 when MeetUp.com swept Governor Howard Dean into the front-runner before the first caucus and primary. MeetUp let people register online to form offline groups that met monthly. By 2006, social networks had evolved to Facebook and MySpace, wildly popular online communities that allow people to create robust personal networks and share all forms of media within it. Indeed, these networks continued to provide offline organizing tools, like MeetUp, but so much more could be done online with them that the impact of the offline activities was boosted considerably, as evidenced by Obama's ability to turn out more than 100,000 volunteers for the Texas primaries and caucuses.[10]

With over 175 million Americans on Facebook, more on MySpace, and hundreds of thousands if not millions of Americans of social networks like BlackPlanet.com (African American), MiGente.com (Hispanic Americans), and Eons.com (seniors), organizing online communities is as important as organizing individual states.

Despite popular perceptions, these communities are not just for kids. At the time of this writing, growth of adult and senior members of Facebook had doubled in recent months, with millions in each age-group having profiles. Facebook now boasts over 11 million members age 25–34, nearly 7 million age 35–54, and nearly a million over 55. And growth is fastest, by far, for the two oldest age-groups.[11]

To the extent that these social networks are where the voters are and to the extent voters prefer to be contacted via them, campaigns must have a strategy for organizing and distributing its message on them.

Social Media

The other side of the social web is social media. Sites like YouTube, Digg, Flickr, and Eventful let people share with the world all types of media they create or find interesting.

YouTube, Google Video, and other sites let people share videos. Given the experiences of Virginia senator George Allen and Montana senator Conrad Burns, getting caught on tape in an embarrassing moment can destroy a campaign, even if the mainstream media ignore the story. George Allen's famous "macacca" video and Conrad Burns falling asleep at an agriculture committee hearing set to music helped derail both incumbents.

During the 2008 presidential campaign, user-generated videos like Obama Girl and 1984/Think Different captured the news cycle and drew popular attention to the Obama campaign. While hardly a decisive factor in his win, these videos took to life in a way that could never have happened before the Internet.

If the media to be shared are photos, then Flickr and Facebook are the tools. Eventful is a popular tool for networked influentials to promote events they are attending. And for all things media, sites like Digg, Reddit, and C2NN allow campaigns and people to promote media content they find online and take advantage of peer reactions to vote the content up or down in the rankings presented on those websites.

By posting content to these sites and then mobilizing supporters to view the content and vote it up, campaigns can better expose positive media coverage of the candidate (or negative coverage of opponents). And, of course, any voter can use these tools to the same effect.

Blogs

The rise of blogs in general and political blogs in particular has dramatically altered the media landscape. As much as any other development online, blogs represent the epitome of the 3-D characteristics of the web. Bloggers have large audiences of devoted readers, engage in cross-blog communication, and are capable of driving the political narrative.

As a result, campaign strategy must adapt. The agenda-setting power of the blogs, A-list blogs and others, means campaigns must implement a comprehensive strategy for monitoring, responding to, and engaging bloggers.[12]

Monitoring blogs using specialized search engines like Technorati .com and Google's blog search (blogsearch.google.com) gives campaigns the ability to identify emerging issues. Technorati.com also provides a measure of a blog's authority (or influence) by indicating how many other websites link to that blog. Other sites like Alexa.com and Compete.com measure the size of a website's audience. Together, these tools allow campaigns to identify which bloggers will have the biggest impact on the race.

Once a campaign identifies blog posts and bloggers that need to be engaged, there are three basic ways to do so. First, a campaign can post comments on the blog in response to an article. It is important that these comments be authentic. If the commenter is a campaign representative, that should be disclosed, to avoid backlash for misrepresentation. If the commenters are volunteers mobilized to post responses by the campaign, those comments should be in the commenters' own words. Otherwise, the appearance of "canned" comments would create backlash from the bloggers.

Second, a campaign can reach out directly to bloggers to ask them to cover a story from the candidate's perspective. When doing this, it is important to remember that bloggers are publishers, editors, and reporters all rolled into one. Because they answer to no one, they must be treated with extra care. Before making contact, preferably one-on-one contact, be sure that the campaign representative is familiar with the blogger's writing. Ensuring a positive, respectful exchange with bloggers is essential to success.

Finally, while there is no *quid pro quo,* if a campaign is advertising on a blog, it is likely that the interactions on particular stories will go more smoothly. Advertising on blogs can be placed using a variety of services. Many blogs use Blogads.com to serve their ads. Others use the Common Sense Media ad network (csmads.com). And still others use Google ads.

Mobile

Perhaps the most exciting tools available to campaigns are the least understood. Mobile devices, especially smart phones, are delivering a combination of voice, text, and Internet communication channels to individuals on the go. While much attention has been focused on the digital divide between rich and poor on the Internet, minority populations that are severely underrepresented on the Internet are overrepresented on mobile networks. According to the Pew Internet and American Life Project, 71 percent of whites have a mobile phone, compared to 74 percent of African Americans and 84 percent of English-speaking Hispanics. Of those owning a mobile device, whites are 73 percent likely to send or receive data on them, while African Americans are 79 percent likely and English-speaking Hispanics are 90 percent likely.[13]

And while early use of basic SMS text messaging over cell phones has been effective at fund-raising, volunteer coordination, demonstration mobilization, and message distribution, perhaps the most powerful applications are those that integrate the Internet with mobile networks. The leading application in this space is Twitter.

Twitter is essentially a microblogging platform that delivers posts via the web and SMS text messaging. Posts are limited to 140 characters, thus developing skills for conveying effective messaging in short bursts, often compared to the art of writing haikus, is the key to success.

While the service is still young and difficult to grasp by many, Twitter offers a few basic features that have enormous flexibility for organizing and driving public discourse. The key to using Twitter rests with its three builts-in methods for creating hyperlinks. The first, and most basic, is the ability to distribute live web links.

Second is the ability to use the "@TwitterName" convention to send a public message to anyone on Twitter. This form of hyperlink not only identifies the conversation partner but also provides a direct link for any reader to explore the posts from that person and allows Twitter users to aggregate and read posts directed at them.

The third type of hyperlink, the hashtag, is perhaps the most powerful. By including in any post "#topicX," users are able to associate their comments to public conversation. Each conversation, by using a common hashtag, effectively creates a group, or community, on Twitter. Each hashtag becomes a hyperlink to search for all posts employing the tag (via http://search.twitter.com).

Developing conventions for the meaning of these hashtags can create powerful organizing effects. For example, an emerging convention is to pair the #p2 and the #digg hashtags with a URL (web address) for an article posted to Digg.com, the social media sharing site. The purpose of this presentation is to alert the progressive community on Twitter (#p2, or possibly other progressive groups like #topprog or conservative groups like #tcot) that people should visit the link, read the article, and then Digg it (give it a "thumbs up" vote). By getting many people to Digg articles this way, those articles can be catapulted up to the top of Digg's most popular articles. This gets the article featured on Digg.com's home page and exposes it to an audience of millions.

Other examples of how mobile networks have been used to shape the outcome of elections include the flash mob demonstration of

900,000 people the day before the incumbent Spanish government lost the election following the al Qaeda train bombing and the use of an audio recording of the president of the Philippines trying to fix the election with the head of the elections commission as a ringtone that spread across the country like wildfire.

With so many people keeping their mobile phones within arm's reach at all times, the ability to connect voters, supporters, and volunteers via mobile networks has become an important part of the campaign landscape. But, unlike advertising on other media, there are concerns that overusing mobile messaging could conceivably turn off the audience and create a political backlash.

Again, the key here is to be respectful of the audience. Since communication channels are becoming disintermediated, the blunt use of them, as we have used broadcast channels, is less effective.

Collaboration

In *The Wisdom of Crowds*, James Surowiecki explores the power of crowd sourcing, of farming out labor to the masses.[14] As we know from generations of survey research and the central limits theorem, on average, the views of the aggregate are more likely to be accurate than an individual or small sample. Elisabeth Noelle-Neumann reported in *The Spiral of Silence* that aggregating who people think will win an upcoming election is a better predictor, especially months out from Election Day, than asking them how they plan to vote.[15]

Tapping into this collective brain trust is made much easier with digital networking technology. Collaboration tools like wikis, platforms that allow large groups of people to collaborate editing a single document, make managing the process of integrating the ideas of thousands of contributors easy. And new variations of wikis that incorporate Digg-like voting tools make the process even more effective.

For campaigns looking to be responsive to constituents as a delegate, in contrast to a trustee relationship, these collaboration tools help make that process manageable. For example, in 2006, when faced with a popular, well-funded incumbent opponent for the Senate, Utah Democratic candidate Pete Ashdown employed such a wiki in his bid to defeat Senator Orrin Hatch. Ashdown gave voters the ability to shape the details of his policy platform with a policy wiki on his campaign website. Such a tactic goes a long way toward deepening relations with voters.

Fund-raising

While incorporating tools into campaign websites to collect donations is a pretty simple concept, the rise of peer-to-peer fund-raising takes the process to a new level. Websites like ActBlue.com, which is set up for Democratic candidates only, allow anyone to create a fund-raising page for any registered candidate. Once the candidate or candidates are selected, a URL is generated that can be distributed to personal networks to ask them to contribute funds.

Fund-raising pages can be set up for slates of candidates, even candidates in other districts. Many campaigns choose to use this platform instead of paying for their own. ActBlue.com takes care of forwarding the donations to the candidate, checks to ensure donors have not exceeded their FEC limits, and provides reporting to the campaigns.

Volunteer Management

In addition to using the various social networks, social media sites, and collaboration tools to organize volunteers, there is software specifically designed to organize volunteers for canvassing and virtual phone-banking. These tools allow campaigns to upload contact databases with addresses and phone numbers. The system then parses out in small batches address and phone lists for either canvassing or phone-banking. Canvassing lists are distributed with walking maps and phone lists are coupled with web forms to report the results of each call.

Conclusion

The range of digital networking tools and strategies for using them will continue to make a big impact on electoral campaigns. That these tools are in the hands of voters as well as campaigns creates a more chaotic environment for spreading campaign messages than in the past. They also provide new solutions to getting the message out and organizing voters and volunteers. To be effective, campaigns must now develop strategies that consider all of the strategic dimensions created by these new technologies. While message and organization remain paramount, digitally networked technology has altered the playing field, not just in scope and scale but in more fundamental ways.

Notes

1 ParkRidge47 is the pseudonym for media political consultant Phillip de Vellis. His YouTube channel, where the Think Different video can be viewed, is www .youtube.com/user/ParkRidge47. Park Ridge, Illinois, is Hillary Rodham Clinton's home-town and 1947 is the year of her birth.

2 Phil de Vellis, "I Made the 'Vote Different' Ad," *Huffington Post,* March 21, 2007, www.huffingtonpost.com/phil-de-vellis-aka-parkridge/i-made-the-vote-differen_ b_43989.html.

3 Justin Hamilton, who is not a professional videographer, "deconstructed" the Think Different video and recreated it with all but one small effect (keeping Clinton's face perfectly framed in the video screen as the camera angle changed) using FinalCut Basic, a $99 software.

4 Alan Rosenblatt, "Obama Girl as a Teaching Moment," *techPresident,* June 14, 2007, www.techpresident.com/blog/entry/399/obamagirl_video_as_a_teaching_moment.

5 Micah Sifry, "The Battle to Control Obama's Myspace," *techPresident,* May 1, 2007, www.techpresident.com/blog/entry/301/the_battle_to_control_obama_s_myspace.

6 See www.techpresident.com/scrape_plot/myspace for a time-series chart of MySpace friends for the candidates.

7 Andrew Kohut, *The Internet Gains in Politics* (Washington, D.C.: Pew Internet and American Life Project, 2008), http://pewInternet.org/PPF/r/234/report_display.asp.

8 Wikipedia, http://en.wikipedia.org/wiki/Eli_Pariser.

9 Other examples include a crew of Swarthmore College students that launched the Genocide Intervention Network and the group of My.BarackObama.com members form-ing a group of 25,000 MyBO members opposing the candidate's vote on the Federal In-telligence Surveillance Act (FISA).

10 Tim Dickinson, "The Machinery of Hope: Inside the Grass-Roots Field Opera-tion of Barack Obama, Who Is Transforming the Way Political Campaigns Are Run," *Rolling Stone,* March 20, 2008, www.rollingstone.com/news/coverstory/obamamachinery ofhope/page/1.

11 Peter Corbett, "2009 Facebook Demographics and Statistics Report: 276% Growth in 35–54 Year Old Users," www.istrategylabs.com/2009-facebook-demographics -and-statistics-report-276-growth-in-35–54-year-old-users/.

12 Kevin Wallsten, "Agenda Setting and the Blogosphere: An Analysis of the Relationship Between Mainstream Media and Political Blogs," *Review of Policy Research* 24, no. 6 (2007): 567–587.

13 John Horrigan, "Mobile Access to Data and Information," March 5, 2008, www.pewInternet.org/PPF/r/244/report_display.asp.

14 James Surowiecki, *The Wisdom of Crowds* (New York: Doubleday, 2004).

15 Elisabeth Noelle-Neumann, *The Spiral of Silence* (Chicago: University of Chicago Press, 1993).

Election Law
Is the New
Rock and Roll

Chris Sautter

In the days immediately following the 2008 U.S. Senate election in Minnesota, a sign appeared in Democrat Al Franken's campaign headquarters: "Election law is the new rock and roll." It was meant to be a welcome sign for the stream of lawyers who were arriving in the state for a pitched Florida-like recount battle in a race where the margin was razor thin. But the slogan could also be said to represent the new status enjoyed by campaign professionals who participate in what had been a backwater specialization. Indeed, some election lawyers have become celebrities, appearing on cable TV programs and being portrayed in the HBO movie *Recount*.

A more telling sign of the growing popular appeal of election law, however, is the burgeoning grassroots voters' rights movement to remove remaining barriers to equal access, as well as the countermovement to protect the integrity of the election process. Campaigns for both major parties and independent groups today routinely integrate a variety of voter and ballot protection activities into their issue and candidate campaigns. Whereas voter protection and recount preparation activities were once an afterthought, now they are an integral part of the campaign. And while these voter and election protection activities have existed for years, they began to explode in numbers and influence during the aftermath of the controversial 2000 presidential election.

Yet behind the popularization of election law is the reality that a political stalemate between the warring factions—Democrats (progressives) and Republicans (conservatives)—is keeping America's election system on a constant meltdown alert. Republicans believe Democrats are aiding and abetting voter fraud and systematically permitting nonvoters to tilt elections while Democrats believe Republicans are trying to suppress and disenfranchise minorities and the poor through modern and sophisticated tactics whose roots can be found in the days of Jim Crow. Until this logjam is broken, our electoral system will remain unworkable and unresponsive to the American electorate.

The 2000 Presidential Recount

The thirty-six-day dispute to resolve the 2000 presidential election was one of the most dramatic events in American political and legal history. The controversy, which kept Americans glued to their televisions watching a live political reality show, exposed a politicized and shoddy underbelly to the election process as well as a partisan side to the U.S. Supreme Court rarely acknowledged. The 2000 Florida presidential recount also proved to be a turning point in American politics. Although many commentators initially expressed doubt about the enduring importance of the Supreme Court's decision, especially after the attacks of 9/11, it is now clear that Florida changed much in the field of law and politics. It is just as true today as it was in 2000 that Florida was a scandal that represents all that is wrong with how elections are run in America. Just as the Watergate scandal created demand and momentum for change and reform, so it was with the 2000 presidential election and the Supreme Court's decision in *Bush v. Gore*.[1] Yet the kind of reform necessary to fix America's broken election system remains elusive.

What made the Supreme Court's decision so unsettling to many is that the Court effectively decided a presidential election in favor of a candidate who did not receive the greatest number of popular votes.

And the Court decided the 2000 election, these same critics would add, by preventing all the votes from being counted. The Court's decision to stop the Florida recount, in the eyes of many, not only lacked a solid legal precedent but was unnecessarily polarizing, punctuating a period in American politics and law that had already become intensely partisan and ideological. But to others, the Supreme Court's decision put a stop to an out-of-control spectacle in which voter intent was being manufactured based on varying opinions of whether "pregnant chads" were or were not real votes. The events of Florida were further proof that liberals were willing to bend rules in order to win an election. To most conservatives, the Supreme Court was stepping in during a national crisis to protect America's constitutional way of government.

But aside from the controversial and some would maintain overtly political manner in which the U.S. Supreme Court decided the 2000 election, the Florida recount exposed serious flaws in the administration of elections generally. Worse, these flaws, administrative snafus, and outright "dirty tricks" were causing the disenfranchisement of thousands of Florida voters and millions of voters nationally, with a disproportionate number being African American.

The most widely observed and often lampooned problem centered on antiquated punch card voting systems that were systematically voiding votes. The problem was inherent in this rather crude form of computerized voting. Every time the cards were fed through a counting device, the reader seemed to come up with a different number. For example, Bush's election night margin of over 1,500 votes was reduced to 537 votes the day after the election when the cards were run through vote tabulators again as the result of a required automatic machine recount. In the punch card voting counties of South Florida, in particular, there were a high number of so-called undervotes, or ballots for which there was no apparent vote in the presidential race. The now infamous chads—the paper squares which were supposed to be punched out by voters—in a large number of instances could not be due to the inability of voters to punch through the chads cleanly. Among other things, chad jams in certain voting machines had prevented clean votes in the punch cards. Ironically, the use of punch card voting was already declining in America in 2000. But punch cards were still used in poorer counties with large numbers of low-income residents because those counties couldn't afford to purchase newer and more expensive voting equipment. Meanwhile, the same punch card equipment was being jettisoned in favor of more modern modes of voting in the wealthier counties in America. In effect, the votes of poor people were being given less weight than votes cast by wealthy voters.

Equally derided was the "butterfly ballot" with its confusing ballot design. It caused many Palm Beach County, Florida, residents to mistakenly mark their ballots for conservative candidate Pat Buchanan when they intended to vote for Democrat Al Gore. Having realized their mistake, more than 6,000 voters, according to an independent study, then punched Gore, thereby voiding them as double votes or overvotes. In addition, it was estimated that another 2,000 votes cast for Buchanan were intended for Gore. In short, the infamous butterfly ballot, which was approved by a Democratic Palm Beach County Supervisor of Elections, almost certainly cost Al Gore the presidency. The butterfly ballot brought public awareness to the fact that defective ballot design can cause voters to be disenfranchised.

One of the more egregious examples of improper and unjust practices used in Florida in the 2000 election was the state's "voter cleansing" program. Under the guise of an antifraud campaign, Secretary of State Katherine Harris hired a firm with Republican ties to help the state purge the voter rolls of felons and deceased voters. In the process, the firm produced an overly inclusive scrub list naming as felons tens of thousands of Floridians with clean records who shared a name and/or address with someone who was a felon. Harris's office then purged the rolls of all those on the list, over 90,000 citizens, the majority of whom were African Americans and nonfelons, preventing them from voting in the 2000 presidential election. Nearly 3 percent of Florida's eligible black voters were on the list.[2]

Another major issue emerging from the 2000 presidential election in Florida involved voters being improperly turned away from the polls on grounds they were not registered. Sloppy administrative record keeping meant that thousands of registered voters were showing up at the polls yet being denied the right to vote because their names had not been transferred to the precinct rosters. While a few states, most notably

California, allowed such voters to cast their votes using "provisional ballots," most states including Florida did not. The problem was most evident in crowded inner city precincts where voters tended to be racial minorities. Long lines at the polls added to the stress, highlighting the fact that most elections have inadequate personnel, especially when voter turnout is high.

Finally, there were numerous reports of voter intimidation, some of which were brought to light through testimony given at on-site hearings held by the U.S. Commission on Civil Rights. Though never fully proven, the impression that minorities were targets of intimidation tactics further cast a cloud over the 2000 Florida election. Some observers point to a history and pattern of voter intimidation going on for years and dating back to passage of the Voting Rights Act of 1965.[3]

The Help America Vote Act (HAVA)

In response to the chaos and irregularities surrounding the 2000 presidential elections, Congress passed the Help America Vote Act (HAVA) in 2002.[4] With HAVA, Congress sought to encourage state and local governments to replace antiquated voting systems that many observers viewed as the principal source of the electoral meltdown in Florida in 2000. In addition, the act sought to make election procedures in general more uniform, outlining, for example, federal standards for voter registration and requiring that voter registration rolls be computerized and updated regularly. HAVA also requires states to allow voters whose names are not on the poll book when they show up to vote to cast provisional ballots that can be counted after the election. In addition, the act mandates states to ensure voters are not discriminated against and to make voting handicap-accessible. And, in a concession to Republicans who were generally unenthusiastic about the reform legislation, the act requires voters who register by mail to show identification the first time they vote.

HAVA changed election administration dramatically. Gone were punch cards and old-fashioned mechanical lever voting machines. State voter rolls were being computerized. But by the 2004 presidential election there was a whole new set of problems, many as a result of the changes brought on by HAVA. The act had offered the states millions of dollars to upgrade voting equipment. Most responded to Washington's offer of big money by embracing expensive touch screen voting machines (DREs). Touch screen voting equipment was touted by the industry as making voting as easy and reliable as withdrawing cash from an ATM. In reality, the technology was still evolving and far from reliable. Computer scientists made headlines poking fun at the expensive equipment and punching holes in industry claims of reliability by demonstrating ways in which the electronic voting machines could be rigged. Critics complained that too many of the machines purchased with HAVA funds failed to produce a paper audit to protect against election fraud. After spending millions on equipment and subjecting themselves to court challenges, many jurisdictions have given up on DREs and moved toward optical scan voting. It combines the voter friendliness of the paper ballot with the speed of an electronic counting device. Optical scan also provides an easy way to check accuracy. In any event, a consensus developed that some paper trail is necessary to check accuracy of results. Many people also insist that voters are entitled to a receipt that would allow them to review and if necessary change their vote before each ballot is cast.

Provisional ballots were meant to provide a fail-safe way for every registered voter to cast a counted vote. Under HAVA, voters whose names are not on the rolls or who lack identification must be given a provisional ballot. Initially proposed by the Congressional Black Caucus to protect the rights of those wrongly purged from or mistakenly left off the voter rolls, the provisional ballot has not been the panacea to voter disenfranchisement many thought it would be. Some observers maintain it has become a catch-all escape clause for election officials to cover up sloppiness and avoid having to bother with putting newly registered voters on the rolls. In some cases, election officials push the provisional ballot onto the voter rather than take the time to address an apparent discrepancy during a busy Election Day.

Further, while HAVA requires states to allow voters whose names do not appear on the voter rolls to cast their votes provisionally, there is no requirement that the provisional ballots actually be counted. In the 2004 election, fully one-third of provisional ballots nationwide were never counted. Nor are there consistent standards regarding which ones to count and how. Instead, the statute defers to local election officials, creating a lack of uniformity among the states. During the 2004 presidential election in Ohio, for example, under order of the highly partisan secretary of state Kenneth Blackwell, otherwise registered voters who showed up at the wrong precinct but within a county would not have their provisional ballots counted. Meanwhile, similar votes were counted in other states. As a consequence, rather than instruct voters on how to take advantage of the opportunity to vote by provisional ballot, campaigns now steer voters away from them.

In addition to problems with new voting equipment and provisional ballots, there is evidence that statewide voter registration databases established pursuant to HAVA have been misused and mishandled. In the weeks leading up to the 2008 election, for example, officials in several states were improperly using Social Security data to verify registration applications for new voters in violation of law, according to news reports.[5] Other states were removing voters from the rolls within ninety days of a federal election, which is prohibited under HAVA except when voters die or inform authorities they have moved out of state. Voter registration and list purging were likely the top voting rights issues of the 2008 election.

Finally, voter identification requirements, which were authorized federally for the first time in HAVA, became the source of one the most contentious partisan struggles in recent years. HAVA requires states to pass laws requiring voter identification for first-time voters who register by mail. Several states, including Indiana, took the opportunity to pass strict laws that would require all voters—not just first-time voters who register by mail—to present identification as a condition of voting. Republicans tend to view such voter ID laws as a legitimate method of curbing fraud. Democrats are convinced voter ID laws are the equivalent of a modern-day poll tax that disproportionately impacts poor, minority, and elderly voters. They argue that such laws are motivated by partisanship and are designed to prevent certain individuals who are more likely to vote Democratic from voting.

The Indiana law was challenged on the grounds that Indiana's voter ID law constituted an unconstitutional barrier to the right to vote rather than an incidental burden justified as a part of the state's regulatory powers, as the state argued. In support of their argument, those challenging the ID law pointed out that there were few if any recent cases of fraud in Indiana or elsewhere involving nonvoters impersonating real voters at the polls. In 2008, the U.S. Supreme Court, in the case *Crawford v. Marion County Election Board*, upheld the Indiana voter identification law as "justified by the valid interest in protecting the integrity and reliability of the electoral process."[6]

At first blush, it might appear that the intimidating effect on minority and elderly voters predicted by critics of voter identification laws did not transpire. Since the 2008 election, conservatives have argued that figures emerging from the election demonstrate that voter ID was a success—or at least it did no harm. They point out that the two states with the strictest voter ID requirements—Indiana and Georgia—enjoyed their highest turnout since 1964 and that African American turnout increased.

Yet the difficulty faced by voters who do not have state drivers licenses has yet to be addressed. In fact, there is growing evidence that Obama's success occurred in spite of losing votes on account of voter identification laws and continued incidents of voter intimidation. The Supreme Court's opinion in *Crawford* makes clear that the Court is likely to side with conservatives for some time to come on issues of voting rights. But the Court's opinion still leaves room to challenge ID laws as applied. For example, there were several nuns who reportedly were prevented from voting on account of Indiana's ID law in the 2008 primary election. Another possibility might be litigation over whether to count certain provisional ballots cast as the result of a voter ID law.

One of the largest issues to go unresolved since the passage of HAVA is continuing and often systematic disenfranchisement of voters who are minority, poor, and elderly. Many states, acting on partisan motives, have adopted registration rules making it more difficult to become eligible to vote. Other states continue to engage in overly aggressive purges that remove otherwise eligible voters from the rolls. This wave of laws and aggressive administrative practices designed to erect new barriers to voting has accelerated since the 2000 Florida presidential recount. By excluding voters who are likely to vote in a certain way, these laws are intended to provide strategic advantage in closely divided elections in which states and regions are defined as "red" or "blue." The lack of resolution on these access issues continues to drive more and more campaigns into the courtrooms.

Litigation Over Voter Access

In the wake of Florida 2000, some legal experts speculated *Bush v. Gore* was a signal that close races would routinely be decided in the courtroom rather than at the polls. These concerns prompted *Wall Street Journal* reporter John Fund to characterize election litigation as the "Floridification" of the voting process. Indeed, according to Loyola law professor Richard L. Hasen, the amount of election law litigation is now more than double the rate before *Bush v. Gore.*[7] Over the past several election cycles, political campaigns have dedicated increasing amounts of staff, time, and money to preparing for postelection challenges. On Election Day, both parties dispatch armies of workers and lawyers to protect their party's voters and the voting process from disruptive activities allegedly carried out by the other side.

Since the 2000 election, acrimonious preelection litigation has also become an integral part of campaign strategy, as the two parties tussle over who is allowed to register to vote and who should be allowed to have access to the polls. Litigation challenging election procedures is rising as each party seeks an advantage that puts its candidate in a stronger position to win.

In Ohio, for instance, Republicans unsuccessfully challenged Ohio's practice of allowing newly registered voters to participate in early voting without waiting the thirty days that would be required if they voted on Election Day. That case and other related cases generated multiple decisions from the Ohio Supreme Court and federal courts, and even one from the U.S. Supreme Court. In Florida, the courts upheld the state's plan to deny regular ballots to voters whose names and addresses fail to match those on Social Security and driver's licenses databases. The decision forced thousands to vote by provisional ballot. In Pennsylvania, Republicans challenged new voters registered by ACORN, the low-income advocacy group known for its aggressive and often sloppy voter registration tactics. The GOP tried to force these new voters to cast provisional rather than regular Election Day ballots.

Preelection litigation focuses on everything from whether students should be required to vote in their home states to whether voting machines are improperly cutting off candidate names. The lawsuits are likely to continue rising so long as the partisan divide on fundamental election issues continues to exist. Democrats believe that there are too many barriers to voting and want to improve access to the polls. Republicans believe the integrity of democracy is endangered by rampant voter fraud. Their respective viewpoints are shaped by the political benefits accruing to them. Greater voter participation by minorities and the poor are likely to benefit Democrats. That's why Democrats are convinced that Republicans' legal tactics are designed to suppress minority voter turnout. Republicans believe Democrats routinely engage in old-fashioned Chicago-style voter fraud, and for a Democrat to win a close election is suggestive of chicanery.

This fundamental difference between the parties and the accompanying overheated rhetoric is likely to continue until there is a more rational and uniform approach to elections. The ongoing partisan legal conflicts are undermining public confidence in the electoral system. Both sides could reduce the level of public cynicism by finding common ground and addressing problem areas well before the election.

Fixing Election Administration

There is growing support for a second and more far-reaching Help America Vote Act, given the ongoing problems with election administration and the constant fear of another major electoral breakdown. HAVA did good things, including a requirement that states switch from inaccurate punch cards to newer, more accurate equipment. There may have been a false start initially, but now most states seem to be on the right track in acquiring reliable voting equipment. Congress needs to pass legislation to require that electronic voting machines produce a voter-verifiable paper trail for each vote so that voters can see that their choices are registered properly. Such a law would go a long way in reestablishing voter trust.

HAVA also aided the process of computerizing voter rolls. The act required every state to implement a statewide voter registration list by 2006. Before HAVA, voter registration was handled locally, sometimes on sheets of paper in the county clerk's office. With registration rolls computerized in a central location, it has been easier to correct errors and eliminate duplication of names. But the massive influx of new voters and problems with chronic computer mismatches has put an almost unmitigated strain on election administration.

A fundamental problem is that America's system of voting is still essentially geared to low voter turnouts, which is why there are continuing problems with long lines, ballot shortages, and machine breakdowns. The last three presidential races have been higher turnout elections, especially in battleground states like Florida and Ohio. Changes need to be made that take into account growing electoral participation.

Policy makers need to allocate sufficient resources and develop creative new approaches to process the volume of voters to avoid breakdowns.

One such approach is early voting. The success of early voting in the 2008 presidential election is leading many to call for its expansion nationwide. Early voting existed in some form in thirty-two states during the 2008 election. The benefit to voters is that it makes voting easier and more accessible, and offers them an opportunity to clear up eligibility questions before the election. Early voting also takes pressure off Election Day administration and provides election officials more time to test new machines and address registration issues. The primary objection to early voting is that a critical event or scandal could occur during the final days of a campaign after many early votes have already been cast. But there is little evidence to support the notion that those who would cast early votes would change their votes based on new information. Extending the right to vote via email for U.S. military is another type of reform that could improve accessibility, although the armed services already seems to do an excellent job turning out the military vote.

The procedures for provisional balloting, which are often used improperly, are in need of reform. Eligibility standards, which get uneven treatment from state to state and even within states, must be standardized. Additional requirements must be placed on election officials to minimize errors in their records to reduce the need for provisional ballots.

Voters should not have their votes discarded due to a technicality. Provisional voting would be much more successful if it were a last resort vehicle rather than a catch-all device.

America's system of voter registration is a vestige of an era when many Americans did not enjoy equal voting rights. The long lines, voter purges, and sometimes complicated registration forms cause headaches for both voters and election officials. Clearly registration reform is needed. The right to vote should not be treated like a club membership. That's why universal registration is gaining support. Anyone who applies for a driver's license or public benefits or who registers for the Selective Service could automatically be registered to vote. Those who favor universal registration say it will improve the administration of voter registration, reduce preelection litigation, and put controversial groups like ACORN out of business. Republicans and other opponents of universal registration argue that it will allow ineligible voters and noncitizens to influence election outcomes. But the current voter rolls are neither complete nor accurate. A move toward universal registration will remove voter registration as an election year partisan battleground for parties, candidates, and independent groups. At the very least, the states need to take a more proactive role in registering voters.

Voter identification requirements should be revisited. Critics argue that voter ID laws (1) disproportionately impact racial minorities and (2) make it unnecessarily difficult for poor people to participate in elections. These concerns are real and should be addressed. Either states should use a single uniform voter ID approach or Congress should overrule the Supreme Court's decision in *Crawford* and ban voter identification laws altogether. States that have voter identification requirements should assume the burden of providing such identification to all voters without cost to them. It does not help that there appears to be a clear partisan benefit to the passage of voter ID laws. If voter ID is to be the election policy of this country, we have to remove the politics from it.

Election reform is never easy. HAVA was the result of a difficult compromise between Democrats and Republicans conducted on the heels of a massive electoral breakdown. The Carter Baker Commission on election reform, though controversial, proposed several good ideas for positive change. The most important recommendation it made for fixing the country's overly politicized, underfunded election system was to turn election administration over to nonpartisan officials (i.e., election officials whose allegiance is to the integrity of the election system rather than to a political party or a candidate). Former Florida secretary of state Katherine Harris personified partisan election administration at its worst. But even good state secretaries are pressured to perform in a partisan manner by party activists who nominate them and provide funding and workers for their election. Elections would be run better if administered by nonpartisan professionals, and election administration would be greatly aided by more extensive training and sufficient funding so that election officials could do their jobs properly. All of these proposed reforms would likely increase voting while improving administration.

The Voting Rights Act

The Voting Rights Act of 1965 (VRA) is one of the most successful pieces of legislation ever to pass through Congress and be enacted into law. But in recent years conservatives have been pushing to eliminate the centerpiece of the act, Section 5, which mandates preapproval from federal officials for electoral changes in places with histories of disenfranchisement on racial grounds. Critics of Section 5 argue that America has entered a new period of postracial politics in which the need for 1960s era civil rights remedies no longer exists. But supporters say Section 5's success in reducing voting discrimination is the very reason to keep the VRA intact.

The VRA was passed to help African Americans realize the guarantees of the Fourteenth and Fifteenth Amendments to the U.S. Constitution. The Fifteenth Amendment specifically prohibits the use of race in determining eligibility to vote. But for almost a hundred years many states circumvented the amendment by establishing voter registration requirements that most blacks could not meet. Jim Crow laws such as poll taxes and literacy tests to deny blacks and other minorities the right to vote were finally outlawed by the VRA. But Section 5 also prohibited "covered jurisdictions"—states mostly in the South plus parts of other states with flagrant histories of discriminatory voting practices—from implementing new voting procedures without receiving approval from a federal judge or the U.S. Attorney General to protect against future racial discrimination.

Congress renewed the VRA with the passage of the Fannie Lou Hamer, Rosa Parks, and Coretta Scott King Voting Rights Reauthorization and Amendments Act of 2006. Though there was considerable concern abut the VRA's future as it came up for renewal, the reauthorized VRA remained largely intact. The sponsors of reauthorization wanted to make sure that African Americans continue to have as much chance as whites to elect their candidate of choice. Support in Congress for VRA extension was overwhelming. But as some observers have noted, several Republicans voted for reauthorization on the assumption that the conservative Supreme Court would rule the VRA unconstitutional.

In early 2009, the U.S. Supreme Court agreed to hear a challenge to the Voting Rights Act brought on behalf of a small water district in Texas by lawyers who called Section 5 the "most federally invasive law in existence." Appellants in the NAMUDNO case, as it is known, argue that Congress failed to adequately substantiate justification for extending the Section 5 provision requiring preclearance.

Longtime critics of the VRA have seized upon the historic election of Barack Obama as further proof that preclearance is an anachronism. "The America that has elected Barack Obama as its first African-American president is far different than when (the Voting Rights Act) was first enacted in 1965," reads the plaintiff's brief.

Indeed, VRA's successes are staggering. In 1964 only three hundred African Americans held public office, including three in Congress. There were no black elected officials in the South. Today there are almost 10,000 black elected officials, including over forty members of Congress. The VRA has also opened the door of political opportunity to Latinos, Native Americans, and Asians. Opponents of Section 5 claim that registration increases among black voters in covered states far exceeded increases of white voters. African American voter turnout increased even in nonbattleground states such as Alabama and Louisiana.

Proponents say that the VRA is still necessary to prevent sudden changes in election rules designed to undercut the rights of African

American voters. The rules requiring approval include the locations of polling places, the places where voters can register, and the boundaries of election districts. There is little doubt that racially polarized voting patterns persist, especially in the states requiring preclearance. Time and again campaigns and officials resort to tactics that play into old racial stereotypes. Performance in these states suggests that large numbers of voters are holding on to outdated racial attitudes. Indeed, Barack Obama performed substantially worse among white voters in the states and regions that require preclearance. Exit polls from the 2008 presidential election show that whites in southern states heavily favored John McCain over Obama. In Texas, 73 percent of whites favored McCain, in Georgia 76 percent, and in Alabama 88 percent. Nationally, the percentage of whites voting for McCain was 55 percent, according to exit polls.

Most observers believe this case could be one of the most important Supreme Court decisions since *Bush v. Gore*. A decision overturning Section 5 of the VRA would be the most dramatic change in U.S. voting laws since the 1960s. States and municipalities would then be free to erect barriers to dilute minority voting power, and undoubtedly some would. On the other hand, the Supreme Court could hand down a narrow ruling exempting jurisdictions in which there has been no recent proof of discrimination rather than completely overturn extension of Section 5. Whatever it does, few expect the Supreme Court to keep the VRA intact as Congress voted in 2006. And few expect voting patterns in covered areas to be the same.

Recounts Since *Bush v. Gore*

For years, election recounts were conducted in obscurity. Occasionally an election dispute would rise to the level of limited national notoriety. Lyndon Johnson famously secured his narrow eighty-seven-vote margin over Coke Stevenson in the controversial 1948 Texas U.S. Senate race as much on the strength of his postelection strategy (which some have characterized as both brilliant and fraudulent) as by his aggressive election campaign. The 1974 U.S. Senate election in New Hampshire between John Durkin and Louis Wyman was so close and contested that the Senate ordered another election. The 1984–1985 recount to resolve a congressional race between Frank McCloskey and Rick McIntyre in Indiana's "Bloody 8th" generated so much ill will on Capitol Hill that House Republicans walked out when Democrat McCloskey was declared the winner by just four votes.

The 2000 Florida presidential election dispute brought the world of chads and butterfly ballots into the nation's living rooms. What most Americans saw watching the recount on television was a surreal circus more akin to a Monty Python sketch than a process to determine which candidate actually carried the state. That image did not appear entirely by accident. The Bush team wanted the public to believe the Florida recount was an out-of-control partisan process. In fact, however, a recount is an adversarial proceeding like any judicial proceeding. Unlike election officials who are (or should be) concerned with accuracy, candidates and their representatives are motivated by outcome: each is trying to win the election. The candidate in the lead wants to convey that he has won and a recount is unnecessary, while the candidate who is behind needs to identify uncounted or miscounted votes. Bush's strategy was to say all the votes had been counted, the election was over, and the public interest in finality outweighed any benefit in recounting votes, especially if the ballots were counted in an uncontrolled, unfair environment. The Bush team also wanted to "run out the clock" by preventing the completion of the recount before the "safe harbor" deadlines seemingly imposed by the Electoral College.

Determining the actual winner of the election would entail a thorough audit of the election; an audit is what any real recount should be. While a thorough audit would not have been in George Bush's interests, it was definitely in Al Gore's interest. That's why the Gore team's failure to seek a statewide hand count of all ballots was so costly. The decision to seek hand recounts in only four Democratic strongholds not only played to Bush's claim that the recount was a sham but also made it more difficult for the Florida Supreme Court to fashion a timely constitutional remedy. Had it done so, the U.S. Supreme Court might not have felt a need to intervene.

The most memorable sentence in the U.S. Supreme Court's opinion in *Bush v. Gore* may have been the most fleeting. "Our consideration is limited to the present circumstances," the majority warned, "for the problem of equal protection in election processes generally presents many complexities." Despite the admonition that the case should be restricted to the facts of the 2000 presidential recount, *Bush v. Gore* seems to be alive and well. The case continues to be the subject of countless law review articles, opinion editorials, and web notes. Lower courts are finally beginning to cite the case, although the Supreme Court has yet to acknowledge it.

If it did nothing else, *Bush v. Gore* introduced the notion that the process of recounting ballots should have rules that are applied evenly and fairly. The basic holding in *Bush v. Gore* is that the use of different counting procedures in a recount violates equal protection. The Court in *Bush v. Gore* found that there was no uniform statewide standard for determining voter intent in Florida. The result, the Court said, was that varying approaches were used county by county causing identical votes to be treated differently—some counted and others not, depending on where the vote was cast. *Bush v. Gore* means that once a state grants the right to vote it may not "by later arbitrary and disparate treatment, value one person's vote over that of another."

Now that elections and recounts are to be conducted under the dictates of the Equal Protection Clause per *Bush v. Gore,* the question is, What amount of perfection is required to satisfy the basic requirement of fairness and equal treatment? What the Justices might have meant in cautioning against reopening the *Bush v. Gore* Pandora's box is that requiring equal treatment in elections is easier said than done. And there is a larger question of whether statewide or congressional district elections can ever be administered in a manner completely compatible with equal protection. There is unequal treatment by election officials in every election. That is the nature of our decentralized system of election administration. Elections can never be held to a standard of perfection. If that becomes the case, there will never be recounts. Instead, close elections will be resolved by special elections that cost millions of dollars.

Several major recounts have been conducted since the 2000 Florida recount, all of them influenced by it to some degree. The 2004 gubernatorial recount in Washington State gained national attention as Christine Gregoire overcame a forty-two-vote deficit to defeat Dino Rossi by 129 votes. The race was marked by controversies over provisional ballots, uncounted absentee ballots, and votes cast by felons. Republicans are still bitter about the outcome, although a Republican judge presided over the election contest trial and even concluded that the few illegal votes identified in the case favored Republican Rossi rather than Democrat Gregoire.

The disputed 2006 election in Florida's 13th Congressional District is another race that garnered national notoriety. In that contest, incumbent Republican congressman Vern Buchanan defeated Democratic challenger Christine Jennings by just 369 votes. However, the official returns revealed an unusually large number of undervotes in Jennings's home county. Jennings argued that some 18,000 votes had disappeared due to malfunctions in the electronic voting machines. The election was contested in the U.S. House of Representatives as well as litigated in the Florida courts. Because the DREs used in Florida did not produce printed records of votes, Jennings was unable to prove her broken machine theory. More likely, the huge undervote resulted from a confusing ballot layout that caused voters to overlook the race. But the suspiciously large number of undervotes in the race heightened the public's unease with electronic voting equipment. Subsequently Governor Charlie Crist ordered that all of the state's touch screen voting machines, which had cost $16 million, be scrapped and replaced with optical scan voting equipment.

The first real test of *Bush v. Gore* in a statewide recount occurred in the 2008 Minnesota U.S. Senate election dispute between Democrat Al Franken and Republican Norm Coleman. On election night, Coleman led by more than 700 votes. However, Coleman's lead shrank during the canvass as election officials found numerous arithmetical mistakes and errors in transposing numbers—all of which reduced Coleman's margin to 215 before the recount even began. During the statewide recount, additional uncounted votes were identified and counted as nearly 3 million ballots were hand-counted. This process gave Franken a lead of 49 votes. Finally, the State Canvass Board overseeing the recount counted an additional 933 absentee ballots which were wrongly rejected on election night, pushing Franken's lead up to 225 votes.

Coleman then filed an election contest claiming errors in the recount. During the contest, the trial court ruled that the statute required the exclusion of certain categories of absentee ballots from review, such as ballot envelopes that were not signed or properly witnessed. But

Coleman claims some absentee ballots defined as illegal by the court were counted in some counties on election night. In other words, Coleman argues that different rules had been applied to the manner in which identical ballots were counted, in violation of *Bush v. Gore*. The trial court in declaring Franken the winner by 312 votes found there was no *Bush v. Gore* violation, so Coleman has appealed to the Minnesota Supreme Court. This book has gone to print before final resolution, but Coleman will have a difficult time persuading the Court to rule for him. In effect, Coleman is asking the Court to either compound equal protection problems by counting more illegal votes, or order a new election although no fraud has been alleged. Neither the Minnesota Supreme Court or the U.S. Supreme Court, if the case goes that far, is likely to be enthusiastic about either remedy.

Elections that require a recount test the election system and serve as a reminder of the continued inadequacies of our system of election administration. Florida 2000 surfaced a host of serious problems. The 2004 Washington State gubernatorial recount uncovered problems with provisional ballots and concerns about counting them after a close election. The Florida 13th Congressional race in 2006 underscored the flaws with touch screen voting and the lack of a paper trail. And the 2008 Minnesota Senate recount revealed how election officials under pressure to complete their work on election night can inadvertently reject hundreds if not thousands of valid absentee ballots. Both Washington State and Minnesota enjoy reputations for fairness and good election administration. Yet it is only when a spotlight is shone on close races that the serious flaws in election administration become evident. Problems will continue to plague our elections until we find a more rational and uniform approach to conducting our elections. But perfection is not a realistic goal. Fundamental fairness and due process are and should be provided in all elections.

Close elections always stir controversy and usually generate reform. Following the controversial McCloskey-McIntyre recount in 1984, Indiana passed an enlightened recount law that the Supreme Court cited as a model in *Bush v. Gore*. The Florida recount led to the passage of HAVA, which, as noted, caused a new set of problems. Washington State improved its handling of absentee and provisional ballots. Florida switched to a more reliable voting system after Florida 13. And Minnesota election officials have already put forward far-reaching election reform proposals. Irrespective of which candidate wins, the voters can be winners if they demand real change and reform.

Reforming Campaign Finance

Our system of campaign finance laws is a product of the Watergate era. The campaign finance reforms passed after the Watergate scandal and amid reports of abuses in the 1972 Nixon campaign provide the basic regulatory framework that has more or less survived to date. The laws are built on principles of disclosure, contribution limits, expenditure limits, and public financing of presidential campaigns. The Watergate reforms notwithstanding, public trust in our political leaders has been declining for most of the past four decades. Like election administration, our campaign finance laws have been burdened by ineffectiveness and unintended consequences. And, as with election administration, the era of Watergate reforms has been marked by sharp partisan debate over the regulation of campaign finance.

The Watergate campaign finance laws have primarily focused on curbing the excesses of candidates, the two major parties, and their surrogates, some of whom masquerade as independent special interests. That means not only protecting against outright corruption but also instilling public confidence in the democratic process by reducing the influence of special interests and leveling the playing field when possible to maintain competitive federal elections.

Of course corruption and influence peddling were not invented during the Nixon years. But politicians are susceptible to being unduly influenced by money because they have to raise large amounts of money to pay for their campaigns. And the high cost of campaigning, which is driven by the cost of broadcast time, serves to heighten the pressure on political candidates to raise money, sometimes putting themselves at risk.

The political and analytical divide in approaching campaign finance law is rooted in the U.S. Supreme Court's 1976 decision in *Buckley v. Valeo*, which upheld spending limits in federal races.[8] But believing that campaign finance laws restrict political speech and therefore the First Amendment, the Supreme Court also held that limits on campaign expenditures were unconstitutional. Since *Buckley,* Republicans and Democrats have gone separate ways on campaign finance issues. Most Republicans oppose federal regulation beyond disclosure requirements while Democrats have pushed for new reform and extensive regulation. But by failing to construct an alternative definition of advocacy and provide new ways to balance the flow of money in and out of campaigns, Congress ensured the eventual demise of the campaign finance system.

In 2002 Congress passed the Bipartisan Campaign Reform Act (BCRA) popularly known as McCain-Feingold.[9] BCRA was the first revision in federal campaign finance laws in almost two decades. The purpose of the act was to ban "soft money," or money not regulated by campaign finance laws, from being contributed to candidates and political parties. Soft money had become a focus for reform because of excesses associated with it during the Clinton administration. McCain-Feingold also prohibited the airing of "nonpartisan" issue ads funded by soft money in the days leading up to elections.

The Supreme Court upheld the constitutionality of the BCRA in most respects in *McConnell v. FEC.*[10] In particular, McConnell upheld the ban on party soft money and the regulation of candidate-specific issue advertising. But by the time the Court revisited McCain-Feingold in *FEC v. Wisconsin Right to Life*, it had two new conservative members in John Roberts and Samuel Alito, swinging the pendulum away from deference to campaign finance regulation and toward deregulation.[11] In *Wisconsin Right to Life*, the Court held as permissible the broadcast of issue advocacy ads paid for by the general funds or special interest groups during the period immediately before a federal election in contravention of the law. This swing away from regulation may eventually take the form of overturning *Buckley* altogether. Such a ruling would likely return campaign finance regulation to the pre-Watergate days unless an acceptable alternative is soon developed.

In 1974 Congress created a system of public funding for presidential campaigns. This was the first attempt at public funding of federal campaigns and at first it was viewed as something of a success. But by the end of the Reagan years, both parties had located loopholes, the greatest being the soft money that was raised by the hundreds of millions in the

1990s. The ban on soft money conveniently coincided with the rise of Internet fund-raising, which first Howard Dean and John Kerry and then Barack Obama used very successfully. In fact, Obama's staggering fundraising successes in the 2008 election may have blown up the system of public financing for presidential elections altogether. Obama was the first candidate to win the presidency without accepting public financing. It is doubtful whether any serious presidential candidate will opt in to the current public financing system. The amounts of money needed to compete are too great and the amounts available from public funding are too limited. But the system could be revived if the public were willing to give greater support to presidential candidates and if the system were retooled to reward small contributors through tax deductions.

The presidential public funding system and the campaign finance system in general are in dire need of a complete overhaul. Public funding of congressional and Senate campaigns, never popular with the public, is likely the only basis for a system that accomplishes all the goals of a successful campaign finance system consistent with Supreme Court dictates regarding the First Amendment. Better regulation of 527s and the bundling of large contributions along with restructuring the Federal Elections Commission are also badly needed reforms.

Conclusion

Election lawyers may be basking in their newly acquired celebrity status, but election law in America is in a state of enormous transition, if not disarray. Since 2000, Congress has passed three major reforms: HAVA (2002), McCain-Feingold (2002), and the Voting Rights Act extension (2006). The first two have not accomplished what they were supposed to, and a conservative Supreme Court is expected to dramatically scale back and perhaps cut out the heart of the Voting Rights Act.

America needs to come to terms with a system that seems on the verge of collapse. The vast amounts of money needed to run a successful campaign are pushing candidates to the edges of corrupt fund-raising activities. Public funding of presidential campaigns in its current form is obsolete, and election administration is incapable of dealing with the volume of voters. A large percentage of voters—usually the poor, the elderly, and minorities—have been left or pushed out by a system that is at best unresponsive.

Dramatic changes have occurred in American politics since the current electoral and campaign finance system was constructed in the wake of Watergate. A bipartisan coalition dedicated to reform and change that is responsive to voters rather than political parties or candidates is required to fix our current broken electoral system.

Notes

1 *Bush v. Gore*, 531 U.S. 98 (2000).

2 Gregory Palast, "Florida's Flawed Voter Cleansing Program," *Salon*, December 4, 2000, http://dir.salon.com/politics/feature/2000/12/04/voter-file/index.html.

3 The Voting Rights Act of 1965, 89 P.L. 110, 79 Stat 437 (1965).

4 The Help America Vote Act, Pub. L. 107–252 (2002).

5 *New York Times*, October 8, 2008.

6 *Crawford v. Marion County Election Board*, 553 U.S. _____ (2008).

7 Richard Hasen, "The Democracy Canon," *Stanford Law Review*, forthcoming (Loyola-LA Legal Studies Paper 2009-6).

8 *Buckley v. Valeo*, 424 U.S. 1 (1976).

9 The Bipartisan Campaign Reform Act of 2002 (BCRA McCain-Feingold Act), P.L. 107–155, 116 Stat 81 (enacted March 27, 2002).

10 *McConnell v. FEC*, 540 U.S. 932 (2003).

11 *FEC v. Wisconsin Right to Life*, 551 U.S. _____ (2007).

11

Campaign Ethics
in a
Changing World

Carol A. Whitney

Introduction

The increasing public distrust of politics and politicians has been well documented in survey data and analyzed by the media. Americans today are cynical about politics. Candidates and political operatives are perceived with suspicion, and incumbent officeholders are equally suspect. Regular reports of legal and ethical violations by elected officials in both political parties only reinforce this impression.

It is difficult to measure ethics in politics, however, when there is no generally accepted definition of ethical behavior in campaign politics. The public as well as campaign professionals judge campaigns based on their own wildly varying ethical and moral standards. Most people don't live up to the standards they profess. We set our standards high with the understanding that we may not always achieve them. So how can we judge whether campaign politics in this country really is as fraught with unethical behavior as the public believes? If it is not, why do campaigns have such a bad reputation? And if it is, what can we do about it?

Who Sets the Boundaries?

Alan Wolfe, in his book *Moral Freedom: The Search for Virtue in a World of Choice*, points out the problems we face in setting moral and ethical boundaries in a world where there is no one overriding moral authority or generally accepted societal norm to define those boundaries for us. We must each struggle to find our own definition of "good."[1]

Establishing ethical standards in campaign politics is difficult, given the varying moral standards by which we live, along with the fact that some practitioners see political standards as different from personal standards.

Some point to the law as the codification of society's ethical standards. But that assumes that the law is unchanging, covers every aspect of ethical behavior, and is always "good." Assuming that we obey the letter of the law, our behavior still may be unethical.

Is it necessary to adhere to the same standards in political activities as in our personal lives? Some argue that the rules of personal morality do not apply in the political world due to the competitive nature of the political game. One could argue, however, that any action justified in politics is a reflection of personal standards; we are still responsible for our actions.

As long as there is no one overriding authority recognized by society, imposition of strict laws and ethical codes will not ensure ethical conduct in campaigns.

Despite efforts to do so, perhaps most notably the Eighteenth Amendment, we cannot legislate morality.[2] Morality in political campaigns must depend on the campaigns themselves—the candidates, staff and advisers, and, to a degree, the candidates' supporters.

Putting It in Perspective:
Historical Precedents

You can't use tact with a Congressman.
A Congressman is a hog.

*You must take a stick
and hit him on the snout.*
—HENRY ADAMS, 1838–1918

Were political campaigns more civil in the past? As far back as George Washington's day, our country's history provides examples of viciousness and questionable ethics in campaign politics. It has always been a rough-and-tumble business, and many practitioners believe it can be nothing else under our particular form of democracy.

In the early eighteen century John Randolph of Roanoke, a distinguished Virginia gentleman, described a fellow member of Congress with the phrase, "he stinks and shines like rotten mackerel by moonlight." In 1884 Grover Cleveland was attacked by Republicans for fathering an illegitimate child; in retaliation, the Democrats produced a rhyme about his opponent: "Blaine, Blaine, James G. Blaine; the continental liar from the state of Maine."

Does this represent a lost age of civility? Does the record of fistfights, shouting matches, canings, and beatings on the floor of the House and Senate speak well for our ancestors? Today these stories seem amusing, and even at the time they made little general impact outside of Washington. Some political observers and historians believe that the rowdiness and exaggeration characterizing old-style politics was a healthy thing and that we have become far more narrow-minded about the process.[3] Is it then our expectations that are at fault? Or is it the greater impact of the news in an age where communication and news delivery are virtually instantaneous?

Scandals at the highest levels of government were as common (if not more so) one hundred years ago, when they received less public scrutiny. Critics of today's negative advertising might consider the girl with the daisy ad run by Lyndon Johnson's 1964 campaign. Although aired only once, it created a media furor.[4] The daisy ad ranks with the most blatantly unethical attack ads from the 1990s.

Is there any reason to believe that today's political campaigns and candidates are really worse than those of the past? Memory of past events blurs over time, so that events from the past do not have the same impact as current events. But even more important for perceptions are the changes brought about by modern communication.

New Tools, Old Problems

The tools of campaign politics have changed dramatically over time, but the ethical dilemmas still revolve around the same basic elements of campaign activity: money, communications, and campaign conduct. The means of achieving the goal may have changed, but the goal remains the same: winning. Every campaign must communicate the candidate's message to the voters, pay for the means of communication, and conduct a campaign to implement that communication.

Money and Ethics

Campaign finance, an ongoing focus of attention and the darling of reformers, is more a legal than an ethical problem. The debate is over what the law should cover, not what is right or wrong. Finance reform has been attempted numerous times over the course of our history in efforts to lessen the power of one special interest or another, but not surprisingly, there has never been full agreement on which groups' power should be curtailed. Since the federal election laws of the 1970s established the Federal Election Commission (FEC), ongoing adjustments and corrections have complicated election law to the point that it is almost impossible for the layman to understand and comply with it. Federal election law has become not the codification of society's ethical standards but the confused result of efforts to legislate fairness.[5]

The most recent effort to lessen the influence of money in campaigns was the Bipartisan Campaign Reform Act (BCRA) of 2002, often called McCain-Feingold after its sponsors.[6] BCRA was designed to remove the influence of soft money from campaigns—funds that fall outside FEC finance regulations. Through soft money contributions, political parties could collect and spend unlimited funds from corporations and unions in "party building" activities—activities that benefitted their candidates.

BCRA has had its benefits. One provision requires that every television ad must include at the beginning or end a visual of the candidate stating his name and that he has approved this communication. The statement must also appear in print on the screen. Since this assigns personal responsibility to the candidate, each ad becomes a statement about the candidate's ethical standards. Radio ads require the inclusion of the statement in the candidate's voice. This requirement was challenged but was approved by the courts and took effect in 2004.[7]

It did not take long to discover the loopholes in the law. Through 527 organizations[8] that are not required to report their contributions and through legal bundling operations,[9] the flow of money continues.

No legal reform has dealt with the basic role of money in a political campaign. The "money is the root of all evil" proponents are convinced that removing money from the process will somehow make campaigns more ethical by removing temptation; the "money is just a medium of exchange" adherents are equally convinced that the desire for victory will be just as strong without financial incentives, and that removing money will not remove the overwhelming need for recognition and the competitive drive that characterize the candidate and the campaign professional. It is true that the cost of political campaigns has reached almost obscene levels. The high cost of communication is responsible for driving up spending, and communicating a message is the main function of a campaign.

No amount of legislation can prevent money from influencing campaign politics. Witness former Illinois governor Rod Blagojovich, who was indicted in December 2008 for attempting to sell the vacant Illinois Senate seat.[10] Certainly this was not ethical, but the fact that it violated the law had no impact on Blagojovich. It is time to recognize that attempts to take the power of money out of the political process have failed.

Ethics and Communications

Ethical questions for political campaigns—as well as the ethical dilemmas most commonly faced in campaign politics—most often center on the main function of any campaign: communication of information, the development and delivery of campaign message(s). Certainly the most blatant violations of accepted ethical standards occur in this area.

Today's campaigns communicate information about their candidates and their opponents emphasizing the superior qualifications of their candidates over the opponents. The most common ethical questions arise out of what information is communicated, and how that communication is crafted and delivered. There may also be ethical dilemmas rising out of the withholding of information; for example, when the information withheld would change the validity or meaning of the message by providing context.

There are four general categories of unethical use of information in campaigns. A fifth, "under the radar" attacks, will be considered in the "New Media" section of this chapter.

Using False Information
The commandment "Thou shalt not lie" is still generally accepted as a guide to moral behavior, no matter how we approach the other nine commandments. Violations include not only lying about the opponent but fudging the facts just a little to make something sound better. Witness the exaggerated résumés published by a few candidates in every election cycle—and caught regularly by their opponents.

Using Negative Personal Information That Is Irrelevant to Job Performance
In this area the boundaries are difficult to define and have changed over time. It can be argued that personal indiscretions are not relevant, and certainly the public has been generous about forgiveness over the past few years. It can also be argued that a pattern of misbehavior, whether extramarital affairs or other moral transgressions, gives an indication of an individual's general honesty and trustworthiness—important criteria for public officeholders. In today's political environment attacks made on the basis of this type of information often don't work unless accompanied by other evidence that the candidate may be unfit to serve.

Using Information to Create a False Impression

This area causes the most arguments among political professionals and leads to the greatest blurring of ethical boundaries. Many believe that "a fact is a fact, and it is perfectly ethical to present any factual information about my opponent and his or her voting record that I choose." However, just as statistics can be manipulated to distort the truth, facts can be used to create a lie—because facts are delivered in a context, and the choice of context can skew the meaning.

The commonest example of this is the use of a series of legislative votes to create a false impression: "he is a dangerous liberal" or "she is a right-wing zealot" are among the most common. Often these votes are simply procedural, moving a bill to the floor for consideration (and possible defeat), or insignificant riders on bills of great importance. The meaning is purposely distorted in order to create a false impression. Is this any different from a lie?

**Using Information to Appeal
to Base Human Instincts**

The most obvious example of this violation of ethical standards is the use of information to elicit racist, homophobic, or other discrimination-based responses. For example, while not openly avowing racist behavior, this approach encourages individuals who have racially based fears to respond in a racist manner.

Other culturally based fears and biases may be triggered in the same manner. Twenty-five years ago, for example, we used to joke about the "tough candidate on a tank with the national guard" television commercials that often appeared when the opponent in a gubernatorial race was a woman. Could we really prove that this was purposely done to remind voters that a woman might not be strong (manly) enough for the position? Of course not; maybe it was just coincidence.

There is little argument among political professionals as to whether this type of communication is wrong. The difficulty occurs in proving it was intended. Making a judgment regarding intent can be difficult. Many of us didn't initially see racism in the infamous Willie Horton ad of 1988, but an ad that played on the public's fear of violent crime. We all need to be more sensitive to and vigilant against advertising designed to reinforce discrimination.

At the same time, it's easy to cross the line into political correctness, where innocent acts become guilty because an observer interprets them in that way. It remains a tough call, but one that has to be made.

Campaign Conduct

Misguided Cleverness

It is amazing what one may be tempted to do in the heat of the campaign. "Dirty tricks," "dumpster diving" for material from the opponent's campaign, tearing down the opposition's yard signs, posting negative comments on the opponent's Facebook page—these and many more may seem clever in the abstract. But whether or not they are ethical, they distract from the real purpose of the campaign and may cause embarrassing media attention. How would you like to see your photo on the front page of the local paper, upside down in a dumpster in front of the opponent's headquarters in the dead of night? How would you explain your arrest for trespassing and theft when you are caught collecting yard signs from front yards? Keep this in mind.

These and more serious forms of questionable campaign conduct are common. A surprising number also violate the law. Campaign operatives have been convicted of federal crimes for activities that seemed clever, such as jamming phone communication to the opponent's campaign.

Should you:

- Put up a fake web page for your opponent that attacks him?
- Follow the opposing candidate with a video cam and annoying questions, hoping to provoke her into a rash statement or an angry reaction?
- Send a spy into the opposition's headquarters?
- Fake a photo for use in campaign materials?
- Fudge the truth on your candidate résumé? (You will always get caught.)

The clever ideas that are generated by exhausted campaign staffers, often late at night, are generally the ones that create problems for the campaign.

The "True Believers" Dilemma

When viewed from outside the process, ethical dilemmas in politics appear easy to resolve. Of course we want to do what is right. If we wouldn't do it in other circumstances, why would we suddenly violate our own ethical standards in a political campaign?

Every one of us *knows* that our candidate is by far the best choice for the job, and that electing the opponent would be a terrible loss to society and the public good. Every candidate *knows* that it is in the public's interest that he or she be elected over the opposition. We (political professionals) want candidates who have that "fire in the belly," an incredible determination to win over all odds, because that intensity not only is necessary to carry a candidate through the incredible stress of the campaign but demonstrates to the public that the candidate really cares. We take the election process seriously in this country and we expect a lot from our candidates. Like it or not, most of us, candidates and consultants alike, are true believers in our cause—whether it be Republican or Democrat. This is why the system works as well as it does.

Little wonder, then, that temptation in a campaign setting is so hard to resist and may masquerade as the opportunity to do what is best for the country/state/community. Is it really so wrong, when victory is a point or two away and the opponent's positions are absolutely wrong (or at least misguided), to shade the facts a little; to attack using questionable information; to insinuate something you cannot prove; to "leak" confidential information on the opponent; or to spread rumors or play on fears through so-called push polling?[11]

It is easy to sit in the office or the classroom and insist that you would do none of the above because they are unethical. It is far more difficult to do so in the heat of the campaign when victory is all-important. In the course of every political campaign, the candidate, the consultant, and the campaign operative face ethical dilemmas and difficult ethical decisions. How can we bring all parties to agreement on a course of action when the media consultant pushes one way, the campaign chair another, and the candidate is too exhausted to focus? A lot of decisions made in the last high-pressure days of the campaign are later regretted.

So how can we be certain the campaign team is equipped to make those tough calls?

Communication and Perception:
The Role of the Media

People who love sausage
and respect the law
should never watch
either of them being made.
—Otto Von Bismarck

The business of government today is conducted in full and immediate view of the people. When people see less than perfect behavior in the process or see their representatives making mistakes, they are disappointed (if not outraged). After all, they expect their elected officials to be better than they (the voters) are at running things. This puts a tremendous burden on those elected. They must be smarter, more capable, and more ethical than the general public, as well as conduct their business (and personal life) in full public view. Is it any wonder the best people often refuse to run?

Add to this the rapid pace of life today. People are accustomed to getting instant answers, finding immediate solutions, having full access to any information they seek. So why, they wonder, can't Congress work that fast? They want action, they expect it fast, and they aren't willing to accept the slow pace of government and legislative decision making.

But voters also have little time to spend thinking about elections and candidates. They are looking for shortcuts to decision making. They turn to the media for answers, and today's media representatives are willing to provide them. You want to choose a candidate but you aren't sure whose advertising to believe? We'll judge it for you; we'll even tell you which candidate is the best choice.

Journalists today see themselves as not only purveyors of information but guardians of public morality. Unfortunately, in the realm of politics they seem to see only immorality. While we understand why they believe it is their responsibility to present to the public every bit of information available on a particular story or the people involved, the media's authority to make judgments on the morality of people and their actions is questionable.

Most journalists know little about the inner workings of the average political campaign, or the purpose of campaign activities. For example, I have been told that my unwillingness to explain to a member of the press just exactly what my campaign strategy is going to be is unduly secretive, that my candidate and I should be willing to share all such information with the public. Excuse me? Does one football team announce to the other their strategy for winning the game—or for specific plays?

We all accept that negative and startling stories are more newsworthy (man bites dog), and that the media seek news that sells. But they are doing a disservice to the people of this country when they focus exclusively on the negative stories—and reinforce the negative assumptions—about politicians and politics. They know full well that they shape public opinion; how can they then decry the sad state of public regard for politics and our leaders?

There are many politicians in *both* parties who have high principles, are excellent role models, and have the best interests of the people at heart. The media needs to acknowledge this, and them. If politics is not considered an honorable calling, at least admit that honorable men suffer through the political process in order to serve.

The Power of the New Media

The Net and Campaign Conduct

The opportunities for delivering campaign messages, coordinating staff and volunteer activities, and raising funds have ballooned through the increasingly sophisticated use of the Internet. Email, social networking sites, and other tools available through today's Internet technology have given campaigns and the public at large the ability to participate in the political process to an unprecedented degree. In Chapter 9 of this volume, Alan Rosenblatt provides a detailed picture of the political uses of the new media.

Increased use of the Internet has also led to new ethical questions. Today's political figure is even more exposed than the politician of the past. Virtually every action may be captured on camera, posted on YouTube, and spread through large interlocking networks of Internet users. Only in today's new media environment could George Allen lose his U.S. Senate seat in 2006 as a result of a single inappropriate remark to a heckler in the crowd. But *macaca* lives on and can still be viewed online.[12] In 2008 numerous young campaigners trailed the opposition with video cameras and tried to provoke rash responses that could be posted online. Is it really ethical to annoy an elected official to the point of anger just to make him look bad? Our representatives are not saints: sometimes, in the heat of the campaign, they respond angrily to rudeness.

Where are the boundaries in this environment? Can any ethical standards be enforced? Does this provide a true picture of our society's standards? We criticize campaigns for negative advertising and are offended by the innuendoes and false impressions provided "under the radar" by political direct mail. But the ethical questions of the new media exist below the surface and are far harder to track and control.

Today a campaign's message can be delivered or subverted by the general public. Increased public participation in politics is a positive outcome. But the World Wide Web remains an uncensored, unpoliced medium for free exchange of information, true or false. Free speech issues have discouraged any efforts at regulation.

What's News and What's Real?

The Pew Center for People and the Press survey in 2008 showed that 13 percent of the public relies on the Internet for news; 26 percent of these "net newsers" read blogs regularly as news sources; 37 percent of the public uses Internet news sources three or more times per week in addition to other sources of news.[13]

But how much of the news on Internet sites is unbiased? Blogs are sources of opinion more than news, and these news sources are not monitored for accuracy. Consequently a relatively large percentage of the public receives information from biased—and sometimes inaccurate—sources

The Persistence of Rumor

Internet-disseminated rumor is becoming an effective tool in the political process—the yellow journalism of the twenty-first century.[14] Thanks to the Internet, rumors and false allegations become a factor in political campaigns. In 2008, there were few who did not hear the false allegations that Barack Obama was a Muslim/Muslim terrorist/secret Muslim who would make this a Muslim country and/or abandon our relationship with Israel and/or make women wear head scarves. These rumors were refuted repeatedly, but many people continued to believe them, and those same rumors about President Obama can still be found on Internet sites and blog postings.

The almost universal use of email and the rapid growth of web-based social networking enables the virtually anonymous distribution of rumors to huge numbers of people almost instantly. Because of the interlocking nature of social networks, those receiving the information are likely to receive it multiple times, thus reinforcing it in their minds. According to current statistics, at least 73 percent of all Americans use the Internet and are targets for this type of false rumor.

This practice is unethical by any standards. It is also common. Shankar Vedantam, in a September 2008 *Washington Post* article, cited new studies showing that false information remains persuasive even after it is refuted. Oddly enough, the study also seems to show that refuting the information actually strengthens it.[15] The problem is that even if the candidate and campaign personnel do not spread such allegations, the campaign's supporters and the public can post anything they like. This is how Barack Obama came to be forced to respond strongly to false allegations.

The persistence of false rumors on the Web lends credence to the negative perceptions of today's ethical standards. That should not mean that those of us involved in politics should abandon our own standards of decency.

Setting an Ethical Course

It makes no difference whether today's political campaigns are or are not less ethical than in the past. The problem lies in the fact that the public believes they are, and this very real problem must be dealt with. Now that our elected representatives are perceived as negatively as candidates and political consultants (somewhere below lawyers and used car salesmen), maybe something can be done about it. Failing that, our representatives will find it hard to do the job they were elected to do.

It will take concerted action to regain the public trust.

The answer does not lie in legislation or regulation. Setting artificial standards will not change human behavior. We will always face ethical dilemmas in the heat of the political campaign, and some people will yield to temptation. There will continue to be political operatives who say that "it all boils down to what you can get away with." Campaign conduct in general, and the public perception of politics, will be changed over the long run only through joint action by the candidates, the political professionals, the media, and the public.

Conclusion: A Code of Ethics or a Call to Action?

There may be no overriding moral or legal authority in a position to establish and enforce a binding code of ethics on the players in the campaign process. But ethical codes can and should govern the actions of every candidate and campaign professional. Ethical behavior inside the profession, however, is not enough to regain public trust.

There is a role for everyone in improving campaign conduct.

1. The Candidates:

Several organizations have tested ethical codes for candidates. The Institute for Global Ethics, for example, tested voluntary compliance with codes of ethics in congressional campaigns in a number of states beginning in 1998.[16] Common Cause, the Alliance for Better Campaigns, and the Project for Excellence in Journalism have worked to develop higher standards for campaigns. But a study by West, Maisel, and Clifton in 1994 demonstrated that none of the reforms had a substantial impact on campaign behavior.[17]

It is my opinion as a political consultant that the strongest step toward better ethical conduct is a higher level of awareness and personal responsibility. Consequently, I ask candidates to sign the following statement:

CANDIDATE CODE OF ETHICS

- I believe that the electoral process demands as high a level of personal integrity as does service in elected office, and that my campaign is a demonstration of my integrity.
- I pledge to provide the voters with accurate information regarding myself and my opponent in order to allow them to make informed choices on Election Day.
- I accept responsibility for the information delivered by my campaign, and the way in which that information is presented.
- I will maintain vigilance over my campaign to ensure that campaign personnel do not misrepresent the facts or mislead the voters, and will make it clear to them at all times that I demand the highest level of integrity from all who represent my campaign.

A candidate who signs this statement is accepting personal responsibility for the conduct of the campaign. It eliminates the excuses and wiggle room ("the consultant didn't tell me . . ." "I couldn't do anything about it . . ."), and consequently candidates who sign this pledge are making a commitment to maintain ethical standards.

2. The Political Professionals:

The American Association of Political Consultants has an official code of ethics. But because membership in the association is voluntary it does not establish an enforceable set of standards for the industry.

Political consultants succeed or fail based on the actions of the public, however, and it is possible that if public awareness is increased, public action will not be far behind. Any consultant with a public reputation for unethical conduct will find work only with candidates who accept unethical behavior, and will be a red flag to the voters.

Professionals in both parties must continue current efforts to define ethical campaign conduct and increase awareness of ethical considerations among new political operatives entering the field. Training in ethical politics, now a curriculum element in a number of universities, as well as partisan and bipartisan political training programs, must be expanded.

Campaign staffers and students should consider following these guidelines:

- Know your ethical boundaries and establish clear standards for yourself. Don't get hung up on judging others. It's enough responsibility to watch yourself.
- Be firm about not violating your personal ethical standards.
- Don't be party to someone else's violating them. Don't split hairs when assessing what others on the campaign are doing, but maintain your basic sense of ethical behavior. It may be difficult to accurately judge intent in others.

In the heat of the campaign you will be tempted. You may give in. If you do, you will eventually forgive yourself but you will never forget.

3. The Media:

Many journalists are trying to encourage greater public scrutiny of campaign advertising practices (and more honesty in advertising) through their "ad watch" programs. But these don't deal with the biggest problem areas. Most of the truly unethical campaign message delivery does not take place on television, but in political mail and activities like push polling, the "under the radar" advertising that is hard to catch. A watch over political mail and the elements of the new media such as social networking sites and YouTube would be even more beneficial to the process.

But the media can do more than promote civility among campaigns. The media can contribute to the civility of public discourse through self-scrutiny and more civil reporting of government, politics, and politicians. Organizations like the Project for Excellence in Journalism, which focuses on "raising the standards of American Journalism through research and education," are a good start.[18] The power of the media can yield positive results when put to good use, and certainly renewed pride in our system of government and elections is a result worth seeking.

4. The Public:

The public has the greatest share of responsibility in a democratic society.

But as our population and our government have grown in size, our connection with our government has diminished. As the workings of government have become more visible, our admiration for our representatives has declined. In an effort to gain control over what they perceive to be a failing system, citizens have tried to bring government down to its lowest common denominator—local and personal control. More and more, they have ignored the electoral process because they see no power in their vote and because all politicians are venal, all campaigns unethical, all elected officials basically corrupt.

In 2008 Barack Obama convinced voters that he too was tired of negative, partisan politics. He pledged to change our political process for the better, and voters turned out to support his election. It is too soon to judge him, but we must remain hopeful that he will indeed lead a positive change in the conduct of politics and government in this country.

The public needs to continue to stand watch. Through education, public awareness of ethics in politics can be increased among students. Through emphasis on ethical behavior on the part of candidates and campaign professionals, the public can be made more aware of the positive work being done inside the profession. Through more equitable media coverage, the positive reality of political behavior can be demonstrated. But the voters also must do their part.

Those of us who work in the profession take pride in our work and our ethical standards. We invite the voters to join us, to participate fully in the political process. That participation can, in the end, provide the solution.

Notes

1 Alan Wolfe, *Moral Freedom: The Search for Virtue in a World of Choice* (New York: Norton, 2001).

2 The Eighteenth Amendment established Prohibition, when the sale of alcohol was illegal in the United States. Prohibition was voided by the Twenty-first Amendment.

3 See "Put the Incivility Back in Politics," *Wall Street Journal*, October 12, 1998.

4 The daisy ad, produced by President Lyndon Johnson's campaign, intimated that Barry Goldwater, if elected, would lead this country into nuclear war.

5 For a review of past campaign finance controversies, see "The Long, Stormy Marriage of Money and Politics," *American Heritage*, November 1998.

6 For full details on BCRA, see www.fec.gov/pages/bcra/bcra_update.shtml.

7 http://electionlawblog.org/archives/000246.html.

8 A 527 is a nonprofit organization formed under Section 527 of the Internal Revenue Code, which grants tax-exempt status to political committees at the national, state, and local level. The term has come to refer to a new form of political organization operating in a gray area of the law. These groups actively influence elections and policy debates at all levels of government, but do not advocate explicitly for election or defeat of candidates.

9 Bundling is the practice of pooling a number of individual contributions to maximize the political influence of the bundler. PACs and party committees that have given the maximum allowed by law often give more money to candidates by bundling individual contributions.

10 For a full text of the indictment, see www.scribd.com/doc/8759869/Blagojevich -Complaint.

11 Push polling is the practice of using phone banks to disseminate negative messages (usually accusations) in the guise of taking a poll. The question is usually phrased something like, "Would you be more or less likely to vote for John Doe if you knew that . . ."

12 www.washingtonpost.com/wp-dyn/content/article/2006/08/14/AR20060 81400589.html.

13 Pew Research Center for the People & the Press, 2008 biennial news consumption survey, http://people-press.org/report/444/.

14 Yellow journalism is defined as biased opinion masquerading as objective fact (library.thinkquest.org).

15 Shankar Vedantam, "The Power of Political Information," *Washington Post*, September 15, 2008.

16 See Institute for Global Ethics, www.globalethics.org.

17 Darryl M. West, L. Sandy Maisel, and Brett Clifton, "The Impact of Reform on Political Discourse," 2004. See www.insidepolitics.org/EvalCampReformPSQ.DOC.

18 www.journalism.org.

12

Madness in Michigan:
A Microcosm of Elections
American Style

David A. Dulio

During the 2008 election cycle, the state of Michigan had just about everything one might expect in a typical American-style campaign. There were spirited debates between candidates, large amounts of money, wall-to-wall television advertisements, volunteers and paid staffers knocking on doors, as well as party infighting, bitter disagreements between voters, political maneuvering and calculation, and, in the end, even a little disappointment. Michigan and its voters are used to being in the spotlight during presidential elections, but 2008 was like no other the state has seen for quite some time.

Typically, Michigan is relatively quiet during the primaries and a hotbed of activity during the general election. In years past, the state arguably had less than its fair share of influence in selecting presidential nominees, but has been front and center in the battle between those nominees to reach the 270 electoral votes needed to win the presidency. During 2008, the focus on Michigan occurred in reverse—Michigan seemed to be omnipresent during the primary phase of the campaign but was little more than an afterthought during the last weeks of the campaign between Barack Obama and John McCain. In this chapter,

I will discuss why Michigan was turned upside down during the 2008 battle for the presidency, and analyze the impact this had on the electoral process as well as what it means for the future of campaigns and elections American style.

The Primary Season:
Battles Between More Than the Candidates

Michigan's important place in the story of the 2008 presidential primary season is not due to a vigorous campaign between candidates over who would best represent their party or a campaign that was over the top in terms of negativity, or, for that matter, some other story line students and observers of our elections are used to seeing. Rather, the story of this primary season is one of process and rules (or rule breaking as the case may be). Indeed, the genesis of this primary does not date to January 15, 2008—the date when over a million Michigan primary voters went to the polls—or to candidates visiting the state to talk to voters, but back many election cycles.

It was Michigan's reaction to one of the most prominent features of the primary process in the United States today—the front-loading of the primary calendar—that was the reason for the state's role in the 2008 primary season. Briefly, front-loading is the result of decisions by states and state parties, over the last several election cycles, to shift the date of their primary or caucus to very early in the nominating calendar. The result is a primary calendar crowded with states in its first few weeks. Why do states and/or state parties move to the beginning? The answer is simple: To increase their chances of being relevant in the process of selecting a candidate for the general election.

Given that nominees are formally chosen by the delegations to each party's national nominating convention during the summer of an election year, delegates are what matters most in the primary process. And since candidates compete for delegates in primaries and caucuses, these delegates are the currency of the modern presidential primary. To win the nomination, a candidate only needs a simple majority of convention delegates. Some states that had previously held their nominating contests later in the primary calendar were irrelevant because a candidate had secured enough delegates to win the nomination before their state even had a chance to vote. Or even if no candidate has garnered an absolute majority of delegates, major rivals might have all dropped out of the race. This is the same problem, however, for states at the end of the primary calendar. Once a presumptive nominee has been identified, a state with a nominating contest at the end of the process is not a relevant part of the nominating process. Trying to get into a position where its voters can affect the nomination process—either by being part of the cluster of states that help a candidate collect the requisite number of delegates or by playing a part in the process of winnowing the number of candidates—is one reason states try to move forward in the calendar.

Another reason states may try to move forward in the nominating process is to attract attention to their state from both the press and the media. This was a crucial piece of Michigan's move to the front of the nominating calendar. Michigan had suffered economically for years before the nation's economic downturn during the last several years of the Bush administration. The Michigan lawmakers who scheduled the state's primary for January 15, 2008, had these factors on their minds. They wanted the candidates who would be fighting to be the next president to hear the concerns of Michigan voters, and scheduling the primary early would help ensure that, or so they thought. Michigan's governor, Jennifer Granholm (D), explained, "Our richly diverse electorate deserves a primary process that requires candidates to address the issues they will be held accountable for in the general election. The January 15th primary in Michigan accomplishes precisely this goal. With our move, we expect that this critical discussion will take place before, not after, party nominations are decided."[1] This was a position held by leaders on both sides of the aisle, as after the initial vote in the state Senate to move the primary, Majority Leader Mike Bishop (R) said, "an early primary will allow all Michigan voters . . . to exert early influence in the presidential nomination process."[2]

Moreover, some in Michigan—most notably Senator Carl Levin and Democratic National Committee (DNC) member Debbie Dingell (wife of Rep. John Dingell, D-MI)—have been on a crusade for years trying to change the nominating calendar of their party. Like many others in states around the country, they have complained about the lock that two states have on the privileged position of leading off the nominating calendar. These states are Iowa and New Hampshire, with Iowa traditionally having the first caucus and New Hampshire holding the first primary a short time later. Levin has been a loud critic of a primary process that has allowed these two states to remain at the front of the line, which gives them a great amount of influence relative to their size in choosing a party's nominee.

Front-loading has become more acute with each passing election cycle as more and more states moved their nominating contest earlier to try and compete with other states to remain relevant and important. After the 2004 election cycle, national Democrats—thanks in part to the urging of Senator Levin—announced they would form a commission to examine the party's process for scheduling primaries. The Commission on Presidential Nomination Timing and Scheduling began meeting in March 2005 and reported back to the Democratic National Committee recommendations for reforms to the primary process, including preserving the privileged positions of Iowa and New Hampshire, adding one or two new caucuses between Iowa and New Hampshire and one or two new primaries between New Hampshire and the opening of the window for all other states on February 5, 2008, and allowing the DNC Rules and Bylaws Committee (RBC) to determine which states should be added. The DNC adopted all of these recommendations.[3]

In July 2006, the DNC Rules and Bylaws Committee met and selected Nevada and South Carolina as the states that would go after Iowa and New Hampshire, respectively. These states were selected because they added diversity along the lines of race and ethnicity, geography, and union density. This set up the first month of the Democratic primary calendar to include Iowa on January 14, Nevada on January 19, New Hampshire on January 22, and South Carolina on January 29. Most importantly for Michigan, the party rules prohibited any other state from going prior to February 5.

The Republican Party also had rules in place limiting when states could begin holding their primaries or caucuses. However, the process for the GOP was much simpler, as a party rule simply states, "No primary, caucus, or convention to elect, select, allocate, or bind delegates to the national convention shall occur prior to the first Tuesday in February in the year in which a national convention is held."[4] Importantly, the RNC provided an exception for New Hampshire and South Carolina so they could "begin their processes at any time on or after the third Tuesday in January in the year in which a national convention is held."[5]

Even in the wake of rules adopted by both parties that did not allow for any state outside of those noted above to hold a nominating contest before February 5, 2008, several states, including California, Florida, Arizona, and several others including Michigan, started to contemplate moving their primary or caucus very early in the year. So many states began to threaten moving their primary to the first weeks of the year that officials in New Hampshire, even though their prime placement was already guaranteed, even talked about moving the primary date into *2007*. When all was said and done, 2008 was the most front-loaded cycle ever, with more than 60 percent of all pledged delegates to both parties' national conventions being selected in nominating contests by the first week of February; as historical context, in 1976, before front-loading had begun, not one primary had even taken place by this time.

Michigan Moves to the Front

On May 3, 2007, the Florida state legislature approved a measure that moved the state's primary election to January 29, 2008, in violation of both parties' rules.[6] This set in motion a series of events that would help define the 2008 presidential election. Roughly three months after Florida's Republican governor, Charlie Crist, made the legislature's move official, on August 21, the Democratic National Committee's Rules and Bylaws Committee voted to strip Florida Democrats of all of their 210 delegates to the 2008 national convention. Stripping Florida of its delegates was viewed as a punishment for breaking party rules, but also as a deterrent to any other state possibly thinking about moving its primary to the front of the line. That failed to work, as on August 22, the Michigan Senate passed a measure of its own setting the state's primary date as January 15, 2008, and the House followed on August 30; Governor Granholm signed the bill on September 4. In the meantime, and at the urging of the national party, New Mexico governor Bill Richardson, and Senators Christopher Dodd, Joe Biden, Hillary Rodham Clinton, Barack Obama, and John Edwards all agreed not to campaign in states that violated party rules by holding early primaries. Moreover, all Democratic candidates save for Clinton, Dodd, and former U.S. senator Mike Gravel (AK) asked the state to remove their names from the primary ballot in Michigan. Finally, on December 1, 2007, the Democratic Party's Rules and Bylaws Committee stripped Michigan of its 156 delegates to the August nominating convention.

Levin and his allies, however, point to the fact that New Hampshire announced in September that it would shift its primary date from January 22 to January 8, also in violation of party rules. There was an important difference here: New Hampshire asked for a waiver to move the date and was granted that waiver; Michigan also asked for a waiver but was denied. The early-primary advocates said the DNC was "selectively enforcing" its own rules.[7]

Officials in Michigan who wanted to be relevant in the 2008 presidential nominating process certainly got their wish. Michigan (and Florida, for that matter) played a significant part in the story of the Democratic primary, but not for the reasons that those who wanted a move to the front of the line wanted. Because of the penalty imposed by the national party, Michigan lost its rather large share of the currency of the primaries—delegates. With no delegates, Michigan Democrats faced the prospect of having a primary that would have no bearing on which candidate eventually won the nomination. Even without delegates, however, Michigan could have benefited from an early position in the calendar because the primary could still have been beneficial for the state—by having candidates visit the state and listen to the concerns of the voters—and important to the process—by potentially having a winnowing effect on the field. But all that was taken away when the party asked candidates not to campaign in the state, and when many of the candidates even went one step further by taking their names off the ballot. What remained was a primary election where no one really knew what the results would mean.

Many discussions and reports of the 2008 Michigan primary focused on the Democrats. What about the Republicans? Michigan also violated the GOP rules for scheduling primaries with a January 15 date, and Michigan Republicans also faced sanctions for violating those rules. However, the GOP race was much less controversial and remained important in the final results. The difference between the two processes lies in the penalties imposed by each national party. While Democrats were stripped of all their delegates and the candidates agreed not to campaign in the state, there was no such ban on campaigning by Republicans and the state was docked only half of its total delegates. Therefore, Republicans were able to retain some influence in the process by moving to the front of the primary calendar.

Republican candidates visited Michigan numerous times, even holding a nationally televised primary debate in the Detroit suburb of Dearborn. All the candidates attended, and the main topic was the economy, the exact issue that the vast majority of Michiganders were worried about. The lead in a *Detroit News* story summed this feeling up nicely: "For once, Michigan is at the center of the national economic story."[8] Moreover, this was the chance to get the GOP presidential candidates focused on issues important to Michigan; chief among these was the economy (Michigan had been in a "one-state recession" for several years already[9]) with more specific issues related to the Big Three automakers, trade (specifically, the North American Free Trade Agreement), and jobs. Getting candidates to focus on these issues *in the state of Michigan* is exactly what the early-primary advocates were hoping for. Michigan-based GOP consultant Denise DeCook was more explicit: "Iowa and New Hampshire have for years been able to press candidates to be very specific about the issues important to them. I don't think it's asking too much of any presidential candidate to be specific about what's helpful to Michigan."[10]

The manner in which the two national parties handled the decision by the Michigan legislature to move the date of the presidential primary before the date allowed by the rules could not have been more different. The consequences of these sanctions—one a slap on the wrist and the other a death sentence—went well beyond impacting the specific contests in Michigan (although that was certainly important) and truly made a large difference in the story of the two primary seasons generally. The GOP decision to take away only half of the state's delegates meant that things could go on nearly as planned: candidates would campaign heavily in the state leading up to the primary date, running television ads, holding events across the state, and organizing volunteers to help make their case. The results of the primary would also be important, both at the convention and in helping shape who would be the eventual nominee. And, as noted above, the concerns of voters in Michigan were heard.

The same cannot be said of the Democrats' process. Because *all* of the delegates were taken away, this set up the confusing, frustrating, and even maddening process that would make the Democratic primary process last until early summer. Michigan went ahead with the primary on January 15, but without most of the candidates who wanted to be president stepping foot in the state and with no meaningful role at the Democratic convention. Beyond that, Michigan was nearly ubiquitous when it came to discussions of and debates about the Democratic primary. But it was not for good reasons. The discussion after the vote was not about which candidate might drop out of the race, who had momentum coming out of Michigan and what that might mean going forward, or even how the candidates had addressed issues important to voters. Rather, there were questions of whether votes in Michigan would even count, what "uncommitted" delegates were, and whether the state parties and state legislature had made a tactical blunder.

The Campaign and the Vote

Once Michiganders were certain that their primary would be held on January 15 and that each party faced sanctions in terms of delegates (Democrats were even banned from campaigning in the state), voters faced a set of choices that were less than ideal. Again, on the GOP side, the primary went along almost as planned. The primary campaign was fairly typical. There were candidate visits, television commercials, and fund-raisers. According to a *New York Times* graphic,[11] John McCain visited Michigan thirty-six times for campaign events between April 2007 and the primary date, while Mitt Romney visited thirty times. Other Republicans held less frequent events in the state; Mike Huckabee and Rudy Giuliani had six and five events, respectively. As noted above, if part of the goal of having an early primary was to get candidates to the state, this objective was met with the two early front-runners making numerous visits to Michigan.[12]

The Republican candidates communicated with voters in Michigan in a number of ways, but as Election Day approached it was television advertising that three of the candidates relied on most. Of all the candidates in the GOP field, only three—Romney, McCain, and Huckabee—went on the air. As Table 12.1 illustrates, Romney spent a great deal more than his rivals in every media market in the state except for the Lansing market where John McCain outspent all Republican candidates. In sum, Romney spent over $2 million on television advertising, while McCain was barely over the $750,000 mark and Huckabee fell short of $500,000. The vast majority of this money was spent on broadcast television buys and not cable; Huckabee was the only candidate to purchase any meaningful time on cable as he spent about one-third of his ad money there while the other candidates spent little (McCain) or no (Romney) money on cable buys.[13]

Table 12.1 Television Ad Spending in Michigan Before GOP Primary, by Media Market

	Romney	*McCain*	*Huckabee*
Detroit	$1,100,215	$358,074	$271,085
Grand Rapids / Kalamazoo	488,590	157,175	87,680
Lansing	48,380	113,885	45,905
Flint / Tri-Cities	220,385	49,630	45,230
Traverse City / Alpena	192,012	65,146	33,700
Marquette	66,699	22,894	14,571
Totals	*2,116,281*	*766,804*	*498,171*

Source: Michigan Campaign Finance Network, "Romney is top TV spender in Michigan GOP presidential primary," http://www.mcfn.org/press.php?prId=52 (accessed January 10, 2009).

Mike Huckabee, a former Arkansas governor, was able to parlay his surprising victory in Iowa two weeks before into some fund-raising success that allowed him to get on the air in Michigan. He had hoped to duplicate his results in Iowa, where he was able to win while being grossly outspent by Romney who relied on millions from his personal fortune to fund his campaign. McCain had rebounded during the latter part of 2007 from a time earlier that year when his campaign was all but left for dead; he managed to raise enough money to allow him to travel to Michigan more than any other Republican, but Romney still outspent him on television by more than 2 to 1.

The candidates who aired television commercials did not get on the air until late. "Romney's TV blitz ran for more than a month, beginning on December 12th. McCain's ads began in out-state markets on January 4th and in Detroit on January 7. Huckabee's ads began statewide on January 9th."[14] In these ads, the candidates discussed the issues most important to Michigan voters—the economy, the economy, and the economy. Huckabee's ads brought his message of economic populism to the state, saying he wanted to be the candidate who reminded voters of a coworker rather than "the guy who laid them off."[15] Romney talked of better trade deals and ways of getting Michiganders back to work.[16] McCain did so as well, but cast the issue as one of job retraining, mainly through community colleges.

Interest groups had a small presence in the GOP primary in terms of advertising. The Club for Growth ran ads the week before the primary against Mike Huckabee's candidacy claiming as governor he supported higher taxes on gas, income, and groceries, among other items.[17] The ad ran only in the last week before Election Day, and the group spent only $186,040.[18] Finally, a committee called Citizens for Small Government made a very small media buy ($2,000) on cable in the Kalamazoo media market in support of U.S. Representative Ron Paul (TX).

Interestingly, all three Republican candidates who campaigned vigorously in Michigan had some kind of advantage they tried to exploit leading up to the primary. Mitt Romney, former governor of Massachusetts, called Michigan home and he campaigned in the state as a "favorite son," taking advantage of his father's popularity as a former governor. Romney placed his national campaign headquarters in Michigan and counted on winning the state on his way to the nomination. Michigan voters had fond memories of John McCain from his 2000 primary victory over George W. Bush. Michiganders also looked favorably on McCain's "maverick" label and his independent streak. Mike Huckabee, while from the South, had a natural constituency in west Michigan with the heavy evangelical population in places such as Holland, Grand Rapids, and Battle Creek.

After all the votes were counted, Mitt Romney won Michigan's Republican primary with 39 percent of the vote to John McCain's 30 percent; Mike Huckabee finished further back with only 16 percent. It is difficult to overstate the importance of economic issues in this primary, however. Exit polls showed that 55 percent of GOP primary voters said the economy was the number one issue, while Iraq came in a distant second with only 17 percent citing it. The difference in the finish between McCain and Romney, however, was without a doubt their attitude toward and response to the question of manufacturing jobs in the state.

Michigan has long relied on the automobile industry for an overwhelming part of its economy; millions of residents, in some way or another, have jobs that are tied to the auto industry. These jobs have been disappearing for years, and as this trend continued in 2008 voters wanted to know what the candidates would do to stop the hemorrhaging. The top two vote getters in the primary gave very different answers to the question. Romney's answer, more than his ties to the state or even his business background, won him votes. In appearances and rallies on both sides of the state McCain said, "I've got to give you some straight talk: Some of the jobs that have left the state of Michigan are not coming back. They are not. And I am sorry to tell you that."[19] But Romney had an answer that appealed to voters who were turned off by McCain's "straight talk." He said, "You know, some jobs have left Michigan that are never coming back. I disagree."[20] McCain's answer was more truthful, but as we see in many campaigns around the nation, that kind of message does not always win votes.

The result had an important impact on the GOP primary race. McCain scored an impressive comeback victory in the New Hampshire primary (his campaign was viewed by many as on its last legs in mid- to late 2007 because of bad poll numbers and low fund-raising totals) on Romney's home turf in the northeast, and he was poised for the knock-out. A McCain victory in Michigan could have meant the end of the Romney campaign. Instead, the former Massachusetts governor lived to fight on. Michigan saved its favorite son from having to drop out for at least a couple of weeks; he ended his campaign on February 7.

In the end, the move to the front of the line of primary states mainly led to the intended consequences: candidates came to the state and discussed voters' worries and those same voters had a role in shaping the field of candidates as the process continued to states with later primaries. Certainly losing half of the delegates to the national convention was not what Michigan Republicans had in mind. However, in the end, the number of delegates has little to do with who wins the nomination. By the time the convention rolled around, Republicans knew that John McCain would be their nominee. This result was not affected by the number of individuals from Michigan on the floor of the convention hall at the GOP convention.

In addition, had Michigan not voted early, the race for the nomination might have looked entirely different. Without a victory in Michigan—Romney's only large-state win (he won caucuses in Wyoming before, as well as Nevada and Maine after the Michigan primary)—Romney may not have had the strength to go on as long as he did. This could have meant that the GOP nomination was in McCain's hands earlier, or it could have united the more conservative wing of the party behind Mike Huckabee and resulted in a more contentious battle. One of the factors that led to McCain's victory was that Romney and Huck-abee split the conservative vote and allowed McCain to garner enough votes to win from the more centrist voters in the primary electorate. In short, Michigan Republicans got mostly what they wanted by breaking party rules and moving their primary up.

The same cannot be said for the Democratic Party. Once all the Democratic candidates, save Clinton, Dodd, Kucinich, and Gravel (with Clinton being the only serious contender), took their names off the ballot, the Michigan Democratic primary was in disarray.[21] There really was no campaign to speak of. The field of candidates had made only a handful of visits to the state before their pledge not to campaign in

Michigan; Clinton and Richardson both held five events while Edwards and Obama each had three.[22] Kucinich was the only Democrat who campaigned in Michigan after the ban; he visited Michigan a total of twenty-six times.[23] Without the front-runner candidates in the state, there was next to no television advertising on the Democratic side. "Dennis Kucinich was the only Democrat to buy television in Michigan. He spent about $10,000 for last minute ads in the Detroit market."[24]

In the wake of the decision by top-tier candidates to take their names off the ballot, there were many questions. What would Democratic voters in Michigan do? Would they vote in their own primary, would they cross over to the GOP primary or not vote at all? If Democrats did vote in their primary, what choices would they have? What about voters who favored one of the candidates who took their name off the ballot? What should they do? On December 10, the Michigan Democratic Party tried to answer some of these questions by issuing a press release indicating that the available choices on primary day would be Clinton, Dodd, Kucinich, Gravel, uncommitted, and write-in.[25] The party also tried to help voters whose favorite candidate would not appear by encouraging them to cast their ballot for uncommitted. This was the best option according to the party because for any write-in ballots to count, the candidate would first have to file additional paperwork with the state, which none did.

While the candidates did not campaign in the state, there was a good deal of activity leading up to primary day by the candidates' supporters. Backers of Barack Obama and John Edwards in particular were encouraging others to cast ballots for uncommitted. Even some grassroots groups popped up to encourage this type of participation, going so far as to get "Vote Uncommitted" lawn signs printed and placed near hundreds of polling places.[26] This was seen as an option for Democrats because as long as uncommitted received more than 15 percent of the votes cast, delegates would be allocated, and those candidates not on the ballot could lay claim to them, if, of course, the state's delegation would be reinstated and seated at the convention in August.

After the votes were counted, Hillary Clinton won the Michigan Democratic primary with 55 percent of the vote. The bigger story, however, was that 40 percent of Democratic primary voters marked uncommitted on their ballot. Turnout was low, as expected. Nonetheless, 594,000 voters turned out to cast ballots.[27] Included in these results were over 75,000 votes for uncommitted in Wayne County, home of Detroit and a large African American population; Clinton beat uncommitted in Wayne County by only 6,000 votes. Presumably, many of these voters were Obama supporters given the makeup of the county. Similarly, in Macomb County north of Detroit, an area with a heavy union presence, most voters selecting uncommitted were likely Edwards supporters.

Exit polls conducted on primary day told a very interesting story. Along with the traditional exit poll questions, those selected to participate in the poll were posed the following question: "If these had been the candidates on the ballot today, for whom would you have voted in the Democratic presidential primary? Hillary Clinton, John Edwards, Dennis Kucinich, Barack Obama, or Bill Richardson." According to the results, Clinton still would have won the primary, but with only 46 percent of the vote, followed closely by Barack Obama with 35 percent, and then John Edwards with just 12 percent.[28] Even more important, these exit polls showed that among those who said they would have voted for Obama, 79 percent marked uncommitted on their ballot; 57 percent of Edwards's would-be support came from uncommitted voters. Many fewer voters who said they would have voted for one of these two candidates reported that they marked their ballots for Senator Clinton. Yes, Hilary Clinton did "win" the Michigan Democratic presidential primary, but the fact that nearly a quarter of a million supporters of other candidates whose names did not even appear on the ballot went to the polls to cast a vote for uncommitted when there was no certainty at the time about what that vote would mean or if it would even count for anything is remarkable, and was a strong signal to the Clinton camp and Democrats nationally.

The Aftermath

Unlike the GOP, Democrats did not achieve their goal of having an impact on the nomination process either by having candidates pay attention to Michigan voters or being part of the delegate selection process.

However, Michigan was not out of the spotlight after the primary. Democratic Party officials nationally and in Michigan knew that a meaningless primary in Michigan could hurt their candidate's chances of winning in November. After all, Michigan is key to Democrats' chances of winning the presidency. This concern was reflected by former Michigan governor James Blanchard (D): "No Democrat has won the White House in sixty years, with one exception, without winning Michigan. You don't want to alienate 600,000 voters to punish some party operatives."[29] While the party rule makers needed to go ahead with the sanctions they imposed so as to not make a mockery of the rules, the idea that Michigan would play no part in the Democrats' nominating convention was seen as a remote possibility by most involved. Even before the decision to strip the state was handed down, party officials in Michigan were confident that the decision would be reversed and the delegates would be seated anyway.[30] National Democrats also knew as time went on, for the reason Governor Blanchard noted, that they could not keep a Michigan delegation from participating in the formal selection process. The state was simply too important for the Electoral College strategy of the presidential candidate to push away or irritate voters in a state that had an affinity for the other party's candidate—John McCain. While they had their own agenda as well, a memo from two Clinton advisers—Harold Ickes and Mark Penn— clearly makes the point: "Democrats barely carried Michigan in 2004 (by only 3 percent—51 to 48). If our party refuses to let them participate in the convention, we will provide a political opportunity for the Republicans to win . . . Michigan."[31]

How to solve this problem dominated much of the discussion as the Democratic primary process moved into its next stages. There was one other factor that kept the status of the delegates from Michigan (and Florida) on the agenda of the primary battle: the fact that the race between Hillary Clinton and Barack Obama was so close for so long. Had the contest between these two rivals not been so protracted, the discussion may have been less important, or at least not as front and center as it was through much of the spring. Several remedies were discussed to solve the problem of the Michigan delegation from having a "redo" primary or caucus to using the results of the exit poll noted above. Of course the two candidates had very different views. Clinton lobbied for the delegates to be counted based on the results of the primary, while the Obama campaign maintained the results were meaningless.[32]

The idea of having another vote actually had a good deal of support from lawmakers in Michigan as well as Democrats nationally. How a do-over would actually work, however, was another matter. Would it be a primary? If so, who would pay for it? Could there be a caucus where Democrats could help pick their nominee as they did four years earlier? What about a mail-in vote, similar to elections in Oregon? In the end, however, hopes for another primary or caucus in Michigan were dashed when the state legislature failed to act in enough time for the do-over contest to be administered.[33] There were also a number of problems with respect to the other options, whether vote by mail, caucus, or primary. Questions over the legality of a do-over, the possibility of lawsuits filed by voters who wished to vote in the new primary but would likely be barred from doing so because they voted in the GOP primary, potential donors privately funding a new primary, and simple logistics were all problems.[34]

In the end, Michigan Democrats were left with no do-over primary and only the opportunity to try and negotiate a deal with the national party and the Clinton and Obama campaigns. Here again, a number of options presented themselves, from using the results of the primary to partly assign delegates to both Clinton and Obama, using only the primary results, splitting the delegates evenly, and even using both the primary results and the national popular vote in all Democratic primaries. The decision was again up to the DNC's Rules and Bylaws Committee, the same body that stripped the state of all its delegates six months earlier. After a day of meetings, testimony, and bickering, the DNC's RBC voted 19 to 8 to reinstate all of Michigan's delegates to the national nominating convention in Denver, but with two important caveats. First, the delegates would only receive one half a vote each; this effectively cut the state's delegation in half.[35] And second, the delegate split would give sixty-nine delegates to Hillary Clinton and fifty-nine delegates to Barack Obama. This was based partly on the results of the January 15 primary, but not completely. The Clinton campaign argued for the strict use of the primary results, which would have given Clinton seventy-eight delegates to Obama's fifty-five (the full number of delegates commensurate with the vote total for uncommitted). The Obama campaign, because its candidate was not on the ballot, argued for an even 64–64 split of the delegates. A group of Michigan Democrats, including Senator Carl Levin and DNC committeewoman Debbie Dingell, proposed the 69–59 allotment because it "splits the difference" between the plans offered by the two campaigns.[36] The result was not without controversy, however, as many Clinton backers at the meeting, including former White House deputy chief of staff Harold Ickes, cried foul. Ickes may have summed up the entire process best when he said, "Was the process flawed? You bet your ass it was flawed."[37]

The General Election: In Like a Lion, Out Like a Lamb

Even before the parties nominated their candidates for the general election, Michigan was on nearly everyone's radar screen as a "battleground" state. This categorization typically means that the result of the contest in that state, and therefore the fate of that state's electoral votes (in this case 17), is in doubt, unlike other states such as New York, Texas, California, or Alabama. Being in this select group of states also means that the candidates will spend a disproportionate amount of their campaign's resources—the candidate's time, money, volunteers, and so on— in these states. Being a battleground state is almost analogous to being one of the first states to hold a nominating contest during the primaries because candidates will be in the state listening to and communicating with voters, hearing their concerns and at least pretending to address these issues. About the only bad thing associated with a battleground state is the onslaught of television ads to which voters are subjected.

In 2008 Michigan had all the makings of a battleground state. First, its electoral history signaled to campaigners and strategists that it could be very competitive on Election Day in the fall. Many of the last several presidential contests in the state were decided by slim margins. Close margins in Michigan date back to 1884, when Republican James Blaine beat Democrat Grover Cleveland by less than 1 percent of the vote. In more modern elections, we can look back to John F. Kennedy's 1960 win over Richard Nixon by two percentage points and Nixon's six-point loss to Hubert H. Humphrey in 1968. After Democratic victories in 1960–1968, Republicans had string of successes from 1972 to 1988 with the slimmest margin of victory being Michigander Gerald Ford's five-point win in 1976. Bill Clinton won the state in both 1992 and 1996, with a margin of over thirteen points in the latter. What is misleading about these figures, however, is the presence of H. Ross Perot in 1992 and 1996 who garnered a large number of votes in both years; indeed, Clinton won the state's electoral votes with only 44 percent and 51 percent of the popular vote in 1992 and 1996 respectively.[38] In 2000 and 2004, the state became entrenched as a battleground state as Democrats Al Gore and John Kerry won the state's popular vote with just over 51 percent.

The second reason for Michigan's potential to be a battleground in 2008 lay in the combination of two factors—the nature of the voters in Michigan and the candidates. First, Michigan's voters can be difficult to predict. After all, Michigan, and specifically Macomb County, which lies about twenty miles north of Detroit, is the home of Reagan Democrats,[39] and Michiganders voted in large numbers for Ross Perot in both of his presidential bids.[40] This unpredictability and independent nature comes from the makeup of the voters. Michigan is a blue-collar state with a heavy union presence, but is also comprised of voters who like their guns, fishing lines, and power boats. As noted earlier, Michigan has been dominated by the auto industry for decades. While the Big Three, their suppliers, and the other related businesses are mainly centered in the southeastern corner of the state, the impact of the auto industry is felt across the state. Millions of Michiganders work for the car companies or work in jobs that are in some way tied to the auto industry, many of which are blue-collar jobs. Michigan is also a state with a heavy evangelical population on the west side of the state in places like Grand Rapids, Holland, Kalamazoo, and Battle Creek. Hunting, fishing, boating, and other outdoor activities are also popular in a state that has the second most miles of coastline next to Alaska.[41] Race is also a big factor in state politics. Many of the first Reagan Democrats were white voters who left Detroit for the suburbs in the 1960s. Detroit, the state's largest city, remains one of the most segregated cities in the nation; the heavy minority population in Detroit is surrounded by much more affluent and white suburbs. With these factors in play many voters tend to feel a lot of cross pressures when confronted with a choice of candidates.

The next factor is the candidates who were running in 2008. As noted earlier, John McCain had a positive history in the state with his primary victory in 2000. McCain won the primary in 2000 in part because there was no Democratic race to speak of (Al Gore had nearly sewn up the nomination before the party caucuses), and it appeared from the turnout in the Democratic caucuses that year (only about 19,000) that more Democrats in Michigan were interested in voting in the GOP race so they could vote for McCain, which they did. McCain appealed to voters in 2000 because he campaigned as a more moderate Republican and an alternative to George W. Bush. Plus, as we also found out in 2008, McCain is a "maverick," which is a quality that many voters in the state admire and respect.

The 2008 campaign between John McCain and Barack Obama was set up to be a closely fought contest because of the factors noted above. McCain's history in the state meant he had a good foundation on which to build a campaign organization, and voters had proven already that he could do well in Michigan. Moreover, on the Democratic side, some voters in Michigan were still smarting from the perceived snub Senator Obama gave them in the primaries. Even more importantly, McCain, it was thought, could do well with a key part of the Democratic coalition—white, working-class voters (the same Democrats Reagan did so well with 28 years earlier). This is a group of voters Obama had difficulty with in the primaries; Senator Clinton seemed to dominate among this group of voters in many primary states. Republicans hoped that McCain could hold the voters Republicans had won in the previous two contests and pick off enough Clinton voters to win the state. Obama, however, was not going to give those votes up without a fight, and he had a huge block of support in Detroit, where African Americans, it was hypothesized, would come out in droves to help elect the first African American president. The general election campaign in Michigan can be broken down into three distinct phases: preconvention, the month of September, and the month of October. The campaigning during each of these three periods differed in ways that were not predicted beforehand.

The Summer Months: A Typical Battleground

Early polling gave McCain supporters some hope, as several surveys showed McCain leading Obama in Michigan through the month of May (Figure 12.1). McCain's lead was slim (the widest margin was 4 points), but Republicans hoped to turn the state red for the first time since 1988. One poll commissioned by the *Detroit News* showed McCain leading 44 percent to 40 percent, but more importantly McCain was leading in key categories. These included being someone voters could trust (45 percent to 30 percent), sharing their values (41 percent to 36 percent), and even a prospective judgment of who would be a better president (41 percent to 38 percent). Moreover, McCain was leading by large margins in important constituencies including Macomb County (51 percent to 35 percent) and among independents generally (42 percent to 28 percent).[42]

Figure 12.1 Real Clear Politics Polling Average: Obama vs. McCain in Michigan

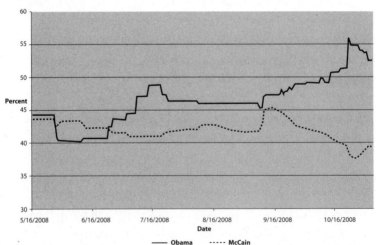

Source: Real Clear Politics polling average, Michigan: McCain vs. Obama, http://www .realclearpolitics.com/epolls/2008/president/mi/michigan_mccain_vs_obama-553.html.

There are important caveats about these polling numbers. First, the data were collected before Obama claimed the nomination (and while the fate of the Michigan delegation at the national convention was still up in the air), and when many Democrats still supported Senator Clinton over Obama. In addition, while McCain irritated Michigan voters earlier in the year with his remark about lost jobs "not coming back," Senator Obama likely caused greater exasperation among the state's voters one year earlier when he gave a speech at the Economic Club of Detroit taking the auto industry to task over fuel economy standards, saying the auto companies were partially to blame for blocking increased fuel efficiency standards.[43] Obama was relatively unfamiliar to Michigan's voters at this time, and his remarks about the auto industry certainly did not endear him to voters, especially those in the key groups noted above.

As the campaign entered the summer, after the dispute over the Democratic delegates was settled and after Obama had clearly won the nomination, Democrats nationwide began to coalesce behind him. And as he began to build a sizable lead in resources, Obama took the lead in Michigan and rarely looked back; he was ahead by about seven points in mid-July.[44] Obama was able to build this lead thanks to several advantages he had in the state. First, and most importantly, Obama had a tremendous fund-raising advantage. In total, Obama raised over $740 million to John McCain's $370 million. This is a shocking differential, especially when one considers that it was only two election cycles before, when George W. Bush, to the chagrin of some, shattered all previous fund-raising records when he raised $100 million. Obama's more than 2 to 1 advantage in fund-raising is slightly misleading because of the two phases of the election. For the primaries Obama raised a total of $414 million; during this same time John McCain raised just $216 million.[45] After they received their party's nomination, the candidates took different funding routes during the general election period. The Obama campaign decided to eschew the public funding system while McCain participated. This allowed Obama to raise as much money as he could, and bypass the spending limits that go along with the public funding. In the month of September alone, Obama raised $150 million, which was nearly twice the amount John McCain was limited to for the entire general election period because of his participation in the public funding system.[46]

This huge monetary advantage is visible when the candidates' expenditures are examined. In Michigan, the Obama campaign held large advantages in two important categories: television advertising and campaign offices that housed both paid staff and volunteers. During the summer months, the two campaigns were on roughly equal footing in terms of television advertising. Between Memorial Day and Labor Day, the McCain campaign aired $6.15 million worth of spots to Obama's $5.5 million (Table 12.2).[47] McCain's advantage here is a bit deceptive because he was on the air about one month before Obama was; McCain began running ads in Michigan immediately after Memorial Day, while Obama went up on June 20 having to wait until he had secured the nomination. On a weekly basis, then, Obama spent more than McCain during this time period, $548,000 per week to McCain's $439,000.[48] Much of the spending on McCain's part late in this period was driven by the fact that he had to spend all of the money he had raised for his primary campaign before he officially accepted the nomination. Because he participated in the public funding system, his $84 million stipend from the government would kick in immediately after the convention and he could not spend any remaining primary funds after this point. So, any free spending by the McCain campaign in Michigan was driven less by how much money he had and more by time constraints. Party organizations and outside groups were on the air during this period to a limited extent. Still, the advertising total in Michigan increased about 40 percent from the same period during 2004.[49]

The importance of Michigan in a Democratic strategy of getting to the magic number of 270 electoral votes can be seen in the allocation of resources to the state in other ways as well. The advantage in resources the Obama campaign enjoyed allowed the campaign to also have an advantage in both field staff and offices throughout the campaign. Even while Barack Obama was still battling Hillary Clinton in primaries in places like Kentucky, Oregon, Montana, and Puerto Rico, the Obama team was setting up field offices in Michigan, gearing up for the general election campaign. By June 10, Obama had fourteen field

Table 12.2 Obama and McCain Ad Spending through October 6

	Obama			McCain		
Media Market	June 20- Sept 1	*Sept 2- Oct 6*	**June 20- Oct 6**	May 28- Aug 31	*Sept 1- Oct 5*	**May 28- Oct 5**
Detroit	$2,555,035	$3,247,810	**$5,802,845**	$2,926,086	$1,918,009	**$4,844,095**
Grand Rapids / Kalamazoo	1,290,769	468,793	**1,759,562**	1,177,494	775,607	**1,953,101**
Lansing	679,154	792,383	**1,471,537**	735,575	218,164	**953,739**
Flint / Tri-Cities	421,966	608,244	**1,030,210**	591,770	394,362	**986,132**
Traverse City / Alpena	541,056	313,511	**854,567**	530,789	291,461	**822,250**
Marquette	126,539	115,837	**242,376**	224,249	85,857	**310,106**
Total	5,614,519	5,546,578	**11,161,097**	6,185,963	3,683,460	**9,869,423**

Source: Michigan Campaign Finance Network, "2008 Michigan Presidential Television Advertising ($s)," http://www.mcfn.org/pdfs/reports/MIPrezTVoct.pdf (accessed January 26, 2009).

offices set up around the state that were mainly conducting voter contact and registration operations.[50] Amy Chapman, Obama's Michigan state director, noted that by mid-July, "progress in Michigan since Senator Obama secured the Democratic nomination has been swift, and we continue growing daily."[51] By this time the Obama campaign had increased the number of field offices in the state to forty, had ninety staffers on the payroll, and was looking to hire eighty more to be field organizers; the 150 total at the time was said to be a minimum. According to Chapman, "These organizers will oversee neighborhood teams, where people will lead the local change in their communities by registering voters, knocking on doors, making phone calls and securing more supporters and volunteers for a Michigan victory. In addition, there are 5 full-time constituency voter coordinators who will oversee the execution of our outreach efforts to a minimum of 13 different constituencies ranging from Women to Veterans."[52] In addition, the Obama campaign worked with the state Democratic Party to recruit over two thousand precinct captains. Democrats bragged that this would be the largest field mobilization effort the state had ever seen.[53] According to a report in *The Hill* newspaper, even at the end of July, "McCain campaign officials [had] yet to report its offices" in Michigan as well as other Midwestern states.[54] However, if the candidates' spending is any indication, the McCain campaign was far behind in field organization. Data compiled by the Center for Responsive Politics showed that as of late July "Obama has spent $35.7 million on staff salaries and benefits and $7.7 million on rent and utilities, while McCain has spent about $11.9 million on staff and about $4 million for office space and utilities."[55]

As both parties' national conventions drew near, the state of the race in Michigan was probably right where most observers thought it would be. Obama was leading but McCain was within striking distance. As he did across the country, Obama was able to connect with voters through his promise of change. But even in the face of difficult times for the Republican brand across the nation, and especially in a state like Michigan where the economy was in such bad shape, McCain supporters had to be pleased with where their campaign stood near the end of August (Figure 12.1). In a survey done by one of the leading polling firms in the state, McCain still led Obama on several important measures of their characteristics: he led by nine points on the question of "someone you can trust" (42 percent to 33 percent), by twenty-four points on experience (63 percent to 19 percent), by twelve points on who "will be a strong leader" (45 percent to 33 percent), and by eighteen points on who "will protect American interests" (48 percent to 30 percent).[56] Still, at this point Obama led by two points in this survey (which was within the margin of error), likely because of the public's feelings about the state of the economy (70 percent of Michiganders said the economy was getting weaker at that time, and 46 percent said the economy was the number one issue) and the nation as a whole (72 percent said the country was "on the wrong track").[57] Again, Obama's promise of change was resonating, and likely trumping any good feelings that the people, at least in Michigan, had for John McCain.

September 2008: Another Comeback?

In the few weeks after the nominating conventions, John McCain had his best chance at overtaking Barack Obama, and possibly winning Michigan's electoral votes (Figure 12.1). Important here were the two vice presidential choices. There has been a good deal of discussion among pundits and journalists about John McCain's selection of Alaska governor Sarah Palin as his running mate and what a disaster it was. Truth be told, the initial reaction to Palin was quite positive, maybe especially in Michigan. In several polls conducted days immediately after the GOP convention wrapped up in St. Paul, Obama's lead was down to one point in Michigan; in one poll McCain led by one point and in another (conducted by a Republican firm) he was up three points.[58] In one of these polls, 45 percent of the respondents said McCain's choice of Palin made it more likely that they would vote for him, with only 35 percent saying it was less likely (a net plus of 10 points); this is compared to 30 percent who said they were more likely to vote for Obama because of his choice of Joe Biden, and 34 percent who said it made it less likely (a net drag of 4 points).

Also, the McCain campaign chose Macomb County—the home of those Reagan Democrats—as the first stop for the GOP ticket after McCain accepted the nomination at his convention. This was noteworthy because of some of the qualities Palin brought to the table, the type of voter the campaign thought she could connect with, and two of the target groups the McCain campaign had their eyes on—blue-collar workers who liked to hunt and fish (like Palin's husband) and women, both of which may have supported Hillary Clinton in the Democratic primary.[59] The rally drew a crowd of about 10,000 and injected some much needed energy into the GOP base.[60] The news was good for the McCain-Palin campaign into mid-September when he was doing well with important constituencies in Michigan: he held a fourteen-point lead with white voters and an eighteen-point lead in the suburbs north of Detroit (an area where George W. Bush did not do as well in the previous two cycles).[61] One Republican poll released on September 20 even showed McCain up three points.[62]

These encouraging poll numbers, however, were short-lived and did not mark good times ahead for the McCain campaign in Michigan or nationally. What turned out to be soft support for the McCain-Palin ticket can be traced to several factors, including the U.S. financial meltdown that hit at roughly the same time as McCain seemed to be gaining ground, and Sarah Palin's difficulties with the press, to name only two. Most students of the 2008 presidential election remember that not long after Palin was wowing Republican crowds, she was roundly criticized regarding her shifting position on Alaska's "bridge to nowhere" (a pork project she loudly denounced as a vice presidential candidate but had supported earlier in Alaska). She had devastating interviews with major news outlets, and, maybe most damning of all, she became a regular target of comedians and satirists on shows like *Saturday Night Live, The Daily Show*, and late night talk shows. Being lampooned to the degree she was would be difficult for anyone to come back from, let alone a candidate many thought was unqualified.

The bigger problem for McCain in Michigan was the financial crisis that seemed to worsen by the day during September. As already noted, Michigan felt the economic downturn earlier and harder than almost any other state thanks in large part to the troubled times of the Big Three automakers. Certainly voters in Michigan were worried about the general state of the economy during the credit crunch that hit in September, but voters in Michigan were a step ahead of the nation when it came to the bailout the auto companies would be asking Congress for in the next few months. This dire economic situation trumped any other issue in the state. Even if voters did think McCain was more experienced and would do a better job on issues like homeland security, the impact of the economic meltdown on the presidential race in Michigan is hard to overstate. And as the crisis deepened, John McCain's chances of winning Michigan disappeared.

By the third week in September, Barack Obama had jumped out to a ten-point lead in some polls, and the trend lines were only getting worse for McCain (Figure 12.1). In addition to the difficulties McCain was having in dealing with the economic problems in the country (it was on September 24 that McCain infamously decided to "suspend" his campaign to return to Washington to work on a solution to the problem in the Senate), he could not keep up with the resources at the disposal of the Obama campaign. In the "air war," Obama significantly outspent—by about $2 million—McCain in September (see Table 12.2). With this advantage in resources, Obama was able to hammer his message—at this time centered mainly on the economy (with some specific focus on the auto industry)[63] and on tying McCain to George W. Bush[64]—and saturate the airwaves with ads. Moreover, Obama dominated areas of the state that were important to him—the Detroit, Flint, and Lansing markets—and stayed close to McCain's spending in areas important for the GOP—Grand Rapids and Traverse City (Table 12.2). In addition, Obama maintained his organizational advantage by opening nearly a dozen more offices around the state than McCain.[65]

October: An Anticlimactic End

As promising as September began for John McCain, it ended just as poorly. By the start of October, McCain was down by seven points in the Real Clear Politics average of polling data (Figure 12.1).[66] The McCain campaign saw the writing on the wall and on October 2 pulled its resources out of the state. What was once a battleground state that gave the GOP a solid chance to turn a blue state red in a year when red states were turning blue, was now judged unwinnable by McCain advisers. Michigan "is the worst state of all the states in play. It's an obvious one . . . to come off the list [of contested states]" said one senior McCain adviser.[67] McCain took his ads off the air, stopped sending direct mail, canceled all upcoming events in the state, and sent most of the limited staff he had there to other states. State Republicans tried to argue that the campaign would still have a presence in the state, but actions speak louder than words, and Michiganders did not see McCain again after the announcement.

The decision to stop competing in Michigan meant that John McCain had almost no chance to win the White House; if he was going to win, he needed to take Michigan from the Democratic column and hold on to other states that had been in the GOP column four years earlier. As the electoral map got filled in on election night, it was clear that McCain would lose not only Michigan but other states he needed, so in the end this one decision did not cost him the election. Instead, it was a sign of larger problems in the campaign, the difficulties faced by all Republicans in a year when the public was clamoring for change, and the strong campaign run by the Obama team.

What caused McCain's exit from Michigan again stems from a disparity of resources between the two campaigns. "Barack Obama's decision to forgo public funding for his presidential campaign helped force John McCain to withdraw from Michigan, abandoning an important strategic objective, said a McCain adviser."[68] NBC News political director Chuck Todd agreed with this assessment: "We are in decision time mode for these campaigns when it comes to money. . . . They have to pick between Michigan and Pennsylvania when it comes to targeting, truly targeting one of these states that [Kerry] carried in '04. They made the decision Pennsylvania over Michigan. It's expensive to do both. If they had the money, they'd be doing both."[69] The fact that the Obama team had access to almost unlimited funds at this point (recall he had raised $150 million in the month of September alone) made it nearly impossible for McCain to keep up, having to ration his completely publicly funded budget of $84 million much more cautiously.

Interestingly, even after McCain left the state, the Obama campaign kept pressing for votes. In September, the Obama field operation swelled to over four hundred paid staffers; after McCain's departure this shrank back to two hundred.[70] While Obama did not appear in Michigan after October 3, his campaign kept opening up field offices around the state. When a campaign has the kind of resources the Obama team did, it can do almost anything it wants—like opening a new field office eight days before the election in a town that would have voted for Obama overwhelmingly anyway. Obama opened an office in Ann Arbor, which voted for Obama by nearly a 5 to 1 margin.[71] Obama spokesman Brent Colburn said about the decision to keep pumping resources into the state: "No matter what the other side decides to do, Michigan is still important to us."[72]

In the waning days of the campaign a group calling itself Our Country Deserves Better PAC bought airtime to run ads that hit on a number of hot-button issues for Michiganders. The ads tried to link Obama to an unpopular governor, Jennifer Granholm, and the former mayor of Detroit, Kwame Kilpatrick, who had recently pled guilty to perjury and other charges; also prominent in the ads were William Ayers, the former domestic terrorist, and Obama's controversial former pastor, Reverend Jeremiah Wright.[73] The media buy around the state was estimated at nearly $500,000.

Analysts in Michigan and nationally also cited McCain mistakes in explaining why he lost a once promising state. Some blamed McCain's stance on free trade in a state hurt by jobs leaving because of the North American Free Trade Agreement (NAFTA).[74] Others argued McCain simply did not have the right message, choosing mainly to attack Obama in his TV ads rather than telling his inspiring story as a war hero.[75] In the end, McCain's inability to steal a state from the Democratic column was a combination of all these factors—an inability to compete financially, an electoral context stacked against him that included a bad year for the GOP brand in the wake of an unpopular president and an economic crisis, and an economic message that was difficult at times to differentiate from his opponent's (e.g., both candidates voted for the Wall Street bailout).

Concluding Thoughts

On Election Day, Barack Obama scored a sixteen-point, 800,000-vote victory in Michigan, something that no one would have predicted two months earlier. Michigan, as it turned out, was a sign of the times as Obama went on to win every battleground state, save Missouri (which he lost by less than 4,000 votes).

There are any number of lessons to take from Michigan in 2008. First, the political context surrounding elections matters a great deal. In some instances it is too much to overcome, as many Republicans found out in 2008. McCain's misfortune of sharing a party affiliation with an unpopular president severely damaged his prospects from the start, although Republicans likely picked the one candidate who had a chance to win in November. Second, resources matter even more. John McCain simply could not keep up with the spending power of the Obama campaign, whether it was on television ads, paid staffers, direct mail, or any other campaign tactic that can be purchased. This is a very important point for those who support the public funding of our presidential elections. There were predictions that after George W. Bush in 2000 and 2004, and John Kerry and Howard Dean in 2004, decided to do without public funding in the primaries, that the public funding system was in danger. The 2008 election cycle moved the system further from being relevant in the next cycle. Third, the messages candidates communicate to potential voters matter as well. John McCain had important problems in Michigan in this regard. Most importantly, he had unpopular stands on issues related to the economy and jobs—the number one issue in Michigan and the nation as a whole.

The campaign in Michigan also illustrated very clearly that our process of choosing candidates for the general election needs an overhaul. It is not that states should not be able to schedule a primary or caucus. Rather, the states and the parties need to get on the same page so that there is less discussion about a rules and bylaws committee and more about candidates and their issue positions. While both parties have decided to convene commissions to investigate possible solutions, it is unclear what those might be. Will Iowa and New Hampshire continue to have a prime place at the beginning of the line? Will states like Michigan be able to attain the relevancy they crave? Will there be a national primary? All of these questions remain on the table.

In the end, the 2008 presidential race in Michigan did not turn out as anyone thought it would. From the first discussions of moving the primary date to Barack Obama's overwhelming victory on November 4, things did not turn out as they typically do in Michigan. But as we approach the 2012 campaign, it is likely that candidates, their advisers, parties, interest groups, and the media will place Michigan back into the column of battleground states and we will start over again.

Notes

1 Governor Jennifer Granholm, quoted in "Granholm Signs Bill Moving Presidential Primary to January 15," September 4, 2007, www.michigan.gov/gov/0,1607,7 -168-23442_21974-175318-,00.html (accessed January 27, 2009).

2 Senator Mike Bishop, quoted in "Bishop, McManus Laud Agreement on Presidential Primary," www.senate.michigan.gov/gop/readarticle.asp?id=723&District=12 (accessed January 27, 2009).

3 Democratic National Committee, Commission on Presidential Nomination Timing and Scheduling, www.democrats.org/page/s/nominating (accessed January 28, 2009).

4 Rules of the Republican National Committee, www.gop.com//images/legal/ 2008_RULES_Adopted.pdf (accessed January 5, 2009).

5 Even though Iowa, Nevada, and Louisiana held nominating contests before February 5, the GOP rules did not affect them because those states did not technically choose their delegates until after that date. Those states formally chose delegates at district or state conventions that occurred after February 5.

6 Adam Goodnough, "Seeking an Edge, Florida Changes Its Primary Date," *New York Times,* May 4, 2007, www.nytimes.com/2007/05/04/us/politics/04florida.html (accessed January 6, 2009).

7 Carl Levin, Carolyn Cheeks Kilpatrick, Ron Gettelfinger, and Debbie Dingell, "Why Michigan Democrats must be seated," *Detroit News,* May 31, 2008, www.det news.com/apps/pbcs.dll/article?AID=/20080531/OPINION01/805310308 (accessed October 8, 2008).

8 Gordon Trowbridge, "GOP Face-off in Dearborn," *Detroit News,* October 9, 2007, www.detnews.com/apps/pbcs.dll/article?AID=/20071009/POLITICS01/710090393 (accessed January 9, 2009).

9 Louis Aguilar, "Worst yet to come for Michigan economy," June 13, 2007, www.detnews.com/apps/pbcs.dll/article?aid=/20070613/biz/706130416/1001 (accessed March 19, 2009).

10 Quoted in Trowbridge, "GOP Face-off."

11 http://politics.nytimes.com/election-guide/2008/schedules/pastevents.html (accessed January 10, 2009).

12 I do not include Rudy Giuliani here because of his (flawed) strategy of waiting until the contest in Florida on January 29 to begin his campaign in earnest.

13 Michigan Campaign Finance Network, "Romney Is Top TV Spender in Michigan GOP Presidential Primary," www.mcfn.org/press.php?prId=52 (accessed January 10, 2009).

14 "Romney Is Top TV Spender."

15 www.youtube.com/watch?v=jMaJ0KtTcr0.

16 www.youtube.com/watch?v=SrIkmrTqEv4.

17 www.youtube.com/watch?v=acwKStKQXGU.

18 "Romney Is Top TV Spender."

19 Sasha Issenberg, "Same State, Different Message for Michigan's Economy," *Boston Globe,* January 14, 2008, www.boston.com/news/nation/articles/2008/01/14/same_state_ different_message_for_michigans_economy (accessed January 13, 2009).

20 Issenberg, "Same State."

21 Dodd dropped out of the race twelve days before the Michigan primary, but his name remained on the ballot; Gravel and Kucinich were mostly minor players in the race.

22 http://politics.nytimes.com/election-guide/2008/schedules/pastevents.html (accessed January 10, 2009).

23 The Ohio House member tried but failed to remove his name from the ballot after a paperwork mistake. Zachary Gorchow, "Kucinich Says He'll Come to Michigan After All," *Detroit Free Press*, January 3, 2008.

24 "Romney Is Top TV Spender."

25 Michigan Democratic Party, "MDP Releases Voter Guide to Help Voters Understand Presidential Primary," www.michigandems.com/121007prs.html (accessed January 5, 2009).

26 Tom Gantert, "Group Lobbies for the 'Uncommitted' Vote," *Ann Arbor News*, January 12, 2008. http://blog.mlive.com/annarbornews/2008/01/group_lobbies_for_the_uncommit.html (accessed January 19, 2009).

27 In 2004 when Democrats had a caucus in early February, only 160,000 Michiganders participated.

28 Exit poll data from MSNBC.com, www.msnbc.msn.com/id/21225987 (accessed January 23, 2009).

29 Lorraine Woellert, "Clinton, Obama Skirmish Over Florida, Michigan Votes," Bloomberg.com, www.bloomberg.com/apps/news?pid=20601103&sid=ajjIJxaoYT4o& refer=us (accessed January 23, 2009).

30 Kathy Barks Hoffman, "Democrats Officially Approve Jan. 15 Primary," *Kalamazoo Gazette*, November 28, 2007, http://blog.mlive.com/kzgazette/2007/11/democrats_officially_approve_j.html (accessed January 23, 2009).

31 Harold Ickes and Mark Penn, "The Path to the Presidency," Clinton campaign memo, www.gwu.edu/~action/2008/clinton/clinton030508memo.html (accessed January 27, 2009).

32 This was a more important battle than it may appear. Near the end of the primary season, Hillary Clinton was trying to make the case to delegates (mainly superdelegates) that they should support her. Part of her reasoning was that she had won many of the biggest states that would be important in the fall. However, two of these states— Michigan and Florida—were not being counted for the reasons described here. Clinton argued that if the voters who turned out in Michigan were included in the total, she would actually be ahead in the popular vote, and as campaign adviser Harold Ickes noted, "Not since 1972 has our party nominated a candidate who was not leading in the popular vote." (Jayson K. Jones and Ana C. Rosado, "The Day After, Clinton Aides Push Delegate Fight," http://thecaucus.blogs.nytimes.com/2008/06/01/the-day-after-clinton-aides-push-delegate-fight/.) However, an important flaw in this argument was that the vote totals they provided gave Obama zero votes from Michigan (since he was not on the ballot). However, according to the totals reported by Real Clear Politics, Clinton would still have been ahead by about 200,000 votes (www.realclearpolitics.com/epolls/2008/president/democratic_vote_count.html [accessed January 28, 2009]).

33 Gordon Trowbridge and Gary Heinlein, "Clinton Turns Up Heat for Do-over," *Detroit News*, March 20, 2008, www.detnews.com/apps/pbcs.dll/article?AID=/2008 0320/POLITICS01/803200382 (accessed January 23, 2009).

34 Gordon Trowbridge, "Obama Camp Criticizes Michigan Do-over Primary Plan," *Detroit News*, March 20, 2008, http://detnews.com/apps/pbcs.dll/article?AID=/ 20080319/METRO/803190442 (accessed January 18, 2009); Gordon Trowbridge and Mark Hornbeck, "Dems Look at Divvying Up Delegates," *Detroit News*, March 22, 2008, www.detnews.com/apps/pbcs.dll/article?AID=/20080322/POLITICS01/803220320 (accessed January 23, 2009).

35 The delegates' full votes were later restored at the request of Barack Obama.

36 Levin et al., "Why Michigan Democrats Must Be Seated."

37 Transcript of DNC Rules and Bylaws Committee meeting, May 31, 2008, http://transcripts.cnn.com/TRANSCRIPTS/0805/31/se.06.html (accessed January 23, 2009).

38 In 1992, Perot won over 19 percent of the popular vote in the state; he got nearly 9 percent in 1996.

39 Democratic pollster Stanley Greenberg conducted a study of Macomb County voters in 1985 in which he analyzed their voting patterns and attitudes. His work was spurred by the fact that 63 percent of the county voted for Kennedy in 1960, but 66 percent voted for Reagan in 1980. His work can be found in Stanley B. Greenberg, *Middle Class Dreams: Building the New American Majority* (New York: Random House, 1995).

40 Perot outperformed his national vote percentage in Michigan in 1992 and was on par with it in 1996.

41 Michigan Department of Environmental Quality, www.michigan.gov/deq/ 0,1607,7-135-3313_3677-15959-,00.html (accessed January 25, 2009).

42 EPIC/MRA Statewide Poll of Likely Voters, May 20–22, 2008, www.epicmra .com/WEB_May08_Freq1.pdf (accessed January 25, 2009); see also SurveyUSA poll, May 27, 2008, www.surveyusa.com/client/PollReport.aspx?g=52d98ca6-6c14-4f4a-9180 -4e7f1fce8a1a (accessed January 25, 2009).

43 Nick Bunkley and Micheline Maynard, "Obama Criticizes Automakers on Fuel Economy," *New York Times*, May 7, 2007, www.nytimes.com/2007/05/07/us/politics/ 07cnd-obama.html (accessed January 25, 2009).

44 This number is based on a Real Clear Politics average of polls at that time, www.realclearpolitics.com/epolls/2008/president/mi/michigan_mccain_vs_obama -553.html (accessed January 25, 2009).

45 Data from the Campaign Finance Institute, "After Holding Financial Advantage in Primaries, Obama Likely to Achieve Only Parity with McCain in General Election," Table 1, www.cfinst.org/president/pdf/Pres08_M9_Table2.pdf (accessed January 25, 2009).

46 Campaign Finance Institute, "McCain Outspent 2–1 by Obama in First Half of October, but Appears Financially Competitive in the Last 20 Days of the Election," www.cfinst.org/president/pdf/Pres08_12G_Table2.pdf (accessed January 25, 2009).

47 Michigan Campaign Finance Network, "Presidential Advertising at $13.6M in Michigan," http://mcfn.org/press.php?prId=69 (accessed January 25, 2009).

48 "Presidential Advertising at $13.6M."

49 "Presidential Advertising at $13.6M."

50 Marc Ambinder, "Obama Campaign Sneaky in Michigan," theatlantic.com, June 10, 2008, http://marcambinder.theatlantic.com/archives/2008/06/obama_campaign_ sneaky_in_michi.php (accessed January 27, 2009).

51 Marc Ambinder, "Obama's Michigan Campaign Will Be 2x the Size of Kerry's," theatlantic.com, July 14, 2008, http://marcambinder.theatlantic.com/archives/2008/07/ obamas_michigan_campaign_will.php (accessed January 27, 2009).

52 Ambinder, "Obama's Michigan Campaign."

53 Ambinder, "Obama's Michigan Campaign."

54 Walter Alarkon and Jordan Fabian, "Obama Takes Advantage in Field Offices," *The Hill*, July 23, 2008, http://thehill.com/campaign-2008/obama-takes-advantage-in -field-offices-2008-07-23.html (accessed January 27, 2009).

55 Alarkon and Fabian, "Obama Takes Advantage."

56 EPIC/MRA, "Statewide Poll of Likely Voters, August 18–21, 2008," www.epicmra .com/WEB_Aug08_Freq1.pdf (accessed January 27, 2009).

57 "Statewide Poll of Likely Voters."

58 Real Clear Politics, "Michigan: McCain vs. Obama" poll averages, www. realclearpolitics.com/epolls/2008/president/mi/michigan_mccain_vs_obama-553.html (accessed January 27, 2009). Public Policy Polling, "Obama Barely Leads in Michigan," September 8, 2008, www.publicpolicypolling.com/pdf/PPP_Release_Michigan_908.pdf (accessed January 27, 2009). PPP is a Democratic polling firm.

59 Tom Curry, "Gauging the Palin Pull in Michigan," msnbc.com, September 9, 2008, www.msnbc.msn.com/id/26629379/ (accessed January 27, 2009).

60 John Hudson, "Palin Choice Revs Up Some Macomb County Activists," *Capital News Service*, September 5, 2008, http://blog.mlive.com/cns/2008/09/palin_choice_ revs_up_some_maco.html (accessed January 27, 2009).

61 *Time*/CNN poll, "Poll: Obama, McCain Split Key States," September 10, 2008, www.time.com/time/politics/article/0,8599,1840327,00.html (accessed January 27, 2009).

62 Real Clear Politics, "Michigan: McCain vs. Obama," www.realclearpolitics.com/ epolls/2008/president/mi/michigan_mccain_vs_obama-553.html (accessed January 27, 2009).

63 Three examples: www.youtube.com/watch?v=00n2IHyQ2lM; www.youtube .com/watch?v=6reQLzgywzk; www.youtube.com/watch?v=nKCkeF6LXVc (accessed January 27, 2009).

64 Two examples: www.youtube.com/watch?v=GV_uryFRPjY; www.youtube.com/ watch?v=8xukbiS8q9s (accessed January 27, 2009).

65 "Obama Leads Better Than 3:1 in Field Offices," www.fivethirtyeight.com/ 2008/08/obama-leads-better-than-31-in-field.html (accessed January 27, 2009).

66 Real Clear Politics, "Michigan: McCain vs. Obama," www.realclearpolitics .com/epolls/2008/president/mi/michigan_mccain_vs_obama-553.html (accessed January 27, 2009).

67 Keith Naughton, "Death of a Battleground," *Newsweek*, November 3, 2008, www.newsweek.com/id/167278 (accessed January 12, 2009).

68 Alexander Bolton, "Public Funding Limits Pushed McCain out of Michigan," *The Hill*, October 4, 2008, http://thehill.com/campaign-2008/public-funding-limits -pushed-mccain-out-of-michigan-2008-10-04.html (accessed January 27, 2009).

69 *The Hotline*, October 3, 2008, www.nationaljournal.com/hotline/hl_20081003_ 8189.php (accessed January 27, 2009).

70 Naughton, "Death of a Battleground."

71 Washtenaw County Canvass Report for President and Vice President, http:// electionresults.ewashtenaw.org/nov2008/canvassreport3.html (accessed January 27, 2009).

72 Naughton, "Death of a Battleground."

73 Kathleen Gray, "Conservative PAC Brings Stop Obama Tour to Michigan," *Detroit Free Press*, October 26, 2008, www.freep.com/article/20081026/NEWS15/810260516/1215/NEWS15 (accessed January 27, 2009); www.youtube.com/watch?v=NEh4dJCcGCc; www.youtube.com/watch?v=GkYmwTFsPQ0.

74 Naughton, "Death of a Battleground."

75 Nolan Finley, "McCain Fails to Tell His Story in Michigan," *Detroit News*, October 8, 2008, www.detnews.com/apps/pbcs.dll/article?AID=/20081005/OPINION03/810050309/1271 (accessed October 8, 2008).

=== 13 ===

Campaigns Matter

Candice J. Nelson

Every four years political scientists predict the outcome of the U.S. presidential election, looking at such things as the current president's job approval rating and the state of the country's economy. The predictions suggest that the campaigns themselves don't matter, that the results are predetermined by conditions outside the control of the presidential campaigns. These predictive models are often correct; in a symposium published in October 2008, seven of the ten participating political scientists predicted that Senator Obama would be elected president on November 4, 2008.[1] However, predictions ignore the actual campaign events that impact the outcome of the election. While the state of the economy and President Bush's approval rating were clearly factors in the 2008 elections, there were many other factors that affected the outcome. As the preceding chapters have shown, the 2008 elections were as much influenced by the campaigns themselves as by the political and economic environment in which they occurred.

Election Rules Matter

The Democratic and Republican parties have one fundamental difference in the way they select their respective party's presidential nominee. Democrats require that delegates to the national nominating convention be allocated proportionally within each state. For example, if a candidate gets 50 percent of the primary or caucus vote, the candidate gets 50 percent of the delegates to the convention from that state, and other candidates contesting the primary or caucus get delegates equal to their percentage of the vote, as long as they get at least 15 percent of the vote. For Republicans, there is no such proportional rule but rather, in many states, a winner-take-all system. That is, a candidate who gets a plurality of the vote in a primary or caucus gets all of the delegates to the convention from that state. The difference in the rules means that Republican candidates seeking the presidential nomination find it easier to amass convention delegates than Democratic candidates do. We can see how this played out in the 2008 nomination process. On Super Tuesday, February 5, twenty-two states had Democratic primaries or caucuses, and twenty-one states had Republican primaries or caucuses. Going into Super Tuesday Senator John McCain had ninety-three delegates, and former Governor Mitt Romney had fifty-nine delegates. For the Democrats, Senator Obama had sixty-three delegates, and Senator Clinton had forty-eight delegates. With so many delegates at stake on February 5, either of the front-running candidates in both parties had the opportunity to come out of February 5 still in contention for the party's nomination.

However, because of the difference in each party's nomination process, the results were very different for the Republicans and the Democrats. As a result of the Republican Party's winner-take-all rules in a number of key states, Senator McCain emerged on February 5 with 704 delegates, over half the 1,191 needed for the nomination. Former governor Romney had only 247 delegates, despite having won 31 percent of the vote in Florida (compared to Senator McCain's 36 percent), 34 percent in Arizona (compared to Senator McCain's 47 percent), 34 percent in California (compared to Senator McCain's 42 percent), and 29 percent in Missouri (compared to Senator McCain's 33 percent).[2]

On the Democratic side, with no winner-take-all provisions, the results after February 5 were quite different. Senator Clinton emerged from the February 5 primaries and caucuses with 814 delegates, only slightly more than Senator Obama's 766 delegates. If the states that were winner-take-all for Republicans on February 5 were also winner-take-all for Democrats, Senator Clinton would have had almost twice as many delegates, 1,026, as Senator Obama, 554. As a result of the election rules, Senator McCain was able to wrap up the Republican nomination on March 4, while Senators Obama and Clinton continued to fight for the nomination all the way through the primary season. Election rules also played a role in the brouhaha over the delegates to the Democratic convention from Michigan and Florida, as David Dulio explains in Chapter 12.

Election rules also matter beyond the presidential nomination process. As Chris Sautter illustrates in Chapter 10, election rules and election laws affect how elections are administered and how votes are counted. Despite the passage of the Help America Vote Act, enacted in the wake of the 2000 presidential election and the subsequent Supreme Court decision in *Bush v. Gore*, there are still widespread discrepancies among the states in registration procedures, voting mechanisms, and other aspects of election administration. Each of these affects election outcomes. For example, four months after the November 2008 elections, the outcome of the Minnesota Senate election still had not been resolved.

Campaign Strategy Matters

In Chapter 2 David Winston discusses the role of election strategy. Certainly the 2008 presidential election illustrates the importance of strategy, and how strategy can affect the outcome of the election. It was widely assumed at the start of the 2008 presidential election that Senator Hillary Rodham Clinton was the front-runner for the Democratic nomination. She was a former first lady, had played a prominent role both nationally and internationally during her husband's administration, and had been reelected to the Senate from New York for a second term with 67 percent of the vote in 2006. Both she and her husband were prolific fund-raisers who seemed perfectly able to raise the prodigious amounts of money that were projected to be necessary to compete for the nomination. Senator Clinton's main competitors for the nomination were expected to be Senator Barack Obama, who, while having received some buzz as a result of his keynote address at the Democratic National Convention in 2004, was a first-term senator who had never been tested in a major competitive race, and former senator John Edwards, who no longer had a political platform and had been the vice presidential nominee on the Democrats' losing ticket in 2004.

Weekly Standard editor and *New York Times* columnist William Kristol epitomized the conventional wisdom surrounding Senator Clinton's candidacy when he stated in December 2006, that "if [Hillary Rodham Clinton] gets a race against John Edwards and Barack Obama, she's going to be the nominee. Gore is the only threat to her, then . . . Barack Obama is not going to beat Hillary Clinton in a single Democratic primary. I'll predict that right now."[3] While Kristol's prediction that Senator Obama would not win a single primary may have been more extreme than some others, his assumption that Senator Clinton would be the nominee was in line with the opinions of other political commentators as the 2008 nomination period began.

The Clinton and Obama teams made two fundamental strategic decisions that clearly impacted the outcome of the Democratic nomination. First, the Clinton campaign, like many political commentators, assumed that Senator Clinton was the front-runner and that the nomination would be decided on Super Tuesday, February 5, because of the front-loading of the nomination process. The Obama campaign, on the other hand, planned for a long, drawn out competition, and put staff in states to organize far in advance of the state primaries and caucuses. As a result, when the nomination was not wrapped up on February 5, the Obama campaign was much better positioned, both organizationally and financially, for the long nomination contest that followed. The second strategic decision that impacted the outcome of the nomination was the Obama campaign's decision to organize in caucus states, even in states that were traditional Republican states, while the Clinton campaign essentially ignored all but the Iowa caucus, focusing instead on large primary states that would likely be battleground states in the general election.

These two strategic decisions combined played a tremendous role in the outcome of the Democratic nomination, particularly because of the party's nominating rules, discussed above. For example, New Jersey, with 107 delegates at stake, and Idaho, with just eighteen, held nomination contests on February 5. Senator Clinton easily won New Jersey's primary with 54 percent of the vote, yet, because of the proportional rules of the Democratic Party, she received fifty-nine pledged delegates, while Barack Obama received forty-eight delegates. Barack Obama received 79 percent of the vote in Idaho's caucus and picked up fifteen of the state's eighteen delegates. Senator Clinton received a net of eleven delegates in New Jersey, while Senator Obama received a net of twelve delegates in Idaho. While Senator McCain easily carried Idaho in the general election, confirming the state's Republican voting pattern, the Republican-leaning states still sent delegates to the Democratic nominating convention, and Senator Obama's strategy of campaigning in those states for the nomination enabled him to slowly build a delegate lead over Senator Clinton.

Following the February 5 primaries and caucuses Senator Clinton lost twelve straight nomination contests. The fallacy of her assumption that winning large states would enable her to win the nomination was acutely evident in the first elections she won after February 5. Senator Clinton won the Ohio primary over Barack Obama by ten percentage points—54 percent to 44 percent—yet received only nine more delegates than he did. In Texas, which Senator Clinton also won, but only by three percentage points, Senators Clinton and Obama each received ninety-two delegates. Senator Clinton's focus on large states may indeed have built the groundwork for success in those states in the general election, but her strategy of ignoring small and Republican-leaning states during the nomination process, coupled with the proportional rules of the Democratic Party, cost her the opportunity to contest the general election.

Senator Clinton's fund-raising strategy also exacerbated her problems, as we saw in Chapter 4. Because Senator Clinton assumed the nomination would be decided on February 5, she focused on raising the bulk of her campaign funds during 2007, and asked donors to max-out their donations to her in the maximum allowed amount of $2300. As we saw in Chapter 4, the conventional wisdom going into the 2008 nomination period was that candidates would need to raise $100 million to be competitive in the primaries and caucuses. Both Senator

Clinton and Senator Obama raised about $100 million in 2007. How-
ever, because Senator Clinton concentrated on maxing out her donors
while Senator Obama raised his money in smaller donations, when the
nomination process extended past February 5, Senator Obama could go
back to his donors and ask them to continue to contribute to his campaign, while Senator Clinton had to cultivate new donors, and even
loan money to her campaign to keep it afloat during the extended nomination process.

The McCain campaign's strategy for winning the nomination was
to "lock up the big money early, round up the best organizers, secure the
shiniest endorsements, and win the label 'inevitable.'"[4] As shown in
Chapters 4–5, when McCain's fund-raising faltered in the first two quar-
ters of 2007, his nomination strategy changed. According to Chuck
Todd in *How Barak Obama Won*, "McCain essentially filed for Chapter
11 and did a massive reorganization. He drastically reduced his staff to
a small band of campaign operatives determined to win the nomination
one early primary state at a time. There was one great illustrative moment in the summer of 2007 of this new campaign, postreorganiza-
tion, when McCain carried his own bags in an airport while traveling
alone to a campaign event in New Hampshire."[5] The McCain campaign
strategy paid off; he won the New Hampshire primary, and two months
later sewed up the Republican nomination.

While McCain's initial approach to winning the Republican nomination was unsuccessful, his opponents' inability to catch fire with Republican primary voters enabled McCain to win the nomination
without much of a fight. Of course, the Republican Party rules for
amassing delegates, discussed above, also helped. Winning the nomination in early March, three months before the Democratic nomination was concluded, should have been a strategic advantage to the
McCain campaign. However, some political observers argue that the Mc-
Cain campaign, for whatever reason, did not take advantage of its early
head start on the general election. Talking about the March to June
period, Chuck Todd observes "this should have been the time for the
McCain campaign to ratchet up his national organization, hone his
general election message, begin the VP vetting process, and raise the
boatload of money he would need to keep up with the financial jugger-

naut that was and still is Barack Obama. As it turns out, McCain apparently did very little of those things."[6]

While political observers question the McCain campaign's strategy during the spring of 2008 after he became the preemptive nominee of the Republican Party, they also question his general election campaign strategy, or even whether he had a campaign strategy. In commenting on McCain's decision to "suspend" his campaign in early October and return to Washington to participate in congressional and administration discussions of how to solve the economic crisis, Evan Thomas writes that "to most commentators, the bizarre rush back to Washington seemed gimmicky—one more tactical gambit in a campaign that seemed to lack any coherent or consistent strategy."[7] Chuck Todd also argues that the McCain campaign was without a general election strategy. "Whether it was the pick of Sarah Palin as running mate, the decision to suspend the campaign, or the introduction of 'Joe the Plumber,' [described in Chapter 7 of this book] the McCain campaign used a series of tactics with no overall strategy."[8]

Strategically, as mentioned above, McCain's campaign managers wanted to position him as the front-runner for the nomination, and then, in the general election, run "a traditional political campaign, going negative and sticking to the sound bites."[9] However, McCain had always been somewhat of a maverick, hanging out with reporters on his Straight Talk Express bus during his 2000 presidential campaign, jousting with the Republican Party on campaign finance reform, and reaching across the aisle to try to forge a compromise on immigration reform. Some question how comfortable McCain was with the strategic decision to run a traditional campaign in 2008. For example, when he first visited his campaign headquarters in Virginia in the early months of 2007 (before the reorganization), his comment was "it's awfully big."[10] Some observers argue that McCain's pick of Sarah Palin as a running mate was a reaction to how his campaign positioned him. "Muzzled and ordered to behave like a regular politician (run negative ads, avoid reporters, just read from the damn teleprompter) McCain had rebelled in his way by picking a fellow subversive."[11] We may need to wait until McCain himself reflects on his campaign to know if these speculations are true. However, a strategic decision to run the campaign in a manner uncomfortable to the candidate clearly could have strategic implications for the success of the campaign.

Campaign Messages Matter

Having a campaign message and having a message that resonates with voters is important to the success of a campaign. As Glen Bolger points out in Chapter 3, campaigns never know when voters are paying attention to the campaign, so when they do, the message they hear should be the one the campaign wants them to hear. The best way to ensure that is to have a focused message. When Obama announced his campaign in Springfield, Illinois, in 2007, and when he spoke at Grant Park in Chicago after he won the election on November 5, his message was remarkably similar. The message of the Obama campaign was change. What change meant may have been tweaked somewhat during the campaign, but anyone who was paying even minimal attention to the 2008 presidential election understood that the overriding message of the Obama campaign was change.

Senator Clinton also had a clearly defined message for most of her campaign: experience. The Clinton campaign illustrates the importance of both having a message and having a message that connects with voters. The Clinton campaign had a message, but it did not resonate with voters. In a year when the incumbent president had approval ratings in the low thirties, at best, when many people in the United States had grown tired and frustrated with the war in Iraq, and when every day posed new economic problems, voters didn't want someone with experience; they wanted a change from the existing political situation. In 2004 a message of experience would probably have been successful, but it wasn't in 2008.

Senator McCain struggled throughout his campaign, particularly the general election campaign, to find a message at all. He too tried to emphasize his experience in public office through his long Senate career, and prior to that his service to the United States in the military, but he too was unsuccessful in connecting his message to the American people.

The McCain campaign was complicated by his support over the years of much, though not all, of the Bush administration policies. His message of experience, in contrast to Barack Obama's inexperience on the national stage, as a first-term senator, was undercut when he named Sarah Palin, the first-term governor of Alaska, as his vice presidential nominee. It became much harder to criticize Senator Obama's lack of experience when the Republican Party's nominee to serve a "heartbeat away from the president" had arguably even less experience than Senator Obama. David Axelrod, the chief strategist for the Obama campaign, described the choice of Palin as "message suicide . . . the McCain campaign had spent the month of August trying to persuade voters to choose experience over celebrity,[12] then in one fell swoop they throw experience out the window."[13]

Campaign Organization Matters

Despite the advances in technology in the past decades, there is still no substitute for a strong grassroots organization. Both Glen Bolger in Chapter 3 and Paul Herrnson in Chapter 8 point out that voter contact is crucial in a close race. No one recognized this better than Barack Obama in 2008. Because of his background as a community organizer, Obama wanted to run a "ground up rather than a top down" campaign.[14] The Obama campaign had thirty-seven field offices in Iowa prior to the Iowa caucus, more than any other presidential campaign.[15] Evan Thomas describes the strength of the Obama campaign organization as follows:

> The power of the Obama organization could be measured: doubling the turnout at the Iowa caucuses, raising twice as much money as any other candidate in history, *organizing* volunteers by the millions . . . At the end of August (2008), as Hurricane Gustav threatened the coast of Texas, the Obama campaign called the Red Cross to say it would be routing donations to it via the Red Cross home page. *Get your servers ready—our guys can be pretty nuts*, Team Obama said. *Sure, sure, whatever*, the Red Cross responded. *We've been through 9/11, Katrina, we*

can handle it. The surge of Obama dollars crashed the Red Cross web site in less than 15 minutes.[16]

In contrast, the McCain campaign's organization was not as strong. "In many states, the McCain campaign was out-organized as well as outspent by Obama."[17] In Chapter 12, David Dulio points out that the strength of the Obama organization continued into the general election. Looking at Michigan, Dulio notes that by mid-June the Obama campaign had field offices set up around the state, and the number of offices increased threefold between mid-June and mid-July. Dulio also finds that the Obama field operation in Michigan towered over the McCain operation, something that was true in other states as well.

The Obama campaign is credited with being in the forefront of new media in the 2008 election. However, new media was not just used to showcase the campaign's expertise in cutting-edge technology; rather, new media was key to the campaign's organization. "We never do something just because it's cool . . . we're always nerdily getting something out of it," said Sam Graham-Felsen, the Obama campaign's blogger.[18] For example, the "Obama '08 iPhone application . . . revealed a sophisticated data-mining operation. Tap the top button, 'call friends,' and the software would take a peek at your phone book and rearrange it in the order that the campaign was targeting states, so that friends who had, say, Colorado or Virginia area codes would appear at the top. With another tap, the Obama supporter could report back essential data for a voter canvass ('left message,' 'not interested,' 'already voted,' etc.). It all went into a giant database for Election Day."[19]

As both Leonard Steinhorn and Alan Rosenblatt point out in their chapters in this book, the Obama campaign invited supporters to be a part of the campaign organization. Be it through online social networks, texting, emails, or other new communication techniques, the Obama campaign encouraged its supporters to adapt the campaign to each supporter's interests, and use those interests and connections to spread the campaign's message and organization. Campaign organization was no longer one-dimensional or two-dimensional, but, as Alan Rosenblatt points out, three-dimensional.

Campaign Management Matters

In the last three presidential elections we have seen clear examples of the importance of campaign management. In the 2000 and 2004 elections the Bush campaign was managed by a staff that had been with Governor George Bush in Texas, ran his presidential campaign in 2000, and ran his reelection campaign in 2004. The discipline this core group brought to the campaign led to a well-run and well-managed campaign that developed a strategy and message early in the election, and stuck with it throughout the election. In 2004 Senator Kerry changed his campaign team three times, and the changes resulted in a faltering campaign strategy and message.[20]

In 2008 it was the Democratic candidate who ran the more disciplined campaign. The Obama campaign had the same senior staff from beginning to end, and maintained a strategy and message discipline that was admired by both Republican and Democratic political operatives alike. Following the November 2008 election, former House Speaker Newt Gingrich, once viewed as a brilliant political strategist for regaining Republican control of the House of Representatives after forty years of Democratic control, said the following of the Obama campaign: "I have to say, as someone who cares how you organize campaigns . . . I will be spending a lot of time over the next year studying the [Barack] Obama campaign because I think it's a watershed campaign . . . I think it's a marvelous case study in 21st century use of technology and the oldest traits of strategy and discipline combined together in a very powerful forum."[21]

Neither Senator Clinton in the primary nor Senator McCain in the primary or general election came close to the consistent campaign management and organization of the Obama campaign. The Clinton campaign seemed beset by personnel clashes almost from the start, with Mark Penn and, to some extent, former president Bill Clinton advocating one strategy and Harold Ickes and Howard Wolfson, among other advisers, arguing a different strategy.[22] Penn was described as "more or less in constant conflict with Hillary's other advisors."[23] One top adviser described the early primary campaign as "a terribly unpleasant place to work. You had seven people on a morning conference call, all of whom had tried to get someone else on the call fired, or knew someone on the call tried to get them fired. It was not a recipe for cohesive team building."[24] After months of internal disagreements Senator Clinton fired her longtime adviser and 2008 campaign manager, Patti Solis Doyle, shortly after the February 5 primary, and later Mark Penn resigned from the campaign. Joshua Green, writing about the internal workings of the Clinton campaign in the September 2008 edition of *The Atlantic Monthly* (and documenting his account with memos from the Clinton campaign), describes Clinton's campaign as "undone by a clash of personalities more toxic than anyone imagined. E-mails and memos . . . reveal the backstabbing and conflicting strategies that produced an epic meltdown."[25]

The McCain campaign didn't fare much better from a management standpoint. As shown in Chapter 4, John McCain, like the Obama and Clinton campaigns, assumed he would have to raise about $100 million in 2007 to be competitive in the 2008 nomination process. When the campaign raised only $12 million in the first quarter of 2007, the fund-raising operation was revamped, but the second quarter figures were just as disappointing, reporting only $11 million raised in the second quarter of 2007. The situation led to backbiting among the campaign's top advisers. "The crystal palace [so named because of its size and its location in Crystal City, Virginia], in the winter of 2007, turned into a snake pit. The Weaver-Nelson [John Weaver, a long-time McCain aide, and Terry Nelson, political director of the Bush Cheney campaign in 2004, and early campaign manager for the 2008 McCain campaign] camp blamed Davis's [Rick Davis, who had managed the 2000 McCain campaign] people in fund-raising for not drumming up enough money; the Davis camp blamed the Nelson-Weaver management for spending money they didn't have."[26] The warring among the staff continued into the primaries, just as it did on the Clinton campaign. "[McCain] hated to fire anyone from his staff. Not unlike Senator Clinton, he resisted stepping in to make personnel decisions, even when they were overdue."[27]

In July 2007 the McCain campaign drastically cut its staff and moved the skeletal staff it still had to concentrate on the New Hampshire primary. McCain won the nomination, but some argued that he then squandered the time between March and June, when the Democratic nominee finally became known. In July 2008 McCain again shook up his campaign organization, and while some argue that Steven Schmitt, the new campaign manager, brought message discipline to the campaign, others questioned the strategy and message that Schmitt promoted.

Conclusion

As the contributors to this book argue, campaigns matter. While the economic crisis in 2008, the unpopular war in Iraq, and President George Bush's low approval numbers clearly contributed to a political environment favorable to any Democratic candidate, the strategic decisions and messages of the Obama campaign undoubtedly contributed to his election as the forty-fourth president of the United States. The early start of the 2008 presidential election, at least two years before the actual election, enabled Obama to slowly improve as a candidate. This was particularly true of his debating skills. In reviewing a tape of his performance in a debate during the summer of 2007, Obama commented, "It's worse than I thought."[28] However, in an interview with a *Newsweek* reporter in May 2008, Obama commented that "in each successive debate [in 2007] my performance had improved to the point where in the final four or five debates before Iowa, I felt that I was performing on a par with Hillary."[29] Given the long nomination process that was to follow, and the many more debates with Senator Clinton, it is no wonder that by the time of the general election debates in October, Obama was prepared. The long, drawn out nomination process enabled Obama to hone his skills as a campaigner and his campaign to refine its operation. The length of the campaign mattered, and in the end probably helped Obama.

Obama's "tortoise and hare strategy" during the nomination process allowed him to slowly rack up delegates until he had a lead that Senator Clinton could not overcome.[30] His fund-raising strategy of appealing to small, medium, and large donors ensured him a steady stream of funds throughout the primary and general elections, enabling him to forgo public funding in the general election, and vastly outspend Senator McCain and the Republican Party. His use of new media, blended with his fund-raising and organizational strategies, allowed him to successfully contest traditionally Republican states such as Virginia, North Carolina, Colorado, and Indiana. The Obama campaign will be studied and analyzed by political operatives for many years because what the Obama campaign did in 2008 mattered, and led to the election of the first African American president of the United States.

Notes

1 James E. Campbell, ed., "Symposium: Forecasting the 2008 National Elections," *PS: Political Science & Politics* 41, no. 4 (October 2008): 681.

2 In the other two winner-take-all states on February 5, Connecticut and New York, McCain received a majority of the vote: 52 percent of the vote in Connecticut and 51 percent of the vote in New York.

3 William Kristol, *Fox News Sunday,* December 17, 2006, as reported in the *Washington Post*, December 28, 2008, B2.

4 Evan Thomas, *A Long Time Coming* (New York: Public Affairs, 2009), 33.

5 Chuck Todd and Sheldon Gawiser, *How Barack Obama Won* (New York: Vintage, 2009), 6.

6 Todd and Gawiser, *How Barack Obama Won*, 16.

7 Thomas, *Long Time Coming*, 137.

8 Todd and Gawiser, *How Barack Obama Won*, 18.

9 Thomas, *Long Time Coming*, 95.

10 Thomas, *Long Time Coming*, 33.

11 Thomas, *Long Time Coming*, 124.

12 The McCain campaign had run an ad mocking the large crowds that had greeted Obama during his European trip in July, likening Obama to celebrities such as Paris Hilton and Brittany Spears. For more on the "celebrity" ad, see Chapter 7 of this volume.

13 Thomas, *Long Time Coming*, 168.

14 Thomas, *Long Time Coming*, 13.

15 Thomas, *Long Time Coming*, 12.

16 Thomas, *Long Time Coming*, 109.

17 Thomas, *Long Time Coming*, 172.

18 Sam Graham-Felsen, speaking to a *Newsweek* reporter. Thomas, *Long Time Coming*, 107.

19 Thomas, *Long Time Coming*, 107.

20 For a more detailed account of the Bush and Kerry campaign organizations, see David A. Dulio and Candice J. Nelson, *Vital Signs: Perspectives on the Health of American Campaigning* (Washington, D.C.: Brookings Institution, 2005), 156–160.

21 Newt Gingrich, "First Person Singular," *Washington Post Magazine,* January 18, 2009, 20.

22 For a more complete account of the Clinton personnel and strategy conflicts, see Joshua Green, "The Front-Runner's Fall," *Atlantic Monthly,* September 2008, www .theatlantic.com/doc/print/200809/hillary-clinton-campaign.

23 Thomas, *Long Time Coming,* 64.

24 Thomas, *Long Time Coming,* 22.

25 Green, "Front-Runner's Fall."

26 Thomas, *Long Time Coming,* 35.

27 Thomas, *Long Time Coming,* 38.

28 Thomas, *Long Time Coming,* 14.

29 Thomas, *Long Time Coming,* 208.

30 Thomas, *Long Time Coming,* 66.

About the Contributors

Glen Bolger is a leading political strategist and pollster for the Republican Party. He is a partner and cofounder of Public Opinion Strategies, a national political and public affairs survey research firm whose clients include leading political figures, Fortune 500 companies, and major associations. Public Opinion Strategies has eighteen U.S. senators, seven governors, and more than forty members of Congress as clients. For its work in the 2002 elections, Public Opinion Strategies won the Pollster of the Year Campaign Excellence Award from the American Association of Political Consultants. Prior to cofounding Public Opinion Strategies, Glen was the director of survey research and analysis for the National Republican Congressional Committee, the political arm of the House Republican Conference. Glen is a graduate of the American University in Washington, D.C. He and his wife Carol have three daughters.

Anthony Corrado is professor of government at Colby College and a nonresident senior fellow at the Brookings Institution. He also serves as chair of the board of trustees of the Campaign Finance Institute, a nonpartisan research organization located in Washington, D.C., and is a member of the American Bar Association's Advisory Commission on Election Law. He is the author or coauthor of numerous books and articles on campaign finance law, political finance, and presidential elections, including *Financing the 2004 Election* (2006) and *The New Campaign Finance Sourcebook* (2005).

David A. Dulio is associate professor of political science at Oakland University in Rochester, Michigan. Dulio has published six books, including *Vital Signs: Perspectives on the Health of American Campaigning* (with Candice J. Nelson, 2005), *For Better or Worse? How Political Consultants Are Changing Elections in the United States* (2004), and *The Mechanics of State Legislative Campaigns* (with John S. Klemanski, 2005). Dulio has also published dozens of articles and book chapters on topics relating to campaigns and elections. During 2001–2002 Dulio served as an American Political Science Association congressional fellow in the office of the U.S. House of Representatives Republican Conference headed by former U.S. Rep. J.C. Watts Jr. (OK).

Paul S. Herrnson is director of the Center for American Politics and Citizenship, professor in the Department of Government and Politics, and Distinguished Scholar-Teacher at the University of Maryland. He has published several books, including *The Financiers of Congressional Elections* (2003), *Voting Technology: The Not-So-Simple Act of Casting a Ballot* (2008), and *Congressional Elections: Campaigning at Home and in Washington*, 5th ed. (2008). Herrnson has advised the U.S. Congress, the Maryland General Assembly, the Federal Election Commission, and various other governmental and nongovernmental organizations on matters pertaining to money and politics, political parties and elections, and political reform.

Dotty Lynch is an Executive in Residence in the School of Communication at American University and a political consultant for CBS News. The 2008 election was her eleventh presidential campaign as a professional journalist and pollster. She was the CBS News senior political editor (1985–2005) and is currently an on-air analyst for CBS Radio and a member of the CBS News Election Decision Desk. She began teaching at American University in 2006 and in 2008 team-taught a class on the presidential primaries that included a five-day field trip to New Hampshire. In the 1970s and 1980s she worked on the polling for the presidential campaigns of George McGovern, Jimmy Carter, and Ted Kennedy as well as dozens of U.S. Senate and gubernatorial candidates. In addition, she developed the concept of the gender gap and is a leading expert on women in politics.

Candice J. Nelson is an associate professor of government and academic director of the Campaign Management Institute at American University. She is the coauthor of *Vital Signs: Perspectives on the Health of American Campaigning* (2005), *Shades of Gray: Perspectives on Campaign Ethics* (2002), *The Money Chase: Congressional Campaign Finance Reform* (1990), and *The Myth of the Independent Voter* (1992). She is a former American Political Science Association congressional fellow. She received her Ph.D. in political science from the University of California at Berkeley.

Alan Rosenblatt is associate director of online advocacy at the Center for American Progress Action Fund. He founded the Internet Advocacy Roundtable in 2005. Alan is an adjunct professor at Johns Hopkins, Georgetown, and American Universities; a blogger at the *Huffington Post*, TechPresident.com, K Street Café, andDrDigiPol.com; a contributing editor to Politics Online; a board member for E-Democracy.org; and a former fellow at George Washington University's Institute for Politics, Democracy, and the Internet. He taught the world's first Internet politics course at George Mason University in 1995. Alan has a Ph.D. in political science from American University.

Chris Sautter, president of Sautter Communications/Sautter Films, is a political media strategist, award-winning filmmaker, and attorney who has gained national notoriety for his work in politics and film. Sautter produced Barack Obama's first political ads and served as a lead attorney in Al Franken's U.S. Senate recount. He coauthored *The Recount Primer* (1994), considered the definitive guide to election disputes. Sautter's first film, *The King of Steeltown: Hardball Politics in the Heartland* (2001) about Chicago-style machine politics, won Best Political Documentary at the New York International Independent Film Festival. Sautter's documentary *So Glad I Made It* (2004), about a struggling singer songwriter, won six top film festival awards and a spot on the Grammy

Awards ballot for Best Music Film. Sautter teaches election law at American University.

Leonard Steinhorn is professor of communication, director of the Public Communication program, and affiliate professor of history at American University. He writes and lectures frequently on politics, media, and the presidency and comments regularly in the press, serving as the political analyst for FOX-5 News in Washington, D.C. He is the author of *The Greater Generation: In Defense of the Baby Boom Legacy* (2006) and coauthor of *By the Color of Our Skin: The Illusion of Integration and the Reality of Race* (1999). Steinhorn's writing has been published in anthologies, textbooks, journals, magazines, and op-ed pages. He lectures frequently at universities and organizations in the United States and abroad, and he serves on the board of the Internet journal History News Network. Previously Steinhorn served as speechwriter and strategist for various politicians and advocacy groups.

James A. Thurber is University Distinguished Professor of Government, founder (1979) and director of the Center for Congressional and Presidential Studies (american.edu/ccps) at American University, Washington, D.C. Under his direction, CCPS organizes biannually the Campaign Management Institute and the Public Affairs and Advocacy Institute over the last two decades. He was the principal investigator of a seven-year grant from The Pew Charitable Trusts to study campaign conduct. He was the principal investigator of a four-year study of lobbying and ethics funded by the Committee for Economic Development. He is a fellow of the National Academy of Public Administration and is a former APSA congressional fellow. He has authored books and articles on Congress, congressional-presidential relations, interest groups and lobbying and ethics, and campaigns and elections. He is an editor of *Rivals for Power: Presidential-Congressional Relations*, 4th ed. (2009), *Congress and the Internet* (with Colton Campbell, 2002), *The Battle for Congress: Consultants, Candidates, and Voters* (2001), *Crowded Airwaves: Campaign Advertising in Elections* (with Candice J. Nelson and David A. Dulio, 2000), *Campaign Warriors: Political Consultants in Elections*

(2000), *Remaking Congress: The Politics of Congressional Stability and Change* (with Roger Davidson, 1995), and *Divided Democracy: Cooperation and Conflict Between Presidents and Congress* (1991). He has co-produced three BBC-TV documentaries on the U.S. Congress and elections.

Carol A. Whitney is a longtime Republican political strategist with particular expertise in message development and delivery. She is an adjunct faculty member who teaches courses in political communications and policy at American University, and also serves as coprogram director of the Campaign Management Institute. She developed the curriculum on ethics in campaign politics distributed to universities in 2000, and teaches a course in ethics in campaign politics.

David Winston has served as a strategic adviser to Senate and House Republican leadership for the past ten years. He was formerly the director of planning for Speaker of the House Newt Gingrich, and advises center-right political parties throughout Europe. Additionally Winston was a senior fellow at the Heritage Foundation where he did statistical policy and econometric modeling. He has served in a senior staff role to four RNC chairmen. Winston is a columnist for the Capitol Hill newspaper *Roll Call* and an election analyst for CBS.

Index